The Philosophical View
of the Great Perfection
in the Tibetan Bon Religion

THE PHILOSOPHICAL VIEW
OF THE GREAT PERFECTION
IN THE TIBETAN BON RELIGION

by

Donatella Rossi

Snow Lion Publications
Ithaca, New York

Snow Lion Publications
P.O. Box 6483
Ithaca, New York 14851 U.S.A.
Telephone: 607-273-8519

www.snowlionpub.com

ISBN 1-55939-129-4

Library of Congress Cataloging-in-Publication Data

Rossi, Donatella, 1958-
   The philosophical view of the great perfection in the Tibetan Bon religion /
   Donatella Rossi.
      p.   cm.
   Includes bibliographical references and index.
   ISBN 1-55939-129-4 (pbk. : alk. paper)
      1. Rdzogs-chen (Bonpo) 2. Bonpo (Sect)—Doctrines. I. Title.

BQ7982.3 .R67 1999
299'.54—dc21

                                                             99-057690

CONTENTS

To my family

ACKNOWLEDGEMENTS

I hereby wish to express my thankfulness to all the people who helped, assisted and encouraged me while I was carrying out the present research. Some of them have passed away in the meantime; as to those whose presence I still enjoy, I hope they will recognize that this token of appreciation is addressed to each of them, even if their names are not all listed here. I would nonetheless like to mention some of those who have been more directly concerned with my endeavour.

First of all, my mentor, Prof. Per Kværne of the University of Oslo, who has supported my research in very many ways from the moment of its inception until its completion. Prof. Katsumi Mimaki of Kyoto University, who made my stay in Japan not only possible but also pleasant, and has kindly followed my work. My friends and colleagues in Japan, who have assisted me with moral and technical support. Prof. Samten G. Karmay, Research Director at the Centre Nationale de la Recherche Scientifique, Paris, Prof. Jens Braarvig of the University of Oslo and Prof. Anne-Marie Blondeau of the École Pratique des Hautes Études, Paris, for their very precious advice, comments and suggestions.

This research has been carried out thanks to the sponsorship of a Special Exchange Programme (SEP) between Japanese and European scholars fostered by the Japanese Ministry of Foreign Affairs and implemented by the Japanese-German Centre, Berlin (August 1993-August 1994); an extraordinary fellowship granted by the Japanese Society for the Promotion of Buddhism (Bukkyo Dendo Kyokai, October 1994-March 1995); and the Centre for Advanced Study at the Norwegian

Academy of Science and Letters, where I worked from August 1995 to June 1996 on the cataloguing of the Bonpo Canon, as member of an international research team directed by Prof. Per Kværne. I am indebted to him, to the Director and the staff of the Centre, to my colleagues Tseyang Changngopa, Dondrup Lhagyal, Dan Martin and Tshering Thar for their kindness and patience, and especially to Geshe Namgyal Nyima Dakar (*dGe bshes* rNam rgyal Nyi ma Brag dkar), whose help and knowledge of Bonpo sources have proved invaluable to me.[1]

My respect and warm gratitude are also extended to Ponlop Trinley Nyima (dPon slob 'Phrin las Nyi ma) of the Tibetan Bon po Monastic Centre, whose assistance has contributed very much to my understanding of the texts and doctrines studied here.[2]

During our working meetings in Dolanji in 1994, he not only generously offered his knowledgeable comments, but also did his best to promote my understanding through lively explanations, extemporary drawings and counter-questions, while offering me boiled eggs and fruit all along.[3]

---

1. For the sake of convenience, Tibetan terms appearing in the text and in the notes will not be preceded by the abbreviation 'Tib.'; non-Tibetan terms will instead be specified as to their linguistic origin. Further, Tibetan textual sources will be referred to by their full or abridged titles, author's name and page number(s). Articles and books in Western languages will be referred to by author's name, year of publication, and whenever deemed appropriate, page number(s). Complete bibliographic references are given in the relevant sections, pp. 273-278 and pp. 278-296 respectively.

2. He belongs to the prestigious Ya ngal lineage of Dolpo, Nepal. For the latter, see the *rGyal gśen ya ṅal gyi gduṅ rabs un chen tshaṅs pa'i sgra dbyaṅs* by Yang sgom Mi 'gyur rGyal mtshan, pp. 1-135.

3. The following information about his life was provided by dPon slob 'Phrin las Nyi ma himself: he was born on the 12th day of the 1st Tibetan month of the year 1963 in Dolpo (for an account about Dolpo see D. L. Snellgrove 1967b). His father was bsTan 'dzin bSam sgrub, his mother bsTan 'dzin chos sgron; she was a *rNying ma* devotee, as was his uncle. When he was young, his name was Tshe dbang sTag lha, a name that he retained until the age of fourteen (1975). According to the tradition of the Ya ngal teachers (*Yang ston pa*), the male spiritual descendants, who are styled *sngags pa*, are supposed to practise in retreat for three years, whereby they engage themselves in preliminary practices (*sngon 'gro*), the practices of the five Yi dam (*yi dam mchog lnga*) of the *Bon* religion (for which see p. 133, n. 1), the practice of mind-consciousness transfer (*'pho ba*) and so on. For what concerns female spiritual descendants, they normally get acquainted with the teachings by residing in or having some degree of interaction with nunneries for a certain period of time. The monastery where Tshe dbang sTag lha pursued his training is named sTar rdzong phun tshogs gling; it is situated south of Tshwa dga' (or Sa dga') and east of bSam gling

Finally, I should like to thank Chogyal Namkhai Norbu (Chos rgyal Nam mkha'i Nor bu), a well-known teacher of the Great Perfection, who was the first person to inspire my interest in these doctrines and the value of the Tibetan culture as a whole.

---

monastery, of which it represents a branch. Until 1978 Tshe dbang sTag lha lived in Dolpo, while in 1979 he moved to Dolanji, India, where he took the full monastic ordination and was subsequently given the name of 'Phrin las Nyi ma. In 1989 he obtained the *dGe bshes* degree. From 1989 to 1992 he was a philosophy teacher at the Dolanji *Bon po* Dialectic School. In 1992 he acquired the title of sMan ri'i dPon slob. At present he mainly teaches philosophy and other aspects of the *Bon* religion. He also travels to various areas, including Mustang, to perform rituals according to the requests of Tibetan *Bon po* believers.

ABBREVIATIONS

abbr.	abbreviated.
AJ	*Acta Jutlandica.*
AM	*Asia Major.*
AO	*Acta Orientalia.*
AOH	*Acta Orientalia Hungarica.*
AS	*Asiatische Studien.*
b.	born.
BEFEO	*Bulletin de l'École Française d'Extrême-Orient.*
BGTC	*Bod rgya tshig mdzod chen mo*, Beijing, 1993.
BIHP	*Bulletin of the Institute of History and Philology.*
BKSR	Bonpo *bKa' 'gyur* Second Reprint.
BSOAS	*Bulletin of the School of Oriental and African Studies.*
Chin.	Chinese.
ed.	editor, edited.
EFEO	*École Française d'Extrême-Orient.*
EW	*East and West.*
HJAS	*Harvard Journal of Asian Studies.*
HR	*History of Religions.*
IIJ	*Indo-Iranian Journal.*
IsMEO	Istituto Italiano per il Medio ed Estremo Oriente.
JA	*Journal Asiatique.*
JIABS	*Journal of the International Association for Buddhist Studies.*
JASB	*Journal of the Asiatic Society of Bengal.*
JRAS	*Journal of the Royal Asiatic Society.*
Lit.	Literally.
LTWA	Library of Tibetan Works and Archives.

MVy	*Mahāvyutpatti,* Sasaki, Tokyo, 1916-1926.
MRDTB	*Memoirs of the Research Department of the Toyo Bunko.*
MS	*Monumenta Serica.*
n.d.	not datable.
OE	*Oriens Extremus.*
RASB	*Royal Asiatic Society of Bengal.*
SCEAR	*Studies in Central and East Asian Religions.*
Skr.	Sanskrit.
SOAS	*School of Oriental and African Studies.*
SOR	*Serie Orientale Roma.*
SPS	*Śatapiṭaka Series.*
TBMC	Tibetan Bonpo Monastic Centre.
TJ	*Tibet Journal.*
TP	*T'oung Pao.*
TR	*Tibetan Review.*

Concerning the notes: For the sake of convenience, notes have been placed at the foot of the page. In the introductory section, the length of some notes prevents them from appearing on the page on which they were cited; however, the reader can find them on the immediately adjoining page.

Part One:

INTRODUCTION

PRELIMINARY REMARKS ON
THE BON RELIGION AND
ON THE TEACHINGS OF THE GREAT PERFECTION

The Bon Religion

The objective of this work is to offer a descriptive analysis of the philosophical view (*lta ba*) of the Great Perfection (*rDzogs pa chen po*, or in short *rDzogs chen*) with particular reference to the Bon religion.[1]

Followers of the Bon religion maintain that its tenets were first expounded as the 'Everlasting *Bon*' (*g.yung drung Bon*)[2] by the Teacher

---

1. The religious phenomenon of Bon has been researched by Western scholars since the end of the last century. See e.g. S. C. Das 1881; B. Laufer 1901; H. Hoffmann 1950; R. A. Stein 1962, pp. 193-210; G. Uray 1964; D. Snellgrove 1967a, which also contains a summarized discussion by Western scholars around the term *bon* and the adjective *bon po* (p. 1, n. 1; p. 20, n. 2); R. A. Stein 1971a; S. G. Karmay 1975a; P. Kværne 1976; G. Tucci 1980, pp. 213-248, where he states (p. 213): "The Bon religion is the indigenous religion of Tibet, which despite all the influences of Buddhism has preserved itself until the present day." Discussions concerning Bon as the indigenous or 'pre-Buddhist' religion of Tibet are found in R. A. Stein 1985a and R. A. Stein 1988. See also T. Skorupski 1990, pp. 273-278; D. Martin 1994, pp. 4-12 in particular. For a fairly recent survey of research on the Bon religion see P. Kværne 1994. For a state-of-the-art discussion about the way in which Western scholars have viewed Bon see P. Kværne 1995, pp. 9-10; cf. the chapter "*Bon dang bon po*" in N. Namkhai 1994, pp. 509-519. D. Martin has compiled a bibliography of all works and articles published so far on the Bon religion.

2. This definition of Bon as 'Everlasting' (*g.yung drung*) does not seem to have been used before the tenth century A.D. Cf. S. G. Karmay 1975a, p. 172.

(*ston pa*) gShen rab Mi bo che, who is considered to have made his appearance on earth much earlier than the Buddha Śākyamuni,[3] and was born in and ruled a country to the West of Tibet known as sTag gzig (or rTag gzigs).[4]

After sTon pa gShen rab entrusted his teachings to worthy successors, the Everlasting Bon is believed to have spread from that country toward the East, reaching India, China, the kingdom of Zhang Zhung and from there Tibet.[5] The kingdom of Zhang Zhung played an influential role in the history and culture of Tibet. With Mount Kailash (Ti se) at its centre,[6] it seems to have covered a vast area to the west and possibly north-east of Tibet.[7] It was divided into three provinces (*sgo phug bar gsum*) where different languages were spoken;[8] one of these, *smar* (or *smrar*),[9] was the language from which numerous texts, including those of the Great Perfection, are said to have been translated into Tibetan. Marriage alliances were established between the royal families of Zhang Zhung and Tibet. Zhang Zhung priests and masters were invited to Tibet to offer their wisdom and their supernatural skills. Eventually, around the seventh/eighth centuries A.D., the kingdom of Zhang Zhung was conquered and annexed to the then expanding Tibetan empire.[10]

Bon enjoyed royal patronage in Tibet until the second half of the eighth century A.D., when Buddhism was adopted as the official creed. Bon lost its recognition and support at the highest level and its followers, particularly within the established religious élite, had no choice but to convert or go into exile. Bonpo texts were hidden so that they could be retrieved and revealed later, at more favourable times.[11]

---

3. See P. Kværne 1989 and also P. Kværne 1995, p. 17. Cf. N. Namkhai 1996, pp. 47-78.

4. According to D. L. Snellgrove and H. Richardson 1968, p. 99, sTag gzig is "vaguely identifiable with Persia." According to G. Tucci 1980, p. 214, sTag gzig is "a name which in Tibetan literature refers to the Iranian (or Iranian-speaking) world". Cf. E. Haarh 1968, p. 9; D. Snellgrove 1987, p. 388 et seq.; P. Kværne 1995, pp. 14-17. On the question of the geographical and sacred origins of Bon, see D. Martin 1998.

5. See S. G. Karmay 1972, p. 21 et seq.

6. See N. Namkhai and R. Prats 1989.

7. See D. L. Snellgrove and H. Richardson 1968, p. 26; S. G. Karmay 1972, p. xxx; G. Tucci 1980, p. 214; P. Kværne 1995, pp. 13-14.

8. See E. Haarh 1968. Cf. the chapter *"Zhang zhung dang bod"* in N. Namkhai 1994, p. 519 et seq.

9. Cf. p. 79, n. 2.

The period following the disintegration of the Tibetan empire (which occurred during the first half of the ninth century) saw a general revival of Buddhism and the gradual rise of doctrinal and philosophical Buddhist tendencies that led to the creation of the well-known schools of Tibetan Buddhism.[12] Bonpos, on their part, did not remain indifferent to that state of affairs, and adapting to the trend of the time, proceeded toward the systematization of their own religion and to the canonization of their scriptures.[13]

This process of adaptation and systematization could not have possibly taken place without interaction with, or inspiration drawn from, the doctrinal milieux that were gradually taking shape. Although it is difficult for us to believe that this process was simply a unilateral one, it thus happened that later Tibetan Buddhist polemics took a very negative stand against the Bonpos, which contributed to the creation of an image of Bon as a decadent unorthodox sect that had plagiarized most of the Buddhist tenets.[14] This image influenced the approach of Western scholarship toward the study of this religion, which for many years remained subject to disdain or biased suspicion.[15] There are unquestionably quite a few aspects of the Bon religion, as it appears today, which do not differ from 'orthodox' Buddhist ones. In this respect Per Kværne has rightly observed:[16]

> In view of the manifest similarities between Bon and Buddhism, one may well ask in what the distinction between the two religions consists. The answer, at least to this author, would seem to depend on which perspective is adopted when describing Bon. Rituals and other religious practices, as well as meditational and metaphysical traditions are, undeniably, to a large extent similar, even identical. Concepts of sacred history and sources of religious authority are, however, radically different and justify the claim of the Bon pos to constitute an entirely distinct religious community.

---

10. About Zhang Zhung see also G. Tucci 1956, pp. 71-75; R. A. Stein 1959, p. 28; G. Uray 1985; L. Petech 1988, pp. 269-270 and pp. 271-272; K. Cech 1992.

11. Cf. S. G. Karmay 1972, p. 94, n. 2.

12. See e.g. G. Tucci 1980 and D. Snellgrove 1987.

13. For which see below, p. 31, n. 67.

14. Cf. e.g. G. Tucci 1980, p. 224.

15. Cf. e.g. D. L. Snellgrove and H. Richardson 1968, pp. 109-110.

16. P. Kværne 1995, p. 13.

In our opinion, it is precisely the value of such concepts and sources that makes Bon not only a fascinating religious phenomenon, but also, if not more importantly, one of the most precious assets of the Tibetan cultural heritage.[17]

Nowadays several thousand Tibetans profess the Bon religion. Bonpos are found in various districts of Western, Central, and Eastern Tibet, and in the Dolpo area of Nepal. Since 1968 a Bonpo lay and monastic settlement has been established by Tibetan refugees in India at Dolanji (Himachal Pradesh).[18]

The Teachings of the Great Perfection

Traditionally speaking, the Great Perfection represents the state of absolute knowledge that is said to exist as a potentiality in all sentient beings. It is also considered to be the essential nature of all phenomena. Teachings that deal with the Great Perfection are esoteric in character. For this reason, they are imparted by teachers who have mastered their meaning only to individuals who are deemed to possess an exceptional capacity of understanding. They provide such individuals with the theoretical and technical means to actualize that absolute state of knowledge within themselves.

---

17. Cf. M. Eliade 1958, p. 26, where speaking about the dialectic of the sacred he states: "The attitude which I have labelled idolatrous is based (whether consciously or not hardly matters) on this view of *all* [his italics] hierophanies as being part of a whole. It would preserve the older hierophanies, by according them value on a different religious level, and the performance of a function there."

18. See P. Kværne 1990c, pp. 114-119 and G. Coleman 1993, pp. 208-210. Cf. P. Kværne 1995, p. 22.

19. The Nine Vehicles of Bon are divided into the so-called Four Vehicles of the Cause (*rgyu'i theg pa bzhi*) and Five Vehicles of the Fruit (*'bras bu'i theg pa lnga*). The Four Vehicles of the Cause are: the Vehicle of the gShen of Prediction (*phywa gshen gyi theg pa*), of the gShen of Appearance (*snang gshen gyi theg pa*), of the gShen of Magic (*'phrul gshen gyi theg pa*), and of the gShen of Existence (*srid gshen gyi theg pa*). The first vehicle is concerned with divination, astrology, diagnostics, healing methods and rituals; the Second is concerned with protection, ransom and exorcism; the Third is concerned with overcoming and elimination of hostile forces; and the Fourth with funerary ritual. For these cf. N. Namkhai 1995. The Five Vehicles of the Fruit are: the Vehicles of Virtuous Devotees (*dge bsnyen gyi theg pa*), of Ascetics (*drang srong gi theg pa*), of the White A (*a dkar gyi theg pa*), of the Primordial gShen (*ye gshen gyi theg pa*), and the Unsurpassable Supreme One (*yang rtse bla med kyi theg pa*). They are respectively

For the Bonpos the teachings of the Great Perfection are the epitome of all the beliefs classified in their Nine Vehicles (*theg pa rim dgu*).[19] The same applies to the *rNying ma pas*, the followers of the Old School of Tibetan Buddhism,[20] although they have also been practised by representatives of other Tibetan Buddhist traditions.[21]

A study of the history and doctrines of the Great Perfection is therefore significant not only in its own right, but also for the understanding of the evolution of Indo-Tibetan Buddhism in general and of the Bon religion in particular.[22]

The historical origins of the Great Perfection cannot be fixed with absolute certainty. Its tenets seem to have taken shape at least around the ninth century A.D.[23] In this respect they can be considered as forerunning the whole evolution and configuration of Tibetan Buddhism. The doctrines of the Great Perfection seem to retain theoretical elements that can be historically traced within the evolution of the higher

---

concerned with rules of conducts and religious practices for lay believers (Fifth Vehicle); rules for fully ordained persons (Sixth Vehicle); tantric practices based on meditative transformation processes (Seventh Vehicle); tantric practices based on the Generation (*bskyed rim*) and Perfection (*rdzogs rim*) stages of meditation (Eighth Vehicle); and the teachings of the Great Perfection (Ninth Vehicle). See D. Snellgrove 1967; P. Kværne 1974, Part One, p. 26; K. Mimaki 1994a and 1994b. Cf. J. Hackin 1924, pp. 31-32; G. Tucci 1949, pp. 109-110. A detailed analysis of the classification of the Nine Vehicles according to the tradition of treasure texts (*gter ma*) is found in a work by Shar rdza bKra shis rGyal mtshan (1859-1934) entitled *Lung rig rin po che'i mdzod blo gsal snying gi nor*, for which cf. S. G. Karmay 1977, p. 171. See also dPal ldan Tshul khrims (1902-1973) *Sangs rgyas g.yung drung bon gyi bstan pa'i 'byung ba brjod pa'i legs bshad bskal pa bzang po'i mgrin rgyan* (hereafter *g.Yung drung bon gyi bstan 'byung*), pp. 393-396.

20. See the *Dam pa'i chos kyi 'khor lo bsgyur ba rnams kyi byung ba gsal bar byed pa mkhas pa'i dga' ston* (abbr. *Chos byung mkhas pa'i dga' ston*) by dPa' bo gTsug lag Phreng ba (1504-1566), pp. 537-651; Dudjom Rinpoche and Jigdrel Yeshe Dorje 1991. See also N. Namkhai 1985; R. Prats 1985; F.-K. Ehrhard 1992; J.-L. Achard 1995 and 1998.

21. To name but one, the Fifth Dalai Lama Ngag dbang Blo bzang rGya mtsho (1617-1682), also known as 'the Great Fifth'. For his hagiography see E. Dargyay 1977, p. 169 et seq. Cf. S. G. Karmay 1988b. The non-sectarian tradition (*ris med pa*) which flourished in Eastern Tibet during the late 19th century was also very much inspired by the doctrinal tenets of the Great Perfection; for this see E. G. Smith 1970.

22. Cf. D. Snellgrove 1967, p. 15; G. Tucci 1980, p. 6; P. Kværne 1983, pp. 367-368; S. G. Karmay 1988a, p. ix; P. Kværne and T. K. Rikey 1996, pp. ix-x.

23. See S. G. Karmay 1988a, p. ix. Cf. H. V. Guenther 1983.

categories of *Tantras* such as Mahāyoga,[24] but they also seem to have been inspired by much earlier philosophical principles.[25]

Although it may be a truism, we do not think that doctrines or spiritual movements originated *ex nihilo* or without regard for actual historical circumstances, be that in the East or in the West. The 'mystery quest' is as old as the human race.[26] The history of religions testifies to the intensity and significance of this quest, which has naturally drawn from beliefs that had already been elaborated at a certain time in history, and which were taken as the basis for further investigation and contemplation.

This quest has certainly been influenced by concrete circumstances. However, since human beings are characterized by a high degree of mobility and adaptability, as well as by curiosity (if not by an overwhelming wish for knowledge), when it comes to addressing questions as vital as one's spiritual salvation or liberation from suffering, a straight line is sometimes very difficult to discover. It is therefore not surprising that similar ideas may have arisen at thousands of kilometers of distance; or that they may have tapped from one another, while concentrating more on the content, rather than the container. For, as an anonymous European mystic put it:

> A thousand miles would you run to speak with another who you knew really felt it, and yet when you got there, find yourself speechless.[27]

---

24. Cf. D. Snellgrove 1985, pp.1354-1359. See also Chou Yi-Liang 1945, Y. S. Hakeda 1967, A. Wayman 1973 and P. Williams 1989. S. G. Karmay (1988a, pp. 41-85) analyzes and translates three documents of Dunhuang, suggesting that they may be considered as "prototypes of the later literature of the rDzogs chen tradition". One of these texts, the *sBas pa'i rgum chung*, has also been edited by N. Namkhai (1984), who provides comments and explanations on specific terms found in the original text.

25. We refer in particular to the doctrine of the Basis-consciousness (Skr. ālaya-vijñāna) as developed within the Yogācāra school, which flourished in India during the fourth century A.D. Cf. discussion below, p. 52 et seq. See K. Mimaki 1982; L. Schmithausen 1987; P. Williams 1989, pp. 77-95; G. Dreyfus & C. Lindtner 1989; G. M. Nagao 1991a; G. M. Nagao 1992; K. Mimaki 1993. Cf. S. D. Ruegg 1980. The theory of the Basis-consciousness has been the object of close philosophical investigation by the well-known teacher and scholar Tsong kha pa Blo bzang Grags Pa (1357-1419) in his work *Yid dang kun gzhi'i dka' ba'i gnas rgya cher 'grel pa legs par bshad pa'i rgya mtsho*. This text has been translated and annotated by G. Sparham (1993). See also D. Snellgrove 1987, p. 398; S. G. Karmay 1988a, p. 178 et seq. Cf. D. Germano 1992, p. 5.

26. See. M. Eliade 1985.

27. See W. Johnston 1973, p. 183.

As far as the Old School (*rNying ma*) is concerned, it is maintained that these doctrines were first propounded by dGa' rab rDo rje, a son miraculously born to the virgin Princess-Bhikṣuṇī of Uḍḍiyāna, Sudharmā.[28] They were subsequently introduced in Tibet from India during the eighth century by the master Vimalamitra.[29] Then, through the intervention of the great master Padmasambhava, who is traditionally considered as the spiritual 'founder' of the Old School,[30] they were entrusted to his disciple Vairocana, who thus became the first lineage holder of the Great Perfection in Tibet.[31] Vairocana reportedly carried out translations into Tibetan of Bonpo works.[32] Moreover, he is said to have hidden some Bonpo texts of the 'Mind Class' (*sems phyogs*, i.e., *rdzogs chen*) before his forced departure from Central Tibet.[33]

---

28. There is no certainty as to when dGa' rab rDo rje actually lived. His name is known from at least the tenth century A.D., since it appears in Tibetan sources such as the *bSam gtan mig sgron* by gNubs chen Sangs rgyas Ye shes (for which see S. G. Karmay 1988a, *passim*). Detailed accounts about dGa' rab rDo rje and the propagation of his teachings are provided by Zhang ston bKra shis rDo rje (1097-1167)—for whom see S. G. Karmay 1988a, p. 209, n. 16 and p. 211—in his *rDzogs pa chen po snying thig gi lo rgyus chen mo*, p. 581 et seq. The historian dPa' bo gTsug lag Phreng ba (1504-1566) in his *Chos 'byung mkhas pa'i dga' ston*, op. cit., p. 565 et seq., states that dGa' rab rDo rje was born about three hundred and sixty years after the Nirvāṇa of Buddha Śākyamuni; (for a discussion about the dates of the Buddha's Nirvāṇa see H. Bechert 1991, pp. 1-23 and pp. 222-236 in particular). Cf. the preface of N. Namkhai to G. Orofino 1990, p. 5 (and the same in the original Italian edition of 1985, pp. 13-14). A. W. Hanson-Barber 1984, pp. 36-38, places dGa' rab rDo rje in the middle of the sixth century A.D. For an account of his life, see E. Dargyay 1977, pp. 19-20 and S. G. Karmay 1988a, p. 19. See also R. Prats 1978, pp. 200-201. For a brief discussion about the Indic original of his name, see D. Germano 1992, p. 4. For the term Uḍḍiyāna, see L. Chandra 1980 and G. Tucci 1980, p. 29.

29. For whom see G. Tucci 1949, p. 198, n. 159; p. 257; p. 381; and p. 611, n. 3; E. Dargyay 1977, *passim*; R. M. Davidson 1981, p. 9, n. 23; L. O. Gómez 1983; F. Faber 1985; F. Faber 1989. Cf. Tulku Thondup Rinpoche 1995, pp. 68-73.

30. For whom see e.g. G. C. Toussaint 1933; A.-M. Blondeau 1971 and 1985; S. G. Karmay 1988a, *passim*. See also U. Loseries 1989. For a traditional account of his life and deeds see T. Thondup Rinpoche 1995, pp. 74-108.

31. See R. Prats 1978, p. 204 et seq.; S. G. Karmay 1988a, pp. 17-37; S. G. Karmay 1985, pp. 272-282. See also E. Dargyay 1985, pp. 283-293. Cf. Tulku Thondup Rinpoche 1995, pp. 103-105.

32. Cf. S. G. Karmay 1972, p. 23.

33. Cf. S. G. Karmay 1972, p. 151. For a discussion about his exile to Eastern Tibet see S. G. Karmay 1988a, pp. 26-29. For the diffusion of the Great Perfection teachings in Tibet according to the Bon religion see below, p. 26 et seq.

It is not uncommon that certain spiritual beliefs may appear as doctrinally inadequate and become unacceptable to the leading forces of a given moment; that is even more so when those spiritual and temporal forces cooperate with each other, as has been the case for Tibet.[34] It has thus happened that both the Great Perfection and the Bon religion as a whole have been no exception to that rule.[35] To give just one example, sPyan snga ba Blo gros rGyal mtshan (1390-1448),[36] a contemporary of Tsong kha pa, did not hesitate in his small treatise about the classification of the *rNying ma pas* and the Bonpos[37] to dismiss their *rDzogs chen* doctrines and related works as carelessly conceived and deceptive,[38] being nothing else, in the case of the *rNying ma pas*, but the outcome of infamous ideas and banned practices expounded in the Mahāyoga *Tantras*, particularly the *gSang ba snying po* (Skt.

---

34. Cf. M. Lalou 1952; A. Macdonald 1971; R. A. Stein 1980; G. Uray 1983; S. G. Karmay 1981 and S. G. Karmay 1983.

35. See S. G. Karmay 1975b. Cf. M. Kapstein 1985.

36. For his dates see G. N. Roerich 1949, p. 317. Cf. L. W. J. van der Kuijp 1986, p. 203, where the dates given are 1402-1472.

37. *rNying ma dang bon gyi rnam gzhag, Collected works of sPyan snga ba Blo gros rGyal mtshan*, Ngawang Gelek Demo, New Delhi 1982, vol. 5, pp. 459-466.

38. *rdzogs chen a ma na se'i chos skor brdzus ma brtsams* / ibid., p. 464,3.

39. *rgyud gsang ba snying po kho na nges pa'i rgyud sogs bsgyur* / ibid., p. 460,3. On this *tantra* and the issue of banned doctrines see S. G. Karmay 1980a and 1980b; see also S. G. Karmay, 1988a, p. ix and pp. 139-140.

40. *rgyal po srong btsan sgam po yan bon med* / *de nas rang bzo byas bon byung* / *khri srong sde* [sic] *btsan dus su hwa shang bskrang kyang slob ma 'gas rdzogs chen brtsams* / *de la brkus nas bon gyis theg pa rim dgu brtsams* / ibid., p. 465,2-3. Cf. M. Lalou 1939, 1953; P. Demiéville 1952, 1970, 1973, 1979; Y. Imaeda 1975; R. Kimura 1981. See also PT 116, fols. 171,1-173,2 and fols. 186,4-187,4 in A. Spanien and Y. Imaeda 1979; S. G. Karmay 1988a, pp. 86-106. Traditional polemics surrounding the *rNying ma pas* and the Bonpos have been the object of quite an extensive and significant literary production. However this question is not elaborated here, since it is not immediately relevant to the doctrines studied. For a most interesting and detailed study concerning the traditional polemics that developed around the Bon religion, see D. Martin 1991. Cf. S. C. Das 1881. Misleading doctrinal identifications have also been attributed *a priori* to the Great Perfection. For example Giuseppe Tucci, following a Tibetan polemical tradition, assumed the presence of Chan elements in the *rDzogs pa chen po*. (See G. Tucci 1958, pp. 21, 45, 60 et seq.; cf. R. A. Stein 1971b and R. A. Stein 1972, p. 23, n. 3). However, on the basis of further research, Samten G. Karmay concluded that: "Even though in rDzogs-chen there may be parallel ideas and practices to those of the Chan, rDzogs-chen must be considered as of Indo-Tibetan origin whilst the tradition of

Guhyagarbha);[39] and in the case of the Bonpos, a self-fabricated system stolen from teachers whose theories had 'officially' been rejected since the time of King Khri srong lDe btsan (b. 742), such as those of Hwa shang (Chin. *he shang*, lit. monk) Mahāyāna.[40]

Chan in Tibet may be studied as an independent tradition." (See S. G. Karmay 1975a, p. 215). When addressing the same question, Per Kværne keenly observed: "Tucci, in spite of his repeated assertions (Tucci 1958, pp. 21, 45, 60) that Ch'an elements are to be found in Rdzogs-chen, nowhere demonstrates that these elements must necessarily, or even preferably, be interpreted as emanating from Ch'an." (See P. Kværne 1983, p. 384). Cf. B. Faure 1991.

THE BONPO GREAT PERFECTION LINEAGES AND THEIR TEXTUAL SOURCES

There are three main systems of transmission related to the teachings of the *rDzogs pa chen po* in the Bon religion. They are known as *A Khrid, rDzogs chen* and *sNyan rgyud*.

The teachings of the *A khrid*—instructions on the absolute state of knowledge symbolized by the letter A—were promulgated by the eleventh-century master rMe'u dGongs mdzod Ri khrod Chen po (1038-1096). They form a full meditative training originally consisting of eighty practice-sessions (*A khrid thun mtshams brgyad cu pa*) lasting two weeks each, which were later reduced to thirty by 'A zha Blo gros rGyal mtshan (1198-1263) and finally to fifteen by Bru chen (or Bru sgom) rGyal ba g.Yung drung (1242-1290), whereby they eventually became known as the *A Khrid thun mtshams bco lnga*.[41]

The system called *rDzogs chen* is based on a textual cycle known as the *rDzogs pa chen po yang rtse klong chen*,[42] which is related to another

---

41. See below, p. 34. Cf. S. G. Karmay 1977, pp. 111-112.

42. The cycle has been reproduced as the *Bla med rdzogs pa chen po yaṅ rtse kloṅ chen gyi khrid gźuṅ cha lag daṅ bcas pa'i gsuṅ pod*, Sherab Wangyal, TBMC, New Delhi, 1973, 2 vols. (hereafter *rDzogs pa chen po Yang rtse klong chen*). Cf. S. G. Karmay 1977, pp. 103-106; S. G. Karmay 1988a, pp. 201-202; P. Kværne 1974, p. 111 and p. 139; P. Kværne 1983, p. 369.

43. For whom see *infra* p. 40, *passim*. For iconographic description see P. Kværne 1995, pp. 25-26, 42-43, 63-64. The cycle has been reproduced as the *rDzogs pa chen po zab lam gnad kyi gdams pa bsgrags pa skor gsum ma bu cha lag daṅ bcas pa*, Patshang Lama Sonam Gyaltsen, TBMC, New Delhi, 1973 (hereafter *rDzogs chen bsGrags pa skor gsum*).

set of teaching traditionally ascribed to the earlier propagation of the doctrine (*snga dar*), i.e., that preceding the abolishment of Bon during the eighth century by King Khri srong lDe btsan.

This set of teachings is called the Three Proclamations, *bsGrags pa skor gsum*, because they were proclaimed in the realms of deities (*lha*), subterranean beings (*klu*) and humans (*mi*) by 'Chi med gTsug phud, an emanation of the deity gShen lha 'Od dkar.[43] They are considered to have been introduced in Zhang Zhung, from sTag gzig, by the master and scholar sNya chen Li shu sTag ring.[44] sNya chen Li shu sTag ring is said to have brought these teachings to Tibet during the eighth century and to have subsequently concealed them at the time of the persecution of Bon carried out during the reign of King Khri srong lDe bstan.[45] Both cycles were discovered by gZhod ston dNgos grub Grags pa, who is considered an incarnation of Li shu sTag ring.[46] He is said to have found them in the statue of Vairocana in the temple of Khom mthing in lHo brag.[47]

The *rDzogs chen yang rtse klong chen* cycle is concerned with expounding the Great Perfection tenets through epistemological and pragmatical means, while that of the Three Proclamations mainly deals with

---

44. Cf. P. Kværne 1971, paragraphs (31) p. 225, (49) p. 227 and (55) pp. 227-228; see also S. G. Karmay 1972, p. 4, n. 1 and pp. 20, 26, 56-57.

45. Cf. various references in S. G. Karmay 1972, and also dPal ldan Tshul khrims (1902-1973), *g.Yung drung bon gyi bstan 'byung*, op. cit., pp. 369-377.

46. The date of this textual discovery is uncertain. The Chronological Table of the sMan ri Abbot Nyi ma bsTan 'dzin (1813-1875), *Sangs rgyas kyi bstan rtsis ngo mtshar nor bu'i phreng*, gives the date 1088 (see P. Kværne 1971, p. 230, par. (87)). Cf. A.-M. Blondeau 1984, p. 89 et seq.; P. Kværne 1988, p. 242. See the *Sangs rgyas bstan pa spyi yi 'byung khung yid bzhin nor bu 'dod pa 'jo ba'i gter mdzod* by Rig 'dzin Kun grol Grags pa (b. 1700), p. 318,1-14; (for Kun grol Grags pa's year of birth cf. A.-M. Blondeau 1984, p. 109, n. 108, where 1718 and not 1700, as inferred from the Chronological Table of Nyi ma bsTan 'dzin, is suggested as being the correct date.) See also *g.Yung drung bon gyi bstan 'byung*, op. cit., pp. 201,5-204,5; S. G. Karmay 1972, pp. 154-156; S. G. Karmay 1977, p. 102; P. Kværne 1983, p. 369; S. G. Karmay 1988a, pp. 201-202, 220.

47. The discovery of both cycles, which is also known as the *lHo brag ma'i skor*, is classified as Central Treasure (*dBus gter*). For the threefold classification of Bonpo treasure texts (*gter ma*) see S. G. Karmay 1972, pp. 190-191. For a short description of the lineage holders, the reason for and the way in which the hiding of the Cycle of the Three Proclamations was carried out, see the colophon of the *Sems don sde bcu'i skor* (text listed in P. Kværne 1974 as K 111, B:6, p. 112, and in S. G. Karmay 1977, as no. 54 (B) 28, p. 101), *rDzogs chen bsGrags pa skor gsum*, pp. 474,2-475,6, and BKSR, vol. 109, pp. 131,1-132,4.

the theoretical aspects of the doctrine. Each Proclamation is divided into three parts styled *rgyud* (tantric teachings), *lung* (precepts) and *man ngag* (essential instructions).[48]

The third system is that of the Aural Lineage of Zhang Zhung (*zhang zhung snyan rgyud*). According to this system, the teachings of the Great Perfection originating from the Primordial Teacher (*ye nyid kyi ston pa*) Kun tu bZang po were mentally transmitted (*dgongs rgyud*) to 'the Nine Well-gone Ones' (*bder gshegs dgu*) and successively received by 'the Twenty-four Individuals' (*gang zag nyi shu rtsa bzhi*) of the kingdom of Zhang Zhung. Starting from the last of these twenty-four masters, Gyer spung sNang bzher sLod po (eighth century),[49] these teachings are said to have enjoyed uninterrupted single transmission (*gcig rgyud*) in Tibet at least until the time of sPa ston bsTan rgyal bZang po, who authored a compilation of the biographical accounts of the teachers of the Zhang Zhung Aural Transmission known as the *rDzogs pa chen po zhang zhung snyan rgyud kyi brgyud pa'i bla ma'i rnam thar*, *The Biographies of the Lineage Teachers of the Zhang Zhung Aural Transmission of the Great Perfection*.[50] An account of the lineages is found in the *History and Doctrines of Bon po Niṣpanna Yoga*.[51] The text relates that until the time of Gyer spungs the teachings of the Great Perfection were not shown in the form of letters but were aurally transmitted through words;[52] they were not suppressed, and therefore were not hidden as textual treasures.[53] According to Bonpo traditional accounts, through

---

48. For a list of texts pertaining to this cycle see S. G. Karmay 1977, pp. 100-103. Cf. P. Kværne 1974, Part Two, pp. 111-112. For the transmission lineage of the Three Proclamations and the biographies of related teachers see *g.Yung drung bon gyi bstan 'byung*, op. cit., vol. 2, pp. 369 et seq. For a discussion and analysis of these two cycles see A.-M. Blondeau 1984, pp. 109-118.

49. Cf. S. G. Karmay 1988a, p. 203.

50. S. G. Karmay (1972, p. 24, n. 4) states that sPa bsTan was a contemporary of Bru chen rGyal ba g.Yung drung (1242-1290). The work was written in the Earth-Pig Year, i.e., 1299 (according to S. G. Karmay 1977, p. 94) or 1419 (according to S. G. Karmay 1988a, p. 203 and p. 234).

51. *SPS*, vol. 73, New Delhi 1968, Section Ka, pp. 1-130. (the volume contains the whole cycle of the *Zhang zhung snyan rgyud* (hereafter *rDzogs pa chen po Zhang zhung snyan rgyud*).

52. Ibid., p. 26,1: *de ltar nyi shu rtsa bzhi ni / gong mas 'og ma la yi ge ris su ma bstan zhing / tshig gis snyan du brgyud de //*

53. Ibid., p. 30,5: *bon zhang zhung snyan rgyud gter du ma nub //*

his magical powers Gyer spungs sNang bzher sLod po was instrumental in negotiating the preservation of Bonpo texts from Zhang
Zhung when King Khri srong lDe btsan invaded that country.[54] The
cycle of the Zhang Zhung Aural transmission is considered to be very
old, if not the oldest, in terms of Great Perfection teachings in the Bon
religion. As to its written form, it doesn't seem to predate the eighth
century, if we are to accept the traditional dates for Gyer spungs sNang
bzher sLod po and the accounts contained in the *Biographies of the Lineage Teachers* by sPa ston bsTan rgyal bZang po.[55]

The cycle is organized into four sections, each dealing with a particular aspect of the teachings transmitted by the master Ta pi Hri tsa
to Gyer spungs. The first section is the external one, expounding the
philosophical view of the Great Perfection (*phyi lta ba spyi gcod*).[56] The
second section is the internal one and contains essential instructions
for the practice (*nang man ngag dmar khrid*). The third section is the
secret one, consisting of meditational instructions involving 'pure
awareness' (*gsang ba rig pa gcer mthong*). The fourth one is the very
secret section, and is focused on teachings meant to disclose the Way
of Being of the Ultimate Nature[57] (*yang gsang gnas lugs phug gcod*).[58]

Although not strictly pertaining to the three transmission lineages
of the Great Perfection, we have to mention two other important cycles
of teachings: the first is that of the *Ye khri mtha' sel*, also known as the
Indian cycle (*rgya gar gyi skor*). This is considered to be the work of the

---

54. See the *rDzogs pa chen po zhang zhung snyan rgyud kyi bon ma nub pa'i gtan tshigs*,
rDzogs pa chen po Zhang zhung snyan rgyud, section Pa, pp. 259-267, translated in D. L.
Snellgrove and H. Richardson 1968, p. 101 et seq. Cf. S. G. Karmay 1972, pp. 97-99.

55. The BKSR, vol. 110, pp. 328-380 contains a text entitled *rDzogs pa chen po zhang
zhung snyan rgyud kyi spyi don gsal ba'i sgron ma* by a Tshe dbang Rig 'dzin, which is
also a genealogy of the Zhang Zhung Aural Transmission teachers, and which seems
to have been written after the above-mentioned *Biographies* of sPa ston, given that
references are made to the latter's work (p. 380,6) as being one of the main sources
utilized by the author for his compilation. This text represents an interesting source
for comparative study.

56. The *rGyud bu chung bcu gnyis* which we have translated and critically edited belongs to this section. See p. 39, *passim*.

57. For these terms see below, p. 43, *passim*.

58. For a list of all the texts associated with the *Zhang zhung snyan rgyud* cycle found
in SPS vol. 73, see S. G. Karmay 1977, pp. 94-97. Cf. P. Kværne 1974, Part Two, pp.
109-111. See also T. Wangyal 1993, pp. 209-212.

eighth-century Zhang Zhung master Dran pa Nam mkha'.[59] These teachings were subsequently transmitted in the eleventh century by a miraculous apparition of Tshe dbang Rig 'dzin, the son of Dran pa Nam mkha', to Lung Bon (or Lung sgom) lHa gnyan (1088-1124 or 1112-1148).[60]

The second one is that of the *Byang chub sems gab pa dgu skor*, which belongs to a series of textual discoveries classified as Southern Treasure (*lHo gter*). The text was found at 'Bri mtshams mtha' dkar in 1017 by gShen chen Klu dga' (996-1035). The latter is traditionally considered as the paramount protagonist of the later diffusion (*phyi dar*) of Bonpo doctrines, which was mainly carried out by means of textual discoveries.[61] The *Byang chub sems gab pa dgu skor* belongs to the Peaceful State cycle (*zhi ba'i don skor*) of the *sPyi spungs Tantras*,[62] and it is considered as a fundamental text of the Bonpo Great Perfection,[63] although it still remains inedited, as do most of the above-mentioned works.

Treasure texts are very important in the Bonpo as well as the *rNying ma* traditions.[64] Reasons for hiding texts could depend on various circumstances: the time for transmission of certain teachings may not be

59. See P. Kværne 1971, par. (41), p. 226; various references in S. G. Karmay 1972; A.-M. Blondeau 1985, pp. 132-143. For the transmission lineage see the *sPyi rgyud ye khri mtha' sel gyi lo rgyus chen mo*, TBMC, Dolanji, n.d., pp. 759-815. For the whole cycle see BKSR, vol. 101. The *Ye khri mtha' sel* is included in the inventory of the Bonpo Canon by Nyi ma bsTan 'dzin (1813-1875)—cf. P. Kværne 1974, K 112, p. 112—as well as in that compiled by Kun grol Grags pa (b. 1700), section Cha, p. 223; but it is notably absent in the *dkar chag* of g.Yung drung Tshul khrims dBang grags, which was composed after that of Nyi ma bsTan 'dzin (cf. P. Kværne 1974, p. 22). See below, p. 32, n. 71.

60. For his dates, cf. P. Kværne 1971, par. (87), p. 230; S. G. Karmay 1972, p. 115, and S. G. Karmay 1977, p. 11.

61. See D. Martin 1991, pp. 224-305; P. Kværne 1971, par. (68), (72) and (75), p. 229; S. G. Karmay 1972, pp. 126 et seq. The *Gab pa dgu skor* has been published by TBMC in *po ti* form, New Delhi, 1967, fols. 1-87. It is listed in P. Kværne 1974, p. 111 as K 109, and in S. G. Karmay 1977, p. 99 as no. 52; it has been reprinted in the BKSR, vol. 99, pp. 10-96.

62. See the *Khro bo dbang chen ngo mtshar rgyas pa'i rnam bshad gsal ba'i sgron ma* by sKyabs ston Rin chen 'Od zer (b. 1353; cf. S. G. Karmay 1972, p. 126, n. 2, and S. G. Karmay 1977, p. 22), contained in the *sPyi spungs khro bo dbang chen gyi 'grel pa dang dbal phur spyi don nyi shu rtsa lnga'i 'grel pa*, Yongzin Sangyay Tenzin, TBMC, New Delhi, 1973; see also the *dkar chag* of Nyi ma bsTan 'dzin, p. 8. Cf. D. Martin 1994, p. 26, n. 99.

63. Cf. S. G. Karmay 1977, p. 99.

favourable; the spiritual conditions of the recipients may not be developed enough; the teachings and their propounders encounter the opposition of political forces. In the case of Bon, it is traditionally maintained that two persecutions have taken place, one at the time of King Gri Gum, and one during the reign of King Khri srong lDe bstan.[65] Some teachings are hidden so that they may be practised in the future and bring spiritual benefit, or also to insure that no corruption takes place after their first promulgation, so that they may preserve their authenticity. Treasure texts can be hidden in natural places (*sa gter*) and even in the mind of realized teachers (*dgongs gter*).[66]

The value attributed to textual treasures by the Bon religion is clearly reflected in their being included in the Bonpo Canon, which was systematized around the fifteenth century.[67] According to the nature of their content, they are grouped under the four canonical sections (*sde*) of *mDo*, *'Bum*, *rGyud* and *mDzod*. The last section contains the teachings of the Great Perfection.[68] This fourfold division is said to have been established by the Teacher gShen rab Mi bo che at the end of his

---

64. See e.g. J. Gyatso 1996. Cf. Tulku Thondup Rinpoche 1986.

65. See S. G. Karmay 1972, pp. xxxi-xxxiii; P. Kværne 1990a, p. 209.

66. Cf. S. G. Karmay 1975a, pp. 187-189.

67. See P. Kværne 1974; S. G. Karmay 1975a, pp. 187-190; S. G. Karmay 1990; P. Kværne 1996, pp. 140-143. Cf. M. Kapstein 1989. So far there have been two reprints of the Bonpo *bKa' 'gyur*, both carried out during the 1980s in Eastern Tibet (present Sichuan Province): the first one (1985) consists of 157 *po ti* volumes printed on cream-coloured paper and tied between red boards; the second one (1989) consists of 192 *po ti* volumes. The first reprint was supervised by g.Yung drung bsTan pa'i rGyal mtshan, also known as Bla ma A g.Yung (b. 1922 at Nyag rong rdzong khong, passed away in 1998); the second one by Bla ma Bon sleb Nam mkha' bsTan 'dzin from rTogs ldan monastery in A mdo rNga ba, and was sponsored by a businessman of the Hui Islamic minority converted to Bon. The Bonpo *bKa' 'gyur* and *brTen 'gyur* have been respectively republished under the supervision of sMon rgyal Lha sras Rinpoche and sPrul sKu bsTan pa'i Nyi ma, in 178 and 380 volumes. Cf. "*g.Yung drung bon gyi bka' 'gyur*", *Bon sgo*, Bon Cultural Centre, Dolanji, 1987, No. 1, pp. 24-34. Six reprints of the *bKa' 'gyur* are at present available in the West: two are preserved at the library of the Shang Shung Institute at Arcidosso, Italy (first and second reprint), one at the Centre d'Études Tibétaines in Paris (second reprint), one at the University of Oslo (second reprint), one at the Library of Congress (first reprint), one at the University of Washington, Seattle (second reprint). One set has also been acquired by the TBMC.

68. For the structure of the Bonpo Canon see P. Kværne 1974, Part One, pp. 23-27.

69. Cf. P. Kværne 1974, Part One, p. 24.

worldly existence.[69] It comprises the primary teachings and precepts belonging to the "Four Portals and the Treasury Counting as Fifth" (*sgo bzhi mdzod lnga*),[70] to the Nine Vehicles, and all the secondary ones.[71]

---

70. For which see D. Snellgrove 1967, pp. 16-19. See also the *'Dul ba gling grags, Sources for a History of Bon*, TBMC, Dolanji, 1972, p. 119,6.

71. At present four main catalogues of the Bonpo Canon are available: the first is the one compiled by Rig 'dzin Kun grol Grags pa (b. 1700), *Zab dang rgya che g.yung drung bon gyi bka' 'gyur dkar chag nyi ma 'bum gyi 'od zer* (Krung go'i Bod gyi Shes rig dPe skrun khang, Xining, 1993). The second is the work of Nyi ma bsTan 'dzin (1813-1875), *bKa' 'gyur brten 'gyur gyi sde can sgrigs tshul bstan pa'i me ro spar ba'i rlung g.yab bon gyi pad mo rgyas byed nyi 'od*, SPS, vol. 37, part II, New Delhi, 1965, for the study of which we refer to P. Kværne 1974. The most detailed one is that written by g.Yung drung Tshul khrims dBang grags (nineteenth century), *rGyal ba'i bka' dang bka' rten rmad 'byung dgos 'dod yid bzhin gter gyi bang mdzod la dkar chags* [sic] *blo'i tha ram bkrol byed 'phrul gyi lde mig* (Bod lJongs Shin hwa Par 'debs bZo grwa, Bod gsar ton yig <93>, no. 019, n.d.), which according to its colophon (p. 1390) was completed in the Iron-Dragon Male Year (*lcags pho 'brug*), probably 1880; the latest one, *g.Yung drung bon gyi bka' 'gyur glog par ma'i dkar chag*, Si khron Zhing chen Mi rigs Zhib 'jug su'o Bod kyi Rig gnas Zhib 'jug khang, 1985, was published when the late Bla ma A g.Yung undertook the first reprint of the Bonpo Canon. We shall note here that in their catalogues, Rig 'dzin Kun grol Grags pa and g.Yung drung Tshul khrims dBang grags refer to the *rGyud* and *mDzod* sections of the Canon as the Section of Formulas (*sngags sde*), and the Mind Section (*sems sde*) respectively.

WESTERN WORKS ON
THE GREAT PERFECTION IN THE BON RELIGION

The Great Perfection in the Old School has been the object of an important study carried out by Samten G. Karmay.[72] His scholarly work elucidates the matter in a very extensive and detailed fashion, both from an historical and a doctrinal viewpoint, and indeed represents a fundamental contribution towards the understanding of this Tibetan tradition. Quite a number of other scholarly studies dealing with the *rDzogs pa chen po* in the *rNying ma* tradition—as well as publications by contemporary Tibetan teachers and Western individuals that are to be considered as more practice-oriented—have come to light during the past twenty years.[73] On the contrary, research works about the Great Perfection in the Bon religion are to date very limited.[74]

In 1967, with the valuable assistance of the Bonpo master Lopon Tenzin Namdak (sLob dpon bsTan 'dzin rNam dag, b. 1926), David L. Snellgrove published *The Nine Ways of Bon*, which contains translated and edited excerpts from the *'Dus pa rin po che dri ma med pa gzi brjid rab tu 'bar ba'i mdo*, "The Precious Compendium, the Immaculate and Glorious Blazing Sūtra", in short referred to as "The Glorious" (*gZi*

---

72. S. G. Karmay 1988a.

73. As an example of how much this kind of literature is becoming popular in the West, one may refer to the numerous titles listed in one of the recent Snow Lion Publications catalogues, Ithaca, New York.

74. S. G. Karmay addresses the Great Perfection doctrines in the Bon religion in 1975a, pp. 213-215, and 1988a, pp. 201-205.

brjid).[75] This is the long-version biography of the teacher gShen rab Mi bo che, the expounder of the Everlasting Bon (*g.yung drung Bon*).[76] *The Nine Ways of Bon* represented the very first conscious attempt carried out in the West to let followers of the Bon religion speak for themselves. The work takes us through the Bonpo cosmological and doctrinal views that form the basis of the Nine Vehicles (*theg pa rim dgu*), the last of which is 'The Unsurpassable Supreme One' (*yang rtse bla med kyi theg pa*), namely the one that deals with *rDzogs chen*.[77] Through the relevant excerpts, we thus get an impression of what *rDzogs chen* for the Bonpos is about.

The first scholarly study strictly dealing with the Great Perfection in the Bon religion was undertaken by Per Kværne in 1973, "Bonpo Studies, the A Khrid System of Meditation", (Part One, *Kailash*, vol. I, no. 1, pp. 19-50 and Part Two, "The Essential Teachings of the A Khrid System", *Kailash*, vol. I, no. 4, pp. 248-332).[78] By analyzing this system, P. Kværne has provided precise and thorough historical and doctrinal references about one of the three main Bonpo systems and lineages of the *rDzogs pa chen po*, and has clarified how this system developed within an interactive environment that involved both Bonpo and *rNying ma pa* teachers.[79]

In 1990 Giacomella Orofino published *Sacred Teachings on Death and Liberation*,[80] a revised version of a research originally published in Italian,[81] which includes an annotated and commented translation of two

75. The text was orally transmitted to Blo ldan sNying po (b. 1360) by sTang chen dMu tsha Gyer med (eighth century; see S. G. Karmay 1972, p. 4, n. 1). Cf. the relevant section of the *gZi brjid* entitled *Bla med kyi theg pa'i don gtan la phab pa'i mdo*, in BKSR, vol. 4, pp. 111-144. It has been reproduced in twelve volumes by the Bonpo Foundation, New Delhi, 1967-1969, on the basis of a manuscript preserved at the monastery of bSam gling in Dolpo, Nepal, which was the source used by Lopon Tenzin Namdak and D. Snellgrove.

76. See D. Snellgrove 1967, pp. 3-9. P. Kværne (1986) has carried out a detailed analysis of the contents of the *gZi brjid*, concurrently with a study of a set of Bonpo paintings depicting the life of sTon pa gShen rab Mi bo che. See also R. A. Stein 1988, p. 43 et seq. and Tr. Sangye Tandar and R. Guard 1992.

77. See D. Snellgrove 1967, pp. 226-255.

78. The work has been revised by P. Kværne with the collaboration of T. Rikey, and published by the LTWA in 1996.

79. See op. cit., Part One, p. 23.

80. Prism press, Bridport.

81. *Insegnamenti tibetani su morte e liberazione*, Edizioni Mediterranee, Rome, 1985.

interesting excerpts, namely the sixth chapter of the *sGron ma drug gi gdams pa* and parts of the *'Chi rtags gsal ba'i sgron ma*. These excerpts contain spiritual precepts, the description of signs and psycho-physical experiences, ransom rituals and releasing methods related to death and the intermediate state after death (*bar do*), presented from the Great Perfection perspective of the Aural (*snyan*) and *rDzogs chen* transmissions.

In 1992 Jean-Luc Achard carried out an interesting monographic research about the practice of *thod rgal*[82] and its related teachings entitled *Le Pic des Visions: Étude sur deux techniques contemplatives de la Grande Perfection dans les traditions rNying-ma-pa et Bon-po*.[83] The work contains extensive translations and analyses of Bonpo textual material related but not limited to that esoteric practice.

Recently Anne Klein and the Bonpo Geshe Tenzin Wangyal (*dGe bshes bsTan 'dzin dBang rgyal*) have undertaken a study and carried out a full translation of the *gTan tshigs gal mdo rig pa'i tshad ma*, a work attributed to the eighth century master sNya chen Li shu sTag ring. The work in question was discovered, among other Bonpo texts, by the three Buddhists of gTsang, Sum pa dBang tshul (alias Sum pa Byang chub), 'Bre Tshul seng and gCer bu dBang phyug, at lHa sa g.yer pa, some time during the fifth *rab byung* (1267-1326). The text, organized in questions and answers, discusses the philosophy of the Great Perfection from the standpoint of logic (*mtshan nyid*).[84]

As far as not strictly scholarly works are concerned, we have to mention the *Bon po Dzogchen Teachings according to Lopon Tenzin Namdak* (transcribed and edited by John M. Reynolds, Bonpo Translation Project, Vidyadhara Publications, San Diego and Amsterdam, 1992), which contains an introduction to *rDzogs chen* and discussions about the position of the Great Perfection with respect to other Buddhist philosophical views.

---

82. For which see below, p. 68.

83. Diplôme de l'École Pratique des Hautes Études, Paris.

84. See S. G. Karmay 1972, p. 152, n. 2, and p. 311,4 et seq.; S. G. Karmay 1977, p. 142. Cf. the *bsTan pa'i rnam bshad dar rgyas gsal ba'i sgron ma* by sPa ston bsTan rgyal bZang po, p. 746,4-7 (the date of composition of this work is not certain; according to S. G. Karmay 1977, p. 117, no. 22, it could be either 1285 or 1345, while according to S. G. Karmay 1988a, p. 233, it was composed in 1405). The Chronology of Nyi ma bsTan 'dzin (1813-1875) compiled in 1842, *Sangs rgyas kyi bstan rtsis ngo mtshar nor bu'i phreng*, is silent about this discovery (see P. Kværne 1971). The text has been published in a collection entitled *Gal mdo*, TBMC, New Delhi, 1972, pp. 47-129, and is also found in *rDzogs chen Grags pa skor gsum*, op. cit., pp. 731-799, as *gTan tshigs nges pa'i gal mdo*.

Further, in 1993, two other works appeared. The first is *Heart Drops of Dharmakaya: Dzogchen Practice of the Bön Tradition* (edited by Richard Dixey with an Introduction by Per Kværne, Snow Lion Publications, Ithaca, New York). It consists of a translation and commentary by Lopon Tenzin Namdak of the *'Od gsal rdzogs pa chen po'i lam gyi rim pa khrid yig kun tu bzang po'i snying tig*, a text written by the Bonpo master Shar rdza bKra shis rGyal mtshan (1859-1934).[85] This publication is the first to be available to Western readers of an entire *rDzogs chen* text, and represents an interesting source of reference based on the oral Bonpo tradition. The same applies to *Wonders of the Natural Mind: The Essence of Dzogchen in the Native Bon Tradition of Tibet* (Station Hill, New York) by Geshe Tenzin Wangyal, which provides historical, philosophical and practical explanations about the Great Perfection based on the textual knowledge and personal experience of the author.

---

85. For his works see S. G. Karmay 1977, pp. 85, 171-183.

A FEW WORDS ON METHODOLOGY

Notwithstanding the distinctive value of the above-mentioned works, there is still need for a comprehensive study of the Great Perfection in the Bon religion. Until an interactive research is carried out on Bonpo and *rNying ma rDzogs chen* literature, many questions are bound to be left in a self-perfected state beyond answer—to paraphrase the doctrines we will be analyzing shortly—particularly with respect to the relevance, influence and 'liability' of the Bonpo Great Perfection doctrines vis-à-vis those embraced by the Old School. The amount of textual sources that remains to be investigated is quite vast, and the present work has no pretense of being exhaustive.[86] As a matter of fact, in embarking on this research, we have felt like Tibetan pilgrims who respectfully throw a little stone onto the heap of a mountain-pass while proclaiming the invincibility of the gods.

We have therefore decided that it was important and appropriate to present in the first place a descriptive analysis of the view of the Bonpo Great Perfection. After having identified textual sources that appeared to be most directly concerned with this view, we have tried to address the question of how its relevant doctrines could have been presented in a way that would have been not only comprehensive and intelligible but also exempt of prejudiced theoretical superimpositions.

---

86. In this respect we think that nowadays it is no longer admissible, from a general scholarly viewpoint, that the role of the Bon religion vis-à-vis the historical and religious developments in Tibet be underestimated or ignored. Hundreds of inedited Bonpo sources contained in the reprints of the Bonpo Canon presently accessible in the West await serious comparative study.

In that respect, we have chosen to avoid the use of Sanskrit equivalents for given Tibetan terms, preferring to render them word for word or to leave them in the Tibetan original.[87] We have also refrained from adopting hermeneutical stands that follow a trend in contemporary religious studies whereby Oriental doctrines are approached from an experiential viewpoint.[88] Such exercises can be very fascinating, but it also seems that they may result in another kind of cultural superimposition, where given doctrines are reformulated according to Western philosophical and psychological frames of reference, rather than being presented on their own terms.[89]

As a general remark, the sources examined appear to be quite technical in nature, notwithstanding the fact that they are for the most part written in verse. They are manuals where the metaphysical and the soteriological, the absolute and the particular, the macrocosmic and the microcosmic, the real and the ideal continuously coalesce, and such a characteristic makes their interpretation at times problematic. Their technical nature is also reflected in the usage of specific terms, all deeply interconnected, which are not merely descriptive, but represent the very core of the doctrine.[90] Many of these terms, which are found in both Bonpo and *rNying ma* literatures, are not new when considered from a broad *mahāyānic* philosophical perspective. But the meaning that they assume in the *rDzogs chen* context is, and this reformulation constitutes one of the fundamental traits of the Great Perfection doctrinal position. A 'correct' interpretation of those terms is virtually tantamount to the understanding of the doctrines under study.

---

87. Generally speaking, we do not think that using Sanskrit to render Tibetan doctrinal or philosophical terms when presenting a translation of a Tibetan source in a Western language is a philologically appropriate solution, although the terms in questions may well be Tibetan translations or interpretations of notions originally formulated in Sanskrit. We also think that such a solution reflects an Indocentric approach towards Tibetan textual materials purported by Western scholarship that does not always render justice to the sources in question. The fact remains that certain given notions or concepts are expressed in Tibetan sources in Tibetan and not in Sanskrit; an effort to translate directly should not therefore be considered worthless or less prestigious. Cf. S. D. Ruegg 1992.

88. Cf. J. Baldick 1989, p. 5 and D. Germano 1992, p. iv.

89. Cf. P. Kværne 1983, p. 385, n. 2; É. Lamotte 1988; R. Thurman 1988, and M. Kapstein 1988.

90. In this work 'technical' terms will be capitalized and hyphenated when translated in English, while terms kept in the Tibetan original will appear in italics.

Moreover, since we believe it necessary to let the sources speak for themselves, if some ground has to be provided for further comparative research, we have discussed and related those terms primarily to the context of the selected *rDzogs chen* textual materials in which they appear.

The remaining part of this Introduction is dedicated to a descriptive analysis of the philosophical view of the Great Perfection, based upon selected excerpts[91] and supported by information drawn from the living oral tradition, particularly from dPon slob 'Phrin las Nyi ma of the TBMC.[92] Further, we will propose a critical edition and translation of two inedited textual sources. We have deemed it useful to present them in their entirety because of the rather comprehensive way in which they elaborate upon the subject-matter, and because they are representative of the literary productions belonging to the respected textual categories of the uninterruptedly transmitted Word (*bka' ma*) and written treasures (*gter ma*).

The first text is *The Twelve Little Tantras from the Zhang Zhung Aural Transmission of the Great Perfection* (*rDzogs pa chen po zhang zhung snyan rgyud las rGyud bu chung bcu gnyis*).[93] The second is *The View which is like the Lion's Roar* (*lTa ba seng ge sgra bsgrags*); it belongs to the Lower of the Three Cycles of Proclamations of the Great Perfection, carried out in the Land of Subterranean Beings (*rDzogs chen bsGrags pa skor gsum, 'Og klu yul du bsgrags pa'i skor*).

The Twelve Little Tantras expounds the precepts of the Great Perfection from the defined setting of a supernatural field[94] through a well-known canonical pattern of question and answer.[95] Altogether, the 'cosmic setting' and the way in which the text presents notions such as those of the Three Bodies (*sku gsum*),[96] the fivefold aspect[97] of the Pure-

---

91. The textual appurtenance of the excerpts will be specified in due course during the presentation. Translations of the selected excerpts appearing in this Introduction will be preceded by the relevant transliteration.

92. His comments on specific terms and expressions appearing hereafter in the notes will be preceded by his name.

93. Hereafter The Twelve Little Tantras.

94. See pp. 81-85.

95. See pp. 85-89.

96. See pp. 129-131.

97. See pp. 99-101.

and-Perfect-Mind (*byang chub kyi sems*),[98] the five poisons (*dug lnga*) transcended as Five Wisdoms (*ye shes lnga*) and the Five Wisdoms themselves,[99] the fivefold representation of the essential points of the teachings as View (*lta ba*), Meditation (*sgom pa*), Conduct (*spyod pa*), Fruit (*'bras bu*) and Realization (*rtogs pa*),[100] of commitment (*dam tshig*) and empowerment (*dbang*),[101] as well as the rhetorical praise of the Great Perfection with respect to all forms of teachings, the classification of the latters[102] and the final invocation-dedication[103] would point to a definite acknowledgement of the tantric notions developed out of mainstream Mahāyāna Buddhism.[104]

The View which is like the Lion's Roar opens without any description of supernatural setting, but with a rather matter-of-fact declaration that the teachings therein contained were bestowed as a blessing by the Compassionate Teacher Kun tu bZang po gShen lha 'Od dkar.[105] It proceeds without further ado in claiming the extraordinariness and superiority of its precepts in terms of real efficaciousness—hence the choice of the metaphor of the lion, symbolizing power and nobility. The complexity of the Great Perfection's view is stressed all along within the text, but in fact this seems more an acknowledgement of the 'difficulty of simplicity' rather than an intended deterrent to the understanding of the doctrines at hand. The text guides the reader, in a very pedagogical way, through the fundamental postulates of Condition (*ngang*), (Ultimate) Nature (*rang bzhin*) and Identity (*bdag nyid*),[106] to that of the Basis of all (*kun gzhi*).[107] And even though it is gShen lha 'Od dkar himself who supposedly speaks in the first person and defines what and in which form he does or doesn't teach, one has the impression of being in the presence of a very human but certainly knowledgeable

---

98. For this term see below, p. 55.

99. See p. 97, n. 4 and p. 129.

100. See p. 137.

101. See p. 133.

102. See pp. 141, 153.

103. See p. 159.

104. Cf. D. Snellgrove 1985, p. 1359 et seq.

105. See p. 169.

106. For which see below, p. 58.

107. For these see below, p. 52, *passim*.

and accomplished instructor, who seems confident in the spiritual capacity of the pupils and provides them, in a simple and straightforward way, with the vital information that will finally allow them to plunge in the dimension of their quintessential being. The fact that the text does not openly refer to notions such as the distinctions of Bodies, Wisdoms and so on is meaningful; it could possibly indicate the character of the target audience, namely one that is not very concerned or does not indulge, either for reasons of education or tendency, in dogmatic speculations. Or also, that these notions are so much taken for granted that there is no need to refer to them at all. It might also be indicative of a point of time in the history of these doctrines when they were presented and practised just as they were formulated, without need for legitimizing superimpositions.[108]

Be that as it may, both texts appear as well structured and coherently devised. In expounding the view of the Great Perfection they reveal traits of universality and atemporality that seem to be shared by many Eastern and Western mystical traditions. In our opinion the view of the Great Perfection represents the culminating point of Tibetan religions in the interpretation of the imponderable Absolute, and deserves an inspiring place of honour within the scope of historico-religious studies.

---

108. For an analysis of the evolution of the *rDzogs chen sems sde* teachings into the more sophisticated and *Tantra*-oriented *sNying thig* system of the *rNying ma* tradition cf. D. Germano 1995.

Mt. Kailash, courtesy of Bya 'Phur Nam mkha' rGyal mtshan (1965-1995).

Do not go abroad. Return within yourself. In the inward man dwells truth. If you find that you are by nature mutable, transcend yourself. But remember in doing so that you must also transcend yourself even as a reasoning soul.

St. Augustine (354-430)[109]

109. "Noli fora ire, in te ipsum redi. In interiore homine habitat ueritas. Et si tuam naturam mutabilem inueneris, transcende et te ipsum. Sed memento, cum te transcendis, ratiocinantem animam te transcendere". *De Vera Religione*, XXXIX, 72, Corpus Christianorum *Series Latina*, vol. XXXII, Aurelii Augustini Opera, Pars IV, I, Turnholti, Typographi Brepols Editores Pontificii, 1962, p. 234. Translated in H. S. Burleigh 1968, p. 69.

THE PHILOSOPHICAL VIEW OF THE
GREAT PERFECTION IN THE BON RELIGION

The View (*lta ba*)

The expression *rdzogs pa chen po'i lta ba*, the View of the Great Perfection, obviously implies the literal connotation of theoretical view or philosophical way of seeing; but as will be shown through this presentation, this 'view' detaches itself from the common Buddhist connotation of theory or (wrong) view[110] to cover the whole gamut of doctrinal, metaphysical and soteriological principles pertaining to the Great Perfection.[111]

The first observation to be made is that the teachings of the Great Perfection are traditionally addressed to individuals who still live in a relative condition, where suffering is concretely experienced, but who are deemed to possess a superior capacity of understanding.[112] Therefore, instead of fostering mere speculative knowledge, the Great Perfection teachings, as they are expounded through the principles related to the Basis (*gzhi*),[113] concentrate uncompromisingly on assisting the individual to transcend the confusion and narrowness that characterize the relative condition, so that one's own Ultimate Nature (*rang*

---

110. Skr. *dṛishṭi*; cf. M. Monier-Williams 1986, p. 492.

111. Cf. The View which is like the Lion's Roar, section 'A, pp. 265-267. On the basis of such an understanding, we prefer not to circumscribe the characterization of this view as philosophical, metaphysical etc., but to refer to it as simply the View.

112. Cf. The View which is like the Lion's Roar, section Dza, p. 251.

113. See below, p. 52, *passim*.

bzhin), which is the self-perfected state of Enlightenment (*sangs rgyas pa*) existing as a potentiality in all beings, may be recognized. When these liberating means are applied through the Path (*lam*), the teachings are centred on actualizing the Awareness (*rig pa*)[114] that the source and the final point of all external and internal phenomena related to the condition of living beings is the unlimited and ineffable state of Reality (*Bon nyid*), which is one with one's own Ultimate Nature. When the teachings describe the Fruit (*'bras bu*), they imply the definitive 'return' to the state of Reality; and since that state is precisely one's intrinsically enlightened Nature, the Fruit is said to already be spontaneously accomplished.[115]

The Reality is called Great Perfection because it is not affected by the limitations that characterize all phenomena, such as their transitoriness, the causes that generate them, and the effects to which they are subjected. It cannot be defined as a meeting of opposite principles, nor as an alternation of forces. It is intrinsically non-dual (*gnyis med*). Therefore, it cannot be identified with the state transcending suffering (*mya ngan las 'das pa*) enjoyed by enlightened beings, nor with the state of transmigration (*'khor ba*), since it encompasses and at the same time transcends them both. It is not a state where distinction or choice is to be made between 'good' and 'bad'. Nor is it a state that can be approached and achieved in a gradual way, by going through successive stages of mental and physical practices.

---

114. On this term cf. G. Tucci 1980, p. 82; p. 264, n. 28.

115. On the question of the Buddha essence (Skr. *tathāgatagarbha*) see D. S. Ruegg 1969; cf. L. Schmithausen 1973; see also P. Williams 1989, pp. 95-115; S. G. Karmay 1988a, pp. 87-88.

116. See the *rDzogs chen bsGrags pa skor gsum*, pp. 278-282. Text listed as K 111, 5.iv = Nya (*lTa ba la shan sgron ma'i luṅ*) in P. Kværne 1974, p. 112, and as no. 54, 17 in S. G. Karmay 1977, p. 100.

117. Kun tu bZang po gShen lha 'Od dkar, see below, p. 49 et seq.

118. dPon slob 'Phrin las Nyi ma: it is not found nor accomplished through the views and practices of the lower eight Vehicles of Bon, although it comprises them. See below, pp. 46-48; cf. The View which is like the Lion's Roar, section Cha, p. 205.

119. dPon slob 'Phrin las Nyi ma: *gnas pa nyid* is an equivalent of *gnas lugs ji bzhin ma*, 'the Way of Being as it is.' For the latter term cf. p. 50 and p. 58.

120. dPon slob 'Phrin las Nyi ma: *bon dang gshen rab med* = *'khor ba dang 'das pa med*, "there is no transmigration nor state transcending suffering"; (gShen rab is representative of enlightened beings).

These ideas are expressed in the *lTa ba la shan sgron ma*, "The Lamp that Clarifies the View" (p. 278,4-7), a short *gter ma* belonging to the cycle of the Three Proclamations:[116]

> *rDzogs pa chen po kun gnas te /*
> *rang bzhin lhun rdzogs chen po nyid /*
> *rdzogs pa chen por ye nas gnas /*
> *thams cad rdzogs pa'i rang bzhin la /*
> *bzang ngan blangs dor gnyis su med /*
> *theg pa lam dang bsgam [sic] bsgrub rtsogs /*
> *rdzogs chen 'di la ngas ma bshad /*
> *rgyu 'bras gnyis su ngas ma bshad /*
> *skye shi med par lhun gyis gnas /*
> *gnas pa nyid la gnyis su med /*
> *des na bon dang gshen rab med /*
> *rgyu 'bras theg par btags pas nor /*
> *lta bas bltas pa 'khrul par snang /*
> *lam gyi rim pa ye nas med /*
> *nye lam bde rdzogs lam gyis [sic] mchog /*
> *'jug lta spyod bsrungs gnyis mi mnga' /*
> *bsgom dang blo yis the tshom med /*
> *des na rdzogs chen nam mkha'i klong //*

The Great Perfection abides (in) everything;
(it is) the great, spontaneously perfected Nature
(which) exists as Great Perfection from the origin.
As to (this Ultimate) Nature which is totally perfected,
(it) has no duality of acceptance (and) rejection, good (or) bad.
(Following) paths (and) vehicles, performing meditation:
I[117] have not proclaimed (that) the Great Perfection (consists) in this.[118]
I have not proclaimed (that it exists) as cause and effect.
It exists spontaneously without birth and death.
As to (that state of) being itself,[119] (it is) without duality;
therefore, (it) has no Bon nor *gShen rab*.[120]
(It is) erroneous to tie (it) to the vehicles of Cause and Fruit.[121]

---

121. In the classification of the Bonpo teachings into Nine Vehicles given by the *gZi brjid* (see D. Snellgrove 1967) and maintained in the group of treasure texts known as the Southern Treasure (*lHo gter*), the teachings of the Great Perfection are considered part of the Five Vehicles of the Fruit (*'bras bu'i theg pa*). See the *g.Yung drung bon gyi bstan 'byung*, op. cit., p. 393 et seq. Cf. S. G. Karmay 1975a, p. 213. On the other hand, the contemporary Bonpo Lama A lags Bon brgya (b. 1935) whom we have once interviewed (see D. Rossi 1994) never referred to the Great Perfection as being the Fifth Vehicle of the Fruit; that seems to be in line, at least from a philosophical standpoint, with the transcendental character of the Great Perfection teachings that we find confirmed in this excerpt.

Investigated through (a specific) view, (it) appears in (a) delusive (way).
From the beginning, (it) has no graduality of paths;
(it is) the best path, the direct path of perfection and bliss.
There is no view (to be) followed, nor conduct (to be) observed.[122]
There is no uncertainty (produced) by thoughts and meditation.[123]
Therefore, (it is) Great Perfection, (it is like) the Expanse of Space.[124]

Taken by itself, the affirmation that this absolute state cannot be found in meditation seems to go against and dismiss the whole range of endeavours that followers of lower Vehicles painstakingly undertake with the aim of reaching the much aspired state that transcends suffering (*mya ngan las 'das pa*). However, in the View of the Great Perfection, meditation is considered as a contingent state, a child's play,[125] because no matter how profound and accomplished that may be, it is nevertheless considered to imply the perception of a subject envisaging its object. Therefore, how can it be possible to actually transcend all suffering by using a means that constitutes the cause, or the emblem, so to speak, of all duality? "The Commentary to The View which is like the Lion's Roar" (*lTa ba seng ge sgra bsgrags kyi 'grel pa, rDzogs chen bsGrags pa skor gsum*, pp. 826,4-7, 827,3-7)[126] briefly describes the way in which the followers of what we can infer to be the Seventh Vehicle of the Fruit[127] endeavour to find the absolute state by practis-

---

122. dPon slob 'Phrin las Nyi ma: the View is the Condition of Kun tu bZang po (*kun tu bzang po'i ngang*, see below, p. 49). If one abides in that state, one's actions will be spontaneously consistent with it, without need for following specific rules such as those which are expected to be observed when one subscribes to the precepts expounded through the lower eight Vehicles. Cf. The Twelve Little Tantras, section Cha, p. 119.

123. That is to say, the state of the Great Perfection is not affected by thoughts nor by the experiences (*nyams*) that may arise through meditation practices. Cf. The Twelve Little Tantras, section Ca, pp. 115-117 and The View which is like the Lion's Roar, section Tsha, p. 245.

124. *nam mkha'i klong*. Depending on the context, the term *nam mkha'* can either be rendered as 'space' or as 'sky'. Cf. The Twelve Little Tantras, section Ja, p. 121. For other interpretations of the term *klong* see D. Snellgrove 1967, p. 262, n. 71 and G. Tucci 1980, p. 219. Cf. D. Germano 1992, p. 937.

125. Cf. The View which is like the Lions' Roar, section Tsha, p. 245.

126. Listed as K 111, section Na, 9 = 3. in P. Kværne 1974, p. 112, and as no. 54, 50 in S. G. Karmay 1977, p. 102.

127. The Vehicle of the White A (*a dkar gyi theg pa*), expounding *tantric* theories as well as meditative processes of transformation. Cf. D. Snellgrove 1967, pp. 170-189.

ing meditation on specific deities; how this view is still maintained in the Eighth Vehicle of the Fruit,[128] although it is approached from a more sophisticated standpoint; and how this view loses its validity when one has realized the 'true' state of meditation:

> *Theg pa 'og ma bas sngags phyi nang gi lugs ni sgom yod du 'dod /*
> *de yang dngos po mtshan ma rang du 'dod ta [*][129] /*
> *zhal yas dang gdan dang yi ge 'bru dang /*
> *sku dang rgyan dang cha lugs sgom pa'o /*
> *theg pa ye gshen pa yang klong du ma gyur bar du sgom du yod par 'dod /*
> *de yang dngos po mtshan ma mi sgom ste /*
> *zhi gnas dang lhag mthong cha mnyam pa de /*
> *ma yengs pa'i ting nge 'dzin gyi sgom pas sgom yod do /*
> *[...] sgom du yod pa'i dus tshod ni /*
> *ma rtogs pa'i dus dang /*
> *rtags [* read rtogs] par bya ba'i thabs kyi dus so /*
> *de la rtogs pa'i dus na sgom du med te [sic][130] /*
> *sgom mi sgom gyi bye brag mi shes pas /*
> *rtags [* read rtogs] pa klong du gyur ba'i dus na yang sgom du med de /*
> *bsgom bya'i yul dang sgom byed kyi blo gnyis ka ban [* read bon] nyid*
>   *dam sems nyid du shes pas so /*
> *yang sgom par bya ba'i yul pha rol na med par rtogs la /*
> *sgom par byed pa'i shes pa tshu ral [* read rol] na med par rtogs pa'i*
>   *sgom med do //*

Lower Vehicles (which follow) the system of outer and inner
    formulas maintain (that it) exists (in) meditation.
By (mentally) assuming the aspect (and) characteristics (of a
    certain deity),
(they) meditate (upon its) countenance, seat, seed-syllable,
body, ornaments and garments.
Also the followers (of) the Vehicle (of) the Primordial gShen
    maintain that

---

128. The Vehicle of the Primordial gShen (*ye gshen gyi theg pa*), explaining the importance of following a qualified teacher, finding the right partners and auspicious sites for meditative practices, the correct preparation of *maṇḍalas*, and the meditation practices involving the stages of Generation (*bskyed rim*) and Perfection (*rdzogs rim*). Cf. D. Snellgrove 1967, pp. 190-225.

129. We have to remark that the text in question appears to be quite corrupted: the vowels *e* and *o* are often absent, as in the cases marked by an asterisk (*) throughout this quotation; it might be a matter of scribal mistakes or of effacement due to time and use of the manuscript. In any case however, the correct affix of the gerund after a final *d* should be *de* and not *te*.

130. See n. 129 above.

as long as (it is) not realized, it is (found) in meditation, (although)
(they) do not meditate (upon) the aspect (and) characteristics (of a
certain deity).
(They say) it is (found in) meditation through the practice of
undistracted meditative absorption (which consists in) equaliz-
ing peaceful-abiding and superior seeing.[131]
When (it is said that) it is (found) in meditation,
it is (either) a method to foster realization
or lack of realization.
In that respect, when one has realized (it), it is not in meditation
since the difference between meditation (and) non-meditation is
not perceived;
also, when realization has fully matured, it is not (found) in meditation
(because) both the mind that performs meditation and the object
that is meditated (upon) are perceived as the Mind-itself,[132] the
Reality.
Moreover it is not (found in) meditation, when (one) realizes (that)
there is no object on one side to be meditated (upon),
(and) no consciousness on the other that performs meditation.

In practice, as said in "The Explanation of the Twelve Little Tantras"
(*rGyud bu chung bcu gnyis kyi don bstan pa*, pp. 187,6-188,1),[133] it is impossible to experience and perceive the absolute state by any other
means than that state itself:

Sems nyid mig dang 'dra ste gzhan gsal rang mi gsal /
rang la rang gis gsang pas rang gsang thabs kyis chod /
thabs gzhan 'khrul cing 'khor ba'i gnas su lhung //

The Mind-itself is like the eye, (without which) other (things)
cannot appear by themselves.
Since it is naturally concealed in itself, it can (only) be discovered
by (entering) its secret (nature).
Other ways are delusive and (make one) fall into the sphere of
transmigration.[134]

---

131. The practice of peaceful-abiding (*zhi gnas*) involves techniques of mental fixa-
tion, with or without an object, aimed at producing a calm state where thoughts are
kept at bay; when that state of calm becomes progressively stable and natural, it
evolves into that of superior seeing (*lhag mthong*), whereby one is able to meditate
without being disturbed by the arising of thoughts. See T. Namdak 1992, p. 78. Cf. G.
M. Nagao 1991b; L. O. Gómez 1983, p. 398.

132. For this term see below, p. 55, *passim*.

133. See the *rDzogs pa chen po Zhang zhung snyan rgyud*, section Cha, pp. 181-192.
Listed in P. Kværne 1974, p. 110 (K 108, 4 = Cha), and in S. G. Karmay 1977, p. 94 (no.
50, Cha.)

In the *lTa ba la shan sgron ma* (op. cit., p. 278,1) we also read that the teachings therein contained have been expounded by the Compassionate Teacher Kun tu bZang po. Instructions of this kind are traditionally not considered as mere verbal expression, but rather as expounded from the state of contemplation (*dgongs pa*),[135] which is referred to as the Condition of Kun tu bZang po (*kun tu bzang po'i ngang*), 'manifesting itself' on a supernatural plane in the form of deities such as gShen lha 'Od dkar. The latter is very often called the Compassionate Teacher (*thugs rje'i ston pa*) in the texts. dPon slob 'Phrin la Nyi ma informs us that the term *kun tu bzang po* can be interpreted as "*dus kun tu (kun tu) dri ma ma bgos pa (bzang po)*", "at all times wearing no stains", and that it refers to the Self-Originated Primordial Wisdom of the Basis (*gzhi'i rang 'byung ye shes*),[136] whereby it is also styled Kun tu bZang po of the Basis (*gzhi'i kun tu bzang po*). He also points out that the term *kun tu bzang po* is interpreted in a twofold way: "*gdags su med pa'i Kun tu bZang po*" and "*gdags su yod pa'i Kun tu bZang po*"; "*gdags su med pa'i Kun tu bZang po*", the inexpressible Kun tu bZang po, symbolizes the Body of Reality (*Bon sku*). The expressible Kun tu bZang po, "*gdags su yod pa'i Kun tu bZang po*", refers, as in the case of our texts, to deities or enlightened beings that are expressible in terms of their attributes and qualifications, such as gShen lha 'Od dkar and Ta pi Hri tsa.[137] These two figures respectively symbolize the Body of Perfection (*rDzogs pa'i sku*) and the Body of Emanation (*sPrul pa'i sku*).[138]

---

134. It is interesting to see how the same idea is expressed in the context of European medieval mysticism (see W. Johnston 1973, p. 92): "...Techniques and methods are ultimately useless for awakening contemplative love. It is futile to come to this work armed with them. For all good methods and means depend on it, while it alone depends on nothing."

135. Cf. the critical edition of the *rGyud bu chung bcu gnyis*, p. 86, 8-9.

136. See below, p. 59 et seq.

137. Ta pi Hri tsa or Ta pi Ra tsa, also called 'Od kyi Khye'u (see S. G. Karmay 1988a, p. 203), is the master who transmitted the teachings of the Great Perfection of the Zhang Zhung Aural Transmission to Gyer spungs sNang bzher sLod po (eighth century). For the former see the *rDzogs pa chen po zhang zhung snyan rgyud kyi brgyud pa'i bla ma rnam thar*, op. cit., pp. 26,5- 27,4, and relevant references in S. G. Karmay 1972. Tulku Thondup 1995, p. 82, contains an interesting statement in this respect: "Guru Rinpoche...even visited Zhangzhung, manifesting as the Tavihṛica [sic] ('Od kyi Khye'u), and taught *Dzogchen Nyen-gyü*, now known as one of the main teachings of Dzogpa Chenpo in the Bön religion..."

138. For the Three Bodies see The Twelve Little Tantras, section Na, pp. 129, 131. See also pp. 81-85, 85 n. 1. On the theory of the Three Bodies cf. e.g. G. M. Nagao 1991c.

The 'personification' of Kun tu bZang po is nevertheless to be understood in a purely symbolic way. Kun tu bZang po is the Primordial Teacher (*ye nyid kyi ston pa*)[139] because 'he' represents the Reality as well as the original recognition of Reality from the part of the individual, a recognition before which, it is said, nothing existed.[140] This Reality is called the Condition of the All-Good (*kun tu bzang po'i ngang*), because it encompasses everything without any selectivity, and because it exists in equality without any extreme or limitation. It is said to be devoid of inherent nature (*rang bzhin med pa*), but at the same time it is endowed with a dynamic potential (*rtsal*) whereby it can manifest itself in all sorts of ways.[141] It may be described through attributes—in order, for instance, to facilitate understanding by the ordinary intellect—but still it remains ineffable and inexplicable even to the Primordial Teacher himself.[142] This Reality exists from beginningless time. It is immutable. It cannot be forged, artificially obtained, manipulated, corrected or modified.

As to the doctrine which refers to this Reality, it is said:

Khyad par chen po'i gzhung /
dngos po'i gnas lugs /
bon thams cad rang bzhin ka dag ye nas sangs rgyas pa yin no //

The doctrine of the Great Difference
is the essential Way of Being,[143]
Primordial Enlightenment, the (Ultimate) Nature (of) all
    phenomena, pure from the beginning.[144]

It is called the doctrine of the Great Difference because of Kun tu bZang po's first realization of the Ultimate Nature of Reality. It is Kun tu bZang po's realization that makes the difference between perceiving everything as the self-perfected Reality, rather than as transmigration or as the state transcending suffering.[145] However, Kun tu bZang po is nothing else but the quintessential state of every individual:

---

139. Cf. The Twelve Little Tantras, p. 81.

140. See The View which is like the Lion's Roar, section Kha, p. 177. Cf. H. V. Guenther 1963; L. Hurvitz 1992-1993.

141. Cf. p. 51 et seq.

142. Cf. The Twelve Little Tantras, p. 143.

143. For the term *dngos po'i gnas lugs* cf. M. M. Broido 1980, pp. 59-66. Cf. D. Germano 1992, p. 15, where *gnas lugs* = abiding reality.

Kun tu bzang po ni rang gi byang chub sems so //

Kun tu bZang po is one's Pure-and-Perfect-Mind.[146]

The way of appearing of the Absolute Reality is also called the Great Manifestation or Great Play (*rol pa chen po*),[147] because all that manifests itself is understood as originating from the unobstructed dynamic potential (*rtsal*) of the Basis.[148] "The Commentary to the View which is like the Lion's Roar" (*lTa ba seng ge sgra bsgrags kyi 'grel pa*, op. cit., p. 821,2-6) specifies that:

Rol pa na [sic] *gnyis te /*
dag pa bon gyi nyid du rol pa dang /
ma dag pa 'khrul snang du rol pa'o /
de yang gzhi rtogs pa la rten nas /
dag pa bon nyid rol pa ni /
sku dang ye shes su shar te /
zhing khams bkod pa phun gsum [sic] *'thogs* [sic] *pa /*
mtshan dang dpe byed [sic][149] *che ba'i yon tan /*
ting nge 'dzin gyi yan lag brgyad cu dang /
'od zer spros bsdu 'jig rten gyi khams gang ba'o //

Manifestation is (of) two (kinds):
the pure (one), manifesting itself as Reality itself, and
the impure (one), manifesting itself as delusive appearance.
Based upon realization of the Basis,

---

144. *Man ngag 'khor ba dong sprugs*, in *rDzogs chen bsGrags pa skor gsum*, p. 673,6 (BKSR, vol. 109, p. 451,4). Listed in P. Kværne 1974 (K 111, B:10, p. 112), and in S. G. Karmay 1977 (no. 54, 45).

145. In our opinion, the expression *khyad par chen po* also entails the idea of the extraordinariness of the Great Perfection doctrine, which through its View allows direct understanding of the Ultimate Nature of Reality. Cf. The View which is like the Lion's Roar, pp. 197, 249.

146. For this term see below, p. 55. Quoted from the *g.Yung drung gsang ba dbang gi rgyud*, the first of the Six *Tantras* (*rGyud drug*) inaugurating the Middle Proclamation in the Land of Human Beings (*bar mi yul du bsgrags pa'i skor*), *rDzogs chen bsGrags pa skor gsum*, p. 422,5 (BKSR, vol. 109, chapter 9, p. 43,5). Text listed in P. Kværne 1974 (K 111, B: 5.i., p. 112), and in S. G. Karmay 1977 (no. 26.i., p. 101).

147. Cf. The View which is like the Lion's Roar, section Pha, p. 231.

148. For which see below, p. 52. In the words of dPon slob 'Phrin las Nyi ma, the Basis has the capacity of manifesting itself as all phenomena. This capacity is called *rtsal*. All that actually appears is called *rol pa*. Cf. T. Namdak 1992, p. 66, where the term *rtsal* is also said to denote the projections conjectured by the ordinary mind (*sems*).

149. The correct form is *byad*, not *byed*.

pure manifestation (as) Reality
arises as Body and Primordial Wisdom,[150]
(as) the perfectly laid out pure fields,[151]
(as) the great qualities (of those) displaying the signs and attributes,[152]
(as) the eighty components of meditative absorption,[153]
(as) the diffusion and retraction of light-rays filling the mundane
    sphere.[154]

Ma dag pa 'khrul snang du rol pa ni /
gnas pa'i sa gsum /
dgos pa'i grong khyer drug /
thun mongs du 'gro ba'i lam lnga /
skye ba'i gnas bzhi /
de la smin pa'i bye brag bzhi bcu rtsa cig ltar rol /
de ltar rol pa shar kyang gzhi'i ngo bor gcig go //

The impure (one), manifesting itself as delusive appearance,
(arises as) the three places of existence,[155]
the six cities of necessity,[156]
the five paths of ordinary beings[157] (and)
the four locations of birth,[158]
which in turn (appear) as the forty-one kinds of fully developed
    manifestation.[159]
Although manifestation arises in those ways, it is one in the
    essence of the Basis.

The Basis of All (*kun gzhi*)

The 'Basis' which is mentioned in the last quotation represents one of
the key notions of the Great Perfection doctrines. The term *kun gzhi* as
understood in that context has a different meaning when compared to
the one previously ascribed to the same term by the Indian Yogācāra

---

150. The Body of Reality (*bon sku*) where Primordial Wisdom (*ye shes*) arises in its
five essential connotations. Cf. The Twelve Little Tantras, section Na, p. 129.

151. Cf. The Twelve Little Tantras, section Na, p. 131.

152. The Wisdom Holders, said to abide at the level of the Body of Perfection (*rdzogs
sku*). Cf. The Twelve Little Tantras, section Na, p. 131.

153. The eighty components of meditative absorption are listed (as eighty-two) in
the *Srid pa'i mdzod phug* (for which see n. 157 below), BKSR, vol. 176, pp. 594,6-602,4,
and (as eighty-five) in the *gZi brjid*, BKSR, vol. 4 pp. 102,3-110; they are described in
their specific characteristics in the *Shes rab kyi pha rol tu phyin pa khams brgyad stong
phrag brgya pa*, (BKSR, vol. 57 (A), chap. 49, pp. 178,7-198,3), a *gter ma* revealed by

school. This philosophical school attributed the name *kun gzhi* (Skr. *ālaya*) to one of the eight kinds of consciousnesses (*rnam par shes pa*, Skr. *vijñāna*) with which it deemed sentient beings to be endowed. In particular the *ālaya-vijñāna*, or basis-consciousness, was thought to contain all sorts of imprints (*bag chags*, Skr. *vāsanā*) produced by causes and actions, and for that reason was considered impure. However, once karmic defilements were purified, this basis-consciousness was believed to disappear altogether to leave room, as it were, for the state of Enlightenment.

According to the View of the Bonpo Great Perfection, the Basis is not simply the container for karmic imprints (*bag chags*), but the receptacle and source of all phenomena of transmigration and the state transcending suffering; for this reason it is also called the Basis of all (*kun gyi gzhi* or simply *kun gzhi*). The Basis of all is the primordial condition which has always been pure (*ka dag*) and spontaneously accomplished (*lhun grub*). It is the source from which everything manifests itself. However, as a mirror impartially reflects all kinds of objects,

gShen chen Klu dga' (listed in P. Kværne 1974 as K 47, *Khams-brgyad gtan-la phab-pa'i 'bum*, pp. 102-103, and in S. G. Karmay 1977, no. 9, ii. 3., p. 8; published in 16 vols. by the TBMC, Dolanji, 1975; BKSR, vols. 42-57).

154. Light being the purest aspect of 'manifestation' at the worldly level.

155. The sphere of desire (*'dod khams*), the sphere of form (*gzugs khams*) and the sphere without form (*gzugs med khams*). Cf. The Twelve Little Tantras, p. 81, n. 5.

156. The six realms of transmigration.

157. The five paths stemming from the five poisons (*dug lnga*): desire (*'dod chags*), aversion (*zhe sdang*), stupidity (*gti mug*), pride (*nga rgyal*), and jealousy (*phrag dog*). Cf. the *bDen pa bon gyi mdzod sgo sgra 'grel 'phrul gyi lde mig*, short title *mDzod sgra 'grel*, p. 225 et seq. (see *mDzod phug: Basic Verses and Commentary*, the Yung Drung Bon Students' Committee, Benares, 1993). The *mDzod sgra 'grel* is a commentary to the *Srid pa'i mdzod phug* attributed to the eighth-century master Dran pa Nam mkha'. According to the Bon religion, the *mDzod phug* was originally translated from the Zhang Zhung language into Tibetan at the time of King Gri gum, and was concealed in the residence of the Zhang Zhung king at Dang ra khyung rdzong during the persecution of Bon carried out by King Gri gum. The discovery of this text is probably to be ascribed to rMa ston Jo lcam, alias rMa lCam me (twelfth century); see S. G. Karmay 1972, p. 8, n. 4; S. G. Karmay 1977, p. 1.

158. Womb (*mngal*), egg (*sgo nga*), heat and humidity (*drod gsher*) and supernatural (*rdzus*). Cf. H. A. Jäschke 1993, p. 29.

159. We were unable to trace any textual reference on the forty-one kinds of fully developed manifestation.

the Basis remains unaffected by the arising of all phenomena. That is why in the previous excerpt it is said that all manifestation is one in the essence of the Basis. It is important to note that the qualifications of the Basis are actually those of the quintessential state of the individual, taken from a macrocosmic perspective. The Basis has an unobstructed capacity of arising in all sorts of ways (*'byung rung ma 'gag pa*); the fact that appearances (*snang ba*) may be perceived as the state of transmigration or the state transcending suffering depends on the understanding of one's Ultimate Nature: if one's Nature is recognized in its essence, which is said to be pure and self-perfected from the origin, that recognition is Primordial Enlightenment (*ye sangs rgyas pa*), the Condition of Kun tu bZang po (*kun tu bzang po'i ngang*). Delusion (*'khrul pa*) and transmigration derive from lack of this recognition, from not acknowledging the mistaken way in which the inferior mind (*dman pa'i sems*) conceives itself and its environment. "The Explanation of the Twelve Little Tantras" (*rGyud bu chung bcu gnyis kyi don bstan pa*, op. cit., p. 182,2-5) elaborates this perspective as follows:

> *gZhi la spyi gcod rnam pa gsum /*
> *sangs gzhi 'khrul gzhi 'byung gzhi gsum /*
> *sangs gzhi ka dag chen po'o /*
> *'khrul gzhi bag chags sogs pa'i gzhi /*
> *'byung gzhi lhun grub lung ma bstan /*
> *'khor 'das kun gyi gzhi ru gyur /*
> *rtogs shing 'khrul te gnas skabs bon /*
> *sems ni rang bzhin 'od gsal la /*
> *rtogs pa'i shes rab skyes pa yis /*
> *rtogs pas kun bzang ye sangs rgyas /*
> *sems ni rang bzhin 'od gsal la /*
> *rtogs pa'i shes rab ma skyes pas /*
> *sems can 'khor bar ye nas 'khrul /*
> *de ma yin la der bzung pas /*
> *thag pa sbrul du 'khrul dang 'dra /*
> *gsum du bstan yang ngo bo gcig /*
> *dbyings chen gcig gis kun la khyab //*

---

160. *'byung gzhi.* Cf. H. A. Jäschke 1993, p. 398.

161. *lung ma bstan;* see BGTC, vol. 2, p. 2789. Cf. L. Chandra 1990, p. 1322, where *lung ma bstan = avyākṛita* (for which see M. Monier-Williams 1986, p. 112). According to T. Namdak 1992, p. 80, the expression *lung ma bstan* also refers to a very deep but at the same time dull and blank mental state that could be experienced during meditation practice, which is not characterized by clarity and awareness, as is the state of contemplation (*dgongs pa*). Cf. The Twelve Little Tantras, section Ca, p. 115.

As to the Basis, (it is) defined in three general ways:
the Basis (of) Enlightenment, the Basis (of) delusion, and the
   Source-Basis.[160]
The Basis (of) Enlightenment is the great primordial purity.
The Basis (of) delusion (is) the foundation of (karmic) imprints
   and so on.
The Source-Basis (is) neutral[161] and spontaneously accomplished.
Transmigration (and) the state transcending suffering occur in the
   Basis of all.
Realization and delusion (are) circumstantial phenomena.
As for the Mind, (its) Nature (is) Clear Light;[162] in this respect,
when the superior knowledge of realization is generated,
(that) realization is Primordial Enlightenment, Kun (tu) bZang (po).
As for the Mind, (its) Nature (is) Clear Light; in this respect,
when the superior knowledge of realization is not generated,
(that is) the original delusion (of) sentient beings (appearing) as
   transmigration.
When it is not that,[163] it is taken as the other,[164]
as (when) a rope is mistaken for a snake.[165]
Even if (the Basis) is explained as threefold, (its) essence (is) one.
(It is) the great, single Dimension[166] encompassing everything.

The Pure-and-Perfect-Mind (*byang chub kyi sems*)

When viewed with respect to living beings, this all-encompassing single
Dimension of the Basis is called the Mind-itself (*sems nyid*)[167] or the
Pure-and-Perfect-Mind (*byang chub kyi sems*). In Western translations

---

162. I.e., not hindered by conceptuality and unlimited in scope. Cf. The Twelve Little
Tantras, section Ka, p. 95, n. 1. On the connection between mind (*sems*) and clear
light (*'od gsal*) cf. G. Tucci 1980, pp. 63-67. See also below, p. 65.

163. dPon slob 'Phrin las Nyi ma: when it is not understood that that is the Way of
Being of the Great Perfection (*rdzogs pa chen po'i gnas lugs*).

164. dPon slob 'Phrin las Nyi ma: when the Nature of the Mind is not understood as
being Primordial Enlightenment, that lack of understanding results in the straying
and illusory state of transmigration.

165. For the rope-snake simile cf. G. M. Nagao 1991d, p. 67; A. Sharma 1997. See also
The View which is like the Lion's Roar, section Tha, p. 219.

166. *dbyings*. See below, p. 59 et seq.

167. We shall note here that when the term Mind-itself (*sems nyid*) is referred to enlightened beings, *sems* is replaced by the honorific *thugs* (*thugs nyid*), and would
seem to be better rendered by 'the very heart', or 'the heart itself'; see The Twelve
Little Tantras, section Ga, p. 103 and p. 145.

this last term is usually rendered by its Sanskrit equivalent, *bodhicitta*.[168] The *bodhicitta* to which *rDzogs chen* doctrines refer to is the 'absolute *bodhicitta*', one of the two kinds of *bodhicitta* that we find already asserted in early Mahāyāna Sūtras such as the *Saṃdhinirmocana*, and which basically indicates the state of Enlightenment.[169] The translation of the term *byang chub kyi sems* with Pure-and-Perfect-Mind is inspired by an explanation contained in *rDzogs pa chen po yang rtse klong chen gyi nges don* (p. 180, 4-5):[170]

> *Byang chub kyi sems de /*
> *byang ste stong nyid skye med ka dag tu gnas /*
> *chub ste snang ba 'gag med lhun grub tu gnas /*
> *sems nyid la gnyis snang dbyer med du gnas so //*

> The Pure-and-Perfect-Mind
> is pure (*byang*), (since it) exists as the primordial purity (of)
>   unborn emptiness;
> it is perfect (*chub*), (since it) exists as the spontaneous
>   accomplishment (of) unobstructed appearance.
> As to the Mind-itself, (it) exists as the inseparable display (of these) two.

Thus, as the passage shows, the Pure-and-Perfect-Mind is represented by the state of inseparability (*dbyer ba med pa*) or non-duality (*gnyis su med pa*) of unborn emptiness, which is primordially pure, and the unobstructed appearance of phenomena, which is spontaneously accomplished. This principle of non-duality of primordial purity and spontaneous accomplishment is a distinctive feature characterizing the View of the Great Perfection.[171] It is precisely through such non-dual modality that the Great Perfection postulates and acknowledges the ontological identity of the Ultimate Nature of living beings and the Reality (*bon nyid*). The *rDzogs pa chen po yang rtse klong chen gyi nges don* (op. cit., p. 179,1-2; 179,3-4; 179,4-180,1) asserts this principle of ontological identity by means of a threefold pattern involving an example (*dpe*), a token (*rtags*) and a meaning (*don*). The example is that of Space (*nam mkha'*); the token is that of the Mind-itself (*sems nyid*); the meaning is the state of Reality (*bon nyid*):

---

168. See e.g. S. G. Karmay 1988a, *passim*.

169. Cf. P. Williams 1989, pp. 197-204. The relative *bodhicitta* consists in the intention of reaching Enlightenment in order to save all sentient beings from suffering.

170. *rDzogs pa chen po Yang rtse klong chen*, op. cit., pp. 167-257. The text in question is listed in P. Kværne 1974, T 256, p. 139, and in S. G. Karmay 1977, no. 55, vol. II, 4, p. 104.

171. Cf. T. Namdak 1992, p. 47.

Nam mkha' stong pa'i ngang nas snang srid sna tshogs su snang /
bon nyid stong pa'i ngang nas bon can mtshan mar snang /
sems nyid stong pa'i ngang nas sems can sna tshogs su snang ngo //

From the empty Condition (of) Space, appearance (and) coming-
    into-being appear in various (ways);
from the empty Condition (of) Reality, phenomena appear with
    (their) characteristics;
from the empty Condition (of) the Mind-itself, sentient beings
    appear in (their) variety.

dPe nam mkha'i ngo bo mtshan mas stong pa bzhin /
don bon nyid kyi ngo bo yang zhen pas stong /
rtags sems nyid kyi ngo bo yang 'dzin rtog gis stong ngo //

Just as the essence of Space, the example, (is) empty in (terms of)
    characteristics,
also the essence of Reality, the meaning, (is) empty in (terms of)
    partiality;
likewise, the essence of the Mind-itself, the token, is empty in
    (terms of) conceptualization and grasping.

sNang srid thams cad nam mkha'i ngang du gnyis med /
bon can thams cad bon nyid kyi ngang du gnyis med /
sems can thams cad sems nyid kyi ngang du gnyis su med de /
des na bon nyid sems nyid nam mkha'i dbyings nyid gsum yang
    gnyis med gcig ste /
rang bzhin med pas stong nyid du gcig /
ma 'gags par 'phyar bas snang ba gcig /
tha dad med pas gnyis med du gcig pa'o //

Since there is no duality between the condition of Space (and) all
    appearance (and) coming-into-being;
(since) there is no duality between the condition of Reality (and) all
    phenomena;
(and since) there is no duality between the condition of the Mind-
    itself (and) all sentient beings,
thus, also the Dimension of Space, the Mind-itself (and) Reality are
    not two (but) one.
Since there is no (inherent) nature, (they are) one as emptiness.
Since (it) arises in an unobstructed way, (it is) one appearance.
Since (appearance and emptiness) are not distinguished, (they) are
    the same as non-duality.

The Pure-and-Perfect-Mind is empty, it is not generated by primary
or instrumental causes (*rgyu dang rkyen*); it cannot be substantially produced. It is primordially pure because from the origin it is not affected

by any sort of delusion and also because any delusion that may arise is spontaneously released.[172] The latter idea can be explained by comparing the arising and releasing of delusion to the arising and releasing of thoughts. When a virtuous, negative or neutral thought arises in our mind, we may follow it, judge, elaborate, translate it into physical actions and so on; but if we simply observe the arising thought and let it be, instead of following or judging it, that thought will eventually dissolve in our mind, since it is not provided with any ground for 'concretization' from its inception.

Although appearance (*snang ba*) as such is generated by causes and is consistent with specific individual perceptions, it represents nonetheless the unlimited way in which the Pure-and-Perfect-Mind may arise. Therefore all appearance is not considered as being completely non-existent in the View of the Great Perfection. Nonetheless, if one investigates appearance, no tangible essence can be produced, because appearance is inherently devoid of a substantiable nature (*rang bzhin med pa*). It has no inherent nature as the Pure-and-Perfect-Mind.[173]

The View of the Great Perfection further acknowledges the ontological identity of the macrocosmic and microcosmic realities through the threefold axiom of Condition (*ngang*), Ultimate Nature (*rang bzhin*) and Identity (*bdag nyid*). The Condition (*ngang*) is the Basis of all (*kun gzhi*)—primordially pure (*ka dag*) and not generated by primary and instrumental causes. It is the origin of all phenomena. The Ultimate Nature (*rang bzhin*) is said to be unaltered (*ma bcos pa*), because the Basis is spontaneously accomplished (*lhun grub*) in terms of its innate potential (*rtsal*) for manifestation (*rol pa*). The non-duality between the Ultimate Nature (i.e., the unaltered appearance of all phenomena) and the Condition (i.e., the Basis of all) is called the Identity (*bdag nyid*).[174] This *unicum* of primordial purity (*ka dag*) and spontaneous accomplishment (*lhun grub*) is the Way of Being (*gnas lugs*) of the Pure-and-Perfect-Mind.

---

172. Cf. The Twelve Little Tantras, section Nya, p. 125.

173. See the *rDzogs pa chen po yang rtse klong chen gyi nges don*, op. cit., pp. 175,1-182,1. Cf. The Twelve Little Tantras, section Ka, p. 95, and The View which is like the Lion's Roar, section Ma, p. 237.

174. Cf. The Twelve Little Tantras, section Nya, p. 123, and The View which is like the Lion's Roar, section Ka, p. 175.

175. For the term *dbyings* cf. G. Tucci 1958, p. 136; D. Snellgrove 1967, Glossary, p. 304; D. S. Ruegg 1971, p. 464, n. 71; P. Kværne 1973, p. 31; D. Germano 1992, pp. 109-

Dimension and Primordial Wisdom (*dbyings dang ye shes*)

Following the above-mentioned threefold axiom, the Basis of all is also referred to as the empty Dimension (*dbyings*)[175] where the Primordial Wisdom (*ye shes*) unfolds and abides. This pair of Dimension and Wisdom is a representation of the Pure-and-Perfect-Mind: the Mind is uniform, like Space (*nam mkha'*); it is unaltered, like the Dimension (*dbyings*) of Space; it is infinite, like the Expanse (*klong*) of Space. Space, Dimension and Expanse are notions used to exemplify the Mind-itself as the unbiased receptacle of its creative potential, just like the universe contains all existing phenomena. The Primordial Wisdom is said to represent the 'clear' or 'appearing aspect' (*gsal cha / snang cha*) of the Mind-itself, and is qualified as active (*g.yo ba*).[176] Let us see how "The Explanation of the Twelve Little Tantras" (*rGyud bu chung bcu gnyis kyi don bstan pa*, op. cit., pp. 185,3-6) elaborates the interrelation of Dimension and Primordial Wisdom:

> *dByings dang ye shes spyi gcod gnyis su bstan /*
> *dbyings ni kun la khyab ste phyogs ris bral /*
> *dbyings nyid rnam par dag ste glo bur dri ma bral /*
> *ngo bo stong par gnas te mtshon du med /*
> *dbyings nas thams cad 'byung ste mtshan ma med //*

> Dimension and Primordial Wisdom are explained in two general ways:
> the Dimension, encompassing everything, (is) without partiality (and) inclination.
> Being pure, the Dimension itself is without accidental defilements.
> Since (in) essence (it) exists as emptiness, (it is) without definition.
> Since the Dimension is (that) from (which) everything originates, (it is) without characterization.

> *Ye shes du mar bstan yang lnga ru 'dus /*
> *de yang bsdus na ci lta ji snyed do /*
> *ye shes ngo bo gsal ba ste /*
> *stong nyid ngang nas gsal bar mtshon /*
> *ngang gis stong pas dbyings zhes bya /*
> *rang bzhin gsal bas ye shes bya //*

---

113 and p. 882. A descriptive analysis of *dbyings* is found in the *mDzod sgra 'grel*, op. cit., pp. 80-91.

176. Cf. the Twelve Little Tantras, p. 83. See also *Sems dang ye shes kyi dri lan* in *Miscellaneous Writings (gSung thor bu) of Kun mkhyen Klong chen pa Dri med 'Od zer* (1308-1363), Sanje Dorje, New Delhi, 1973, vol. 1, pp. 377,2-393.

Primordial Wisdom is explained as manifold, and (is also)
    reduced to five;[177]
but when (one) draws (them all) together, there are (about)
    as many as (one may) conceive.
Primordial Wisdom is clear (in) essence,
(it) clearly comes forth from the Condition (of) emptiness.
Being naturally empty, (the Condition) is called Dimension;
Being clear, the (Ultimate) Nature is called Primordial Wisdom.

gNyis su med pas spros dang bral /
spros dang bral ba de nyid las /
rang bzhin gsal bas rang 'byung ye shes yin /
de ltar rtogs pas rang rig ye shes yin /
rnam rtog ngang gis dag pas mi rtog ye shes yin /
spros dang bral bas dbyings shes gnyis med do /
ngo bo gnyis med thig le nyag gcig go //

Being non-dual, (Dimension and Wisdom) (are) not diversified.[178]
When out of that non-diversification
(the Ultimate) Nature shines forth, (it) is the Self-Originated
    Primordial Wisdom.
The realization (that it is) in that way[179] is (called) the Primordial
    Wisdom of Self-Awareness;
naturally purified (from) conceptuality, (it) is the Non-conceptual
    Primordial Wisdom.
Being without diversification, Dimension and (Primordial) Wisdom
    do not exist (as a) duality.
The essence (is) non-dual, it is the Single Essence.[180]

---

177. Cf. The Twelve Little Tantras, section Na, p. 129.

178. For *spros pa* as equivalent of Skr. *prapañca* see M. Monier-Williams 1986, p. 681, F. Edgerton 1953, vol. II, Dictionary, p. 380 and also D. T. Suzuki 1934, p. 119. Cf. R. A. Stein 1983, p. 155, n. 15. D. Germano 1992, p. 864, translates *spros pa* with 'discursiveness'. According to dPon slob 'Phrin las Nyi ma, *spros pa = 'gul ba, g.yo ba*, to move, act, change, alter (cf. BGTC, vol. 1, p. 496), and when followed by *bral (spros bral)* = *mtshan ma* (Skr. *nimitta*, see M. Monier-Williams 1986, p. 551, F. Edgerton 1953, p. 297) *med pa*, without characterization, or also *nyon mongs med pa*, devoid of afflictions.

179. dPon slob 'Phrin las Nyi ma: the realization that the Dimension and the Self-Originated Primordial Wisdom exist inseparably. Cf. The View which is like the Lion's Roar, section Ba, p. 233.

180. *thig le nyag gcig*. This is a very frequent expression occurring in the texts of the Great Perfection (see The Twelve Little Tantras, *passim*). It is used in a poetical and laudatory way to denote the state of non-duality that characterizes the Basis or the Mind-itself. "The Explanation of the Twelve Little Tantras" (op. cit., p. 187, 1-2) interprets the expression *thig le nyag gcig* in the following way: "*Thig* is the Primordial Wisdom of Emptiness; *le* is the Dimension of Clarity; *nyag gcig* is (their) unification.

The Beginning of Transmigration

As we have seen, the Basis of all is the empty Dimension of Reality where the Self-Originated Primordial Wisdom abides. This Primordial Wisdom represents the state of Enlightenment (*sangs rgyas pa*), which is the ultimate, transcendental state of being. The Ultimate Nature and attributes of the Basis mirror, so to speak, those of the Mind-itself. They constitute the theoretical premise through which an individual is hooked to the Ultimate Nature of the Mind (*sems kyi rang bzhin*). When there is clear understanding of the View, this understanding is supposed to be integrated in every moment of one's existence, so that one may eventually realize one's full potential, which the texts define as that of Body (*sku*), Speech (*gsung*), Mind (*thugs*), Qualities (*yon tan*) and Activity (*phrin las*).[181]

dPon slob 'Phrin las Nyi ma specifies that with respect to an individual who follows the View of the Great Perfection, the Self-Originated Primordial Wisdom (*rang 'byung ye shes*) is also called 'the Clear Light which is the meaning' (*don gyi 'od gsal*), and it is styled the 'mother' (*ma*); the Primordial Wisdom of Self-Awareness (*rang rig pa'i ye shes*), which is the recognition of one's Ultimate Nature, is called 'the Clear Light which is the example' (*dpe'i 'od gsal*),[182] and it is styled the 'son' (*bu*).[183]

For people who have mastered the practice of contemplation, the actual recognition of one's Ultimate Nature occurs in the intermediate state after death (*bar do*), and it is thus compared to the encounter of 'mother' and 'child'.[184]

Thig is absence of birth; *le* is absence of interruption; *nyag gcig* is absence of birth and interruption. It is the non-dual Body of Reality, pure from the beginning." (*thig ni stong pa'i ye shes so / le ni gsal ba'i dbyings nyid do / nyag gcig gzung du 'jug pa'o / thig ni skye ba med pa'o / le ni 'gag pa med pa'o / nyag gcig skye 'gag gnyis med do / gnyis med bon sku ka dag go //*) *Thig le*, which means sphere, dot, and when used in modern Tibetan, zero, also represents the potentiality of the non-dual state, and as the form of the sphere suggests, it denotes infiniteness, lack of borders, perfection from within. It also has a strictly technical connotation inasmuch as it refers to spheres appearing as visions when certain practices are performed. See below, pp. 68-69. Cf. p. 217, n. 2.

181. Cf. The Twelve Little Tantras, section Kha, pp. 99, 101.

182. For a discussion of *dpe'i 'od gsal* and related notions in the Buddhist context see D. S. Ruegg 1966 n. 2, pp. 58-64. Cf. Tucci 1958, p. 60-64.

183. Cf. the View which is like the Lion's Roar, section Da, p. 223.

184. See R. A. Stein 1970; P. Kværne 1985; Sogyal Rinpoche 1994, p. 263 et seq.; G. Orofino 1990, *passim*. It is interesting to note the different ways in which the teachings of the intermediate state are classified in the *dkar chag* of Rig 'dzin Kun grol

This metaphor of the meeting of mother and child is quite an idyllic and vivid comparison: a child has immediate recognition of its mother and is never mistaken in that respect; through the perception of her presence, it experiences complete trust and security. If we view it in broader terms however, this metaphor in our opinion also entails a subtle implication. A child cannot remain a child forever. Eventually, it will have to find its own identity; it will have to discover 'the mother and son' that exist inseparably within itself. Awareness of one's own identity will then constitute the demarcating point between turning to the very source of happiness, or perpetrating attempts to seek happiness in the belief that it will be found outside oneself. If the individual realizes that his or her 'identity' is the state that in its emptiness and clarity exists in a non-dual and inseparable way, that will become the real emancipation, the state of true Enlightenment.[185] Without such an awareness, the individual will get lost in the delusive meanderings of particularization and dichotomy. According to the Great Perfection, such lack of awareness (*ma rig pa*) becomes the starting point of transmigration. As is said in the *Byang chub sems gab pa dgu bskor* (pp. 50,2-6):[186]

> gZha' tshon sgyu ma 'di la dpyad du med /
> sgyu mas sgyu ma bslus pas gzhan dbang mngon sprul thob /
> kun bzang ngang la ye med kun mnyam ste /
> 'khrul pa'i blo yi sgyu ma dang du blangs /
> gzung 'dzin sgyu ma de ni zo chu'i rgyun ma 'dra /
> bag chags de la zhen pas kun 'byung rang la shar /

Grags pa, Nyi ma bsTan 'dzin and g.Yung drung Tshul Khrims dBang grags: the first includes them in the Section of Formulas (*sNgags sde*, vol. Du, op. cit., p. 204, *Dam pa rang grol gyi zhi khro bar do thos grol*). The second considers them as *bKa' brten* or teachings that support the Word (cf. P. Kvaerne 1974, T 124, p. 123, *Bar do thos grol*). Also g.Yung drung Tshul Khrims includes them in the Section of Formulas; however, many titles referred to as *bar do* teachings appear in various volumes of the Mind Section (*Sems sde*) as well (op. cit., pp. 1158-1281). Such an occurrence seems justified, if nothing else, by the fact that during the *bar do* one is supposed to have the opportunity of concretely realizing the state of the Great Perfection.

185. Cf. The View which is like the Lion's Roar, section Pa, p. 229.

186. We have used a microfilmed reproduction of the text published by the TBMC, Dolanji, 1967, pp. 19-192, preserved at the Library of the Toyo Bunko, Tokyo. We hereby wish to express our gratitude to Mr. Y. Fukuda, Research Member of the Tibetan Seminar at the Toyo Bunko, for having kindly assisted us in obtaining this reproduction.

187. dPon slob 'Phrin las Nyi ma: the mirage of existence experienced by the ordinary mind.

kun 'byung rang la shar bas bdag dang gzhan du bzung /
'khrul pa de yis mnyam pa'i don la sgribs /
shes rab gsal bas 'khrul pa med par bya /
bdag dang gzhan du mi bzung kun 'byung bdag /
bag chags de la zhen pa'i zo chu'i rgyun ma bcad /
zo chu'i rgyud ma bcad pas sgyu ma brgyad du rtogs /
sgyu ma bslu ru med pas kun bzang ngang la mnyam //

This mirage[187] is indefinite[188] (like a) rainbow.
When mirage is deceived by mirage,[189] (that) results (in) manifest dependency.[190]
As for the Condition of Kun (tu) bzang (po), there is no (such thing from the) beginning, since it is totally equalized.[191]
The mirage of the deluded mind is acknowledged;
that mirage of grasping (and) grasped is like the flowing of water-buckets;[192]
since (one) is biased with respect to that imprint,[193] all (that) arises (seems) to come forth by itself.
Since all (that) arises (seems) to come forth by itself, (it is) conceived as self and other;[194]
through that delusion, the state of equality is obscured.
When superior knowledge shines forth, delusion is annihilated;
all (that) arises (is) the self, (it is) not conceived as self and other, (and)
the flowing of water-buckets of (one's) bias toward that imprint is discontinued.

---

188. dPon slob 'Phrin las Nyi ma: it cannot be defined since it does not possess any inherent or concrete nature.

189. dPon slob 'Phrin las Nyi ma: when the ordinary mind is caught by its delusions.

190. dPon slob 'Phrin las Nyi ma: the dependency of the mind with respect to the objects of its delusion.

191. dPon slob 'Phrin las Nyi ma: in the Condition of *Kun tu bZang po* everything is equalized inasmuch as it is perceived as being empty in nature.

192. *zo chu'i rgyun ma*. L. Chandra 1990, p. 2072 has *zo ba'i 'khrul 'khor = ghaṭi-yantra*. M. Monier-Williams 1986, p. 375 explains *ghaṭi-yantra* as "the buckets of the well or any machine for raising water", and compares it to *ara-ghaṭṭa*, which is described (p. 86) as "a wheel or machine for raising water from a well". Prof. Jan Nattier of Indiana University has kindly pointed out to me another interesting reference in F. Edgerton 1953, vol. 2, p. 162 in connection with the term *aupapādukāḥ* (Divy. 300.17: *aupapādukāḥ sattvā ghaṭiyantraprayogena cyavamānā upapadyamānāśca*), "falling and being reborn in the manner of a bucket-machine".

193. dPon slob 'Phrin las Nyi ma: the imprint of grasping and grasped.

194. About the notion of *bdag* and *gzhan* cf. e.g. T. J. F. Tillemans 1988.

When the chain of water-buckets is not severed, the mirage is
perceived as eightfold.[195]
Being not deceived (by) mirage(s), the Condition (of) Kun (tu)
bZang (po) (remains) equalized.

What is the 'genetic' cause that prevents recognition of the Ultimate Nature? According to the texts, it is the so-called 'non-awareness simultaneously born' with sentient beings (*lhan gcig skyes pa'i ma
rig pa*).[196] It is this non-awareness (*ma rig pa*) of the Way of Being of the
Basis/Mind-itself which consolidates into dichotomic perceptions and
makes sentient beings miserable, until they are taught about their
Nature and 'return' to it.

As it is said:[197]

gZhi yi gnas tshul gnyug ma'i bon /
ye sangs rgyas pa yin bzhin du /
de ma shes te ma rig rmongs
lhan gcig skyes pa'i ma rig pa'o /
de nas phyin ci log gi blo /
de ma thag tu myur la rags /
bdag dang bdag gis 'dzin cing ltas /
kun tu rtags (read *brtags*) *pa'i ma rig pa'o //*

The Manner of Being of the Basis, the pristine phenomenon,
is just Primordial Enlightenment;
that not being known, (one is) confused (by) non-awareness;
(this) is the non-awareness simultaneously born.
Then, the fallacious mind
suddenly and quickly gets coarse
by investigating and conceiving through the I and mine;
(this) is the non-awareness that defines everything.[198]

When viewed from the absolute standpoint of the Basis however,
this inherent non-awareness is an accidental (*glo bur*) phenomenon,
because even if one is overpowered by the limitations of the deluded
mind (*'khrul pa'i blo*), one is in fact never separated from one's Ultimate Nature.[199]

---

195. dPon slob 'Phrin las Nyi ma: the eight views of the lower Vehicles.

196. Cf. P. Kværne 1975, G. Tucci 1980, p. 65.

197. *g.Yung drung yang rtse gsang ba'i rgyud*, BKRS, vol. 106, p. 226,4-6. Text listed in
S. G. Karmay 1977 as no. 13, 6., p. 13. Reproduced in *Collected Tantras of Bon* by T.
Namdak, TBMC, New Delhi, 1972, 3 vols., vol. 3, pp. 90-99.

Turning Back to the Source

Kun gzhi stong pa rgyu med las /
sgra ni dbyings kyi rtsal du shar /
rig pa stong pa rgyu med las /
'od ni ye shes rtsal du shar /
dbyer med stong pa rgyu med las /
zer ni thig le'i rtsal du shar /
sgra 'od zer gsum rkyen byas nas /
ma rtogs lus ngag yid du 'khrul /
'bras bu khams gsum 'khor bar 'khyams //

From the Basis (of) all, empty (and) without cause,
sound, the dynamic potential of the Dimension, arises.
From the Awareness, empty (and) without cause,
light, the dynamic potential (of) Primordial Wisdom, appears.
From the inseparability, empty (and) without cause,
rays, the dynamic potential of the Essence, appear.
When sound, light and rays are taken (as) instrumental causes[200]
(that) ignorance (turns into) the delusion of body, speech (and) mind;
the result (is) wandering in the circle (of) the three spheres.[201]

As we can understand from this passage, sound, light and rays together represent the dynamic potential through which all circumstantial appearance, all phenomena come into being. When related to the
Basis, sound, light and rays are styled 'the spontaneously accomplished
sound, light and rays of the Basis' (*gzhi la lhun gyis grub pa'i sgra 'od zer
gsum*). When related to the perception of living beings, they are defined as 'the ordinary sound, light and rays arising through instrumental causes' (*'phral du rkyen gyis 'char ba'i sgra 'od zer gsum*). When
perceived during contemplative practices, they are called 'the sound,
light and rays arising as experiences on the path' (*lam rtags nyams la
'char ba'i sgra 'od zer gsum*). Finally, when their appearance is experienced in the intermediate state after death (*bar do*), they are 'the sound
light and rays appearing at the time of the intermediate state' (*bar do*

---

198. Cf. BGTC, vol. 1, p. 17, *kun tu brtags pa'i mtshan nyid.*

199. Cf. The View which is like the Lion's Roar, section Ca, p. 203.

200. dPon slob 'Phrin las Nyi ma: when they are not understood as being the innate
potential of the Mind-itself.

201. *rGyud bu chung bcu gnyis kyi don bstan pa*, op. cit., p. 186,1-2.

dus su 'char ba'i sgra 'od zer gsum).[202] The quality, if we may say so, of these three great appearances (*snang ba chen po gsum*)[203] is, once again, determined by the perception of the individual: if Reality appears as the above-mentioned delusion of body, speech and mind, as suffering and transmigration, that depends exclusively on the lack of recognition of the Way of Being of one's Ultimate Nature.

In this respect we will mention that the *'Khor lo bzhi sbrags* (*The Four Wheels Combined*), a text belonging to the cycle of the *rDzogs pa chen po Zhang zhung snyan rgyud*,[204] elaborates these notions by describing how the phenomenal and pure dimensions, as well as living creatures, their sensory and physical aggregates, passions and so on, come respectively into being from each of the five elements (*'byung ba lnga*), space, wind, fire, water and earth. The essence of the five elements is said to be light, which represents, as we have seen, the specific dynamic potential of Primordial Wisdom.[205] Further, the *'Khor lo bzhi sbrags* also contains a metaphor which we deem relevant to the present discussion; referring in passing to a 'King of Self-Knowledge' (*rang shes rig gi rgyal po*), the text states:[206]

> *sNang ba gsum dang /*
> *rang shes rig gi rgyal po zung du 'brel pas... //*

> The three appearances and
> the King of Self-Knowledge are interrelated...[207]

---

202. See the *rDzogs pa chen po zhang zhung snyan rgyud kyi spyi don gsal ba'i sgron ma* by Tshe dbang Rig 'dzin (cf. p. 29, n. 55), p. 365,2-4. This text is not included in *SPS* vol. 73, New Delhi, 1968 (cf. P. Kværne 1974, pp. 109-111), while it is reproduced in the BKSR (vol. 110, pp. 328-380).

203. This is how they are referred to in the *'Khor lo bzhi sbrags*, p. 451,1. See discussion below.

204. Op. cit., section Zha, pp. 449-464. Listed in P. Kværne 1974 as K 108, 8=Zha, p. 110, and in S. G. Karmay 1977 as no. 50, Zha, p. 96.

205. We shall note that the origin of the phenomenal world is also presented from an esoteric perspective recalling Great Perfection tenets in the *gSang mchog ma rgyud thugs rje nyi ma'i rgyud*, a *gter ma* revealed by Guru rNon rtse, alias A Ya Bon po lHa 'bum (b. 1136); see the *gZhi ye sangs rgyas pa'i rgyud*, the *Lam mngon sangs rgyas pa'i rgyud* and the *'Bras bu rdzogs sangs rgyas pa'i rgyud*—listed in P. Kværne 1974 as K 81, p. 107 and in S. G. Karmay 1977 as no. 21,ii, Ka, Kha and Ga, p. 19; published within the collection entitled *Ma rgyud sangs rgyas rgyud gsum rtsa 'grel*, TBMC, New Delhi, 1971. A study of the Mother *Tantras* in the Bon religion has been carried out by D. Martin (1994). Cf. S. Dietz 1988.

Tshe 'dir bla mas ngo sprad pas sgra 'od zer gsum rang snang yin par shes /
rang shes rig gi rgyal po'i gnas lugs mngon par shes so //

Having received the teacher's introduction during this life, one has
   the precognition (of) sound, light (and) rays as being one's (own)
   appearance,
(and) one has the precognition (of) the Way of Being of the King of
   Self-Knowledge.[208]

In our opinion, if we take *rang shes* in *rang shes rig gi rgyal po* as a
contraction of *rang snang yin par shes* (known as being one's own appearance), the expression 'King of Self-Knowledge' could also be interpreted as a condensed technical description of the Mind-itself, focused on Awareness as its inborn, determinant qualification.[209]

In order to be able to actualize the understanding of one's Ultimate
Nature, to become 'the King of Self-Knowledge', one has to be introduced by a qualified teacher to the principles of the View and integrate them with one's own existence by practising methods that will
allow one to acquire deeper and deeper familiarity with the state of
the Great Perfection. Without such integration, the mere knowledge
of one's Nature as being that of Primordial Enlightenment is quite
useless (*go mi chod pa*), particularly during the intermediate state, the
most crucial moment when one will have the opportunity to eventually perceive one's Nature and be released from the relative condition, or else fall back again into duality. As it is said:

Grol 'khrul gnyis kyi so mtshams ni bar do la thug pa'o //

It is in the intermediate state (that) the border between deliverance
   (and) delusion is reached.[210]

---

206. These are not all the instances where this expression appears in the text; we are
quoting the following ones as illustrative examples.

207. Op. cit., *gnas pa gzhi'i 'khor lo* (the Wheel of the abiding Basis), p. 451,3.

208. Op. cit., *bar do 'dus kyi 'khor lo* (the Wheel of the time of the intermediate state), p.
463,3-4. The knowledge of sound, light and rays originating from oneself, and that of
the Way of Being mentioned in this passage represent two of the six precognitions
(*mngon shes drug*) said to arise together with the six subsequent recollections (*rjes dran
drug*) during the intermediate state. Through these precognitions and recollections one
is supposed to reach deliverance; see op. cit., *bar do 'dus kyi 'khor lo*, p. 463, 2-5.

209. Cf. S. G. Karmay 1988a, pp. 203-205, and S. G. Karmay 1998.

210. *'Khor lo bzhi sbrags*, op. cit., p. 464,3.

The most important and distinctive practices reputed to promote real understanding of the state of the Great Perfection are those of *khregs chod* and *thod rgal*. The first is said to be practised in order to dissolve the rigidity of one's dualistic perception, and to learn to integrate one's Awareness with all aspects of one's life and being, without necessarily striving to perform any specially devised meditation or assuming any specific form of behaviour. The second implies, at least in its first stages, specific physical postures and ways of gazing; it is practised in order to overcome one's dualistic perception by concretely realizing the Ultimate Nature of the Mind-itself through the arising of visions;[211] the practice of *thod rgal* is also said to represent a preparation for dealing with the different manifestations that will appear during the intermediate state.[212] As a result of having performed these practices during one's lifetime, the *rDzogs chen pa*, the follower of the Great Perfection, should be able to achieve the Fruit of his or her realization after death. In particular, those individuals who are endowed with excellent spiritual capacity (*dbang po rab*) will attain liberation (*thar pa*) without having to go through the intermediate state.[213] They will show their realization in the form of the so-called rainbow body

---

211. Cf. S. G. Karmay 1988b, *passim*.

212. These two practices are undertaken after a preliminary training meant to achieve distinct perception between the way of functioning of the ordinary mind and the Mind-itself. Cf. T. Namdak 1992, pp. 69-84. A thorough mastery in the practice of *khregs chod* is required before one may approach and benefit from the practice of *thod rgal*; the former is traditionally recognized as being so determinant to the latter that it is said: *khregs ma chod na thod mi rgal*, "without cutting the rigidity there can be no transcendence". Cf. T. Namdak 1993, pp. 51-113, T. Wangyal 1993, pp. 164-174. See also J.-L. Achard 1992. For the terms *khregs chod* and *thod rgal* cf. D. S. Ruegg 1966, p. 76; J. May 1967; D. Snellgrove 1967, p. 139; R. A. Stein 1971, pp. 23-28; G. Tucci 1980, pp. 85-87, and p. 264, n. 31; S. G. Karmay 1972, p. 53, n. 1; P. Kværne 1973, p. 44, n. 9; E. Dargyay 1977, p. 217, n. 115 and p. 230, n. 374; S. G. Karmay 1988a, pp. 193, 213-214 and 215.

213. Cf. the 'Khor lo bzhi sbrags, op. cit., p. 462,4.

214. Cf. S. G. Karmay 1972, p. 53, n. 1; S. G. Karmay 1975b, p. 155; G. Tucci 1980, p. 86; N. Namkhai 1985, p. 1021-1022; S. G. Karmay 1988a, p. 190-196.

215. According to dPon slob 'Phrin las Nyi ma, hair and nails do not disappear because they are insensitive parts of the body (*tshor ba med pa*). Sogyal Rinpoche 1994, p. 168 says that: "...Only the hair and nails, the impurities of the body, are found." According to Western physiology, hair and nail are not considered to be living tissues because they do not contain any DNA. One of the most recent, publicly known examples of rainbow body in the Bonpo tradition is that of the famous master and

('*ja' lus*),[214] a process through which the aggregates of the physical body will progressively be reabsorbed into the essence of the five elements, that is to say light, so as to eventually disappear altogether, leaving only hair and nails behind.[215]

---

prolific scholar Shar rdza bKra shis rGyal mtshan (1859-1934). For a translated account of this event see T. Namdak 1993, pp. 26-29. Cf. S. G. Karmay 1972, p. xv-xvi and also BGTC, vol. 2, p. 3290. See also the '*Khor lo bzhi sbrags*, op. cit., pp. 462,4-464,3, and the *Bar do'i ngo sprod kyi gdams pa* in the *rDzogs pa chen po Yang rtse klong chen*, op. cit., pp. 667-725.

Part Two:

THE TWELVE LITTLE TANTRAS FROM THE ZHANG ZHUNG AURAL TRANSMISSION OF THE GREAT PERFECTION

NOTE TO THE CRITICAL EDITION OF THE
RGYUD BU CHUNG BCU GNYIS

The text used as the basis for this critical edition is that contained in the section marked with key-letter *Ca* in the *rDzogs pa chen po zhang zhung snyan rgyud, History and Doctrine of Bon-po Niṣpanna-Yoga*—a reproduction of a xylographic edition made from the blocks of sMan ri monastery, and published by Lokesh Chandra and Tenzin Namdak as vol. 73 of the Śatapiṭaka Series, International Academy of Indian Culture, New Delhi, 1968 (ff. 1-6, pp. 169-179; marginal title: *rGyud bu chung*; first folio, 1 line (title); second folio, 5 lines; remaining folios, 6 lines; *dbu chen* script).[1]

The text has been collated with:

+ the *rDzogs pa chen po zhang zhung snyan rgyud las rGyud bu chung bcu gnyis*, contained in the *rDzogs pa chen po zhang zhung snyan rgyud kyi gsung pod*,[2] (section marked with key-letter **Ca**, ff. 1-6, pp. 231-241; marginal title: *rGyud bu chung*; first folio, 1 line (title); second folio, 5 lines; remaining folios, 6 lines; *dbu chen* script);

---

1. The text is indexed in P. Kværne 1974 as K 108,4 = Ca, p. 110, and in S. G. Karmay 1977 as no. 50, Ca., p. 94.

2. According to dGe bshes rNam rgyal Nyi ma Brag dkar, who worked as a librarian at the TBMC from 1989 to 1995, the reproduction of this text in a single volume, as well as that of the *g.Yung drung bon gyi bka' dang bka' rten* (2 vols., see Note to the Critical Edition of the *lTa ba seng ge sgra bsgrags*, p. 165), was printed in India during the 1980s, through the support and sponsorship of the late Khyung po rTse drug mKhan po brTson 'grus rGyal mtshan, alias rTse drug Rinpoche (1914-1985).

♦ the *rDzogs pa chen po zhang zhung snyan rgyud kyi lta ba spyi gcod kyi rtsa ba'i glad don rGyud bu chung bcu gnyis,* contained in the first and second reprint of the Bonpo Canon[1] (section marked with key-letter Nga, ff. 1-9, pp. 98-106; marginal title: *sPyi gcod;* first folio, 1 line, recto (title), 5 lines, verso; ff. 2-8, 7 lines; folio 9, recto, 3 lines; *dbu med* script);

♦ the *g.Yung drung tshig rkang bcu gnyis,* contained in the *rDzogs pa chen po zhang zhung snyan rgyud* cycle, manuscript originating from Dolpo, Nepal, from the Snellgrove collection preserved at the British Library, Oriental and India Office Collections (ff. 1-10, no page numbering;[2] marginal title: *Tshig rkang;* first folio, 1 line, recto (title), 7 lines, verso; ff. 2-9, 8 lines; folio 10, recto, 4 lines; *dbu med* script).[3]

---

1. *mDzod sde* section, vol. 1/Ka and vol. 110 respectively. Both versions are identical, contextually and in terms of page and folio numbering. I am grateful to S. Meinheit of the Library of Congress for having provided me with a photostatic copy of the text of the first reprint, and to the library of the Shang Shung Institute, Italy, for that of the second.

2. Two folios are equally numbered as 6. In this critical edition the second folio no. 6 will be called 6 bis a/b.

3. I am grateful to P. Kværne for having put the relevant microfilm at my disposal.

LEGENDA:[1]

ZN 169,1:
ZN = *rDzogs pa chen po zhang zhung snyan rgyud*
169 = page number
1 = line number

SP 231:
SP = *rDzogs pa chen po zhang zhung snyan rgyud kyi gsung pod*
23 = page number

KS 98a:
KS = versions contained in the first and second reprint of
the Bonpo *bKa' 'gyur*
98 = page number
a/b = recto/verso

TK 1a:
TK = *g.Yung drung tshig rkang bcu gnyis*, text preserved at
the British Library
1 = page number
a/b = recto/verso

---

1. The *legenda* and the technical details related to the critical apparatus apply, with due differences in the abbreviations of texts names and page/folio numbers, to both the Twelve Little Tantras and the View which is like the Lion's Roar.

①	= line starting point in ZN
[231]	= page starting point in SP
{98a/b}	= folio recto/verso starting point in KS
(1a/b)	= folio recto/verso starting point in TK
> <	= in text addenda
{ }	= in text corrigenda
?	= unclear reading
om.	= omission, omitted
incl.	= inclusion, included
***	= missing
ego	= presumed reading reconstituted by us when the manuscript is unclear

Notes appearing in the Tibetan text are written in italics and are kept within parentheses in the main body of the critical edition. They are also written in italics but kept within square brackets in the translation.

Verses are separated by a double slash (//); differences in the separation of the verses among the various versions are reported in the notes.

Sentences that are too long to be kept on one line are split into two parts and do not carry any separation mark (//).

Verses are counted by five in both the critical edition and translation; the latter carries the page numbering of ZN, which was chosen as the basis for the critical edition.

When the syllables of a verse are contextually linked through a series of dots, or are treated as separate verses altogether, that will be reflected accordingly in note after the separation mark.

With respect to the translation, we have adopted a better reading in the critical edition whenever deemed suitable, indicating in the notes the readings of the texts examined.

All contracted/hidden words (*bsdus yig/skung yig*)[1] have been resolved in the transliteration. We would like to remark that whenever the *da log dra* sign (ᡆ) is used in place of the consonant-group -*gs*, the

---

1. For which cf. A. Csöma de Kőrös 1834; J. Bacot 1912; Nor brang O rgyan, *"Bod kyi skung yig gi rnam gzhag chung ngu"*, Bod rig pa'i ched rtsom gces bsdus, Bod ljongs Mi dmangs dPe skrun khang, Xining, 1987, pp. 413-483; R. Prats 1991; see also Namkha Gyal tsen (Cha-Phur), *Yig gzugs du ma'i ma phyi gzhon nu mdzas pa'i lang tsho*, Mu khri bTsan po'i Rig gzhung zhib 'jug khang, Bonpo Monastic Centre, Dolanji, 1994.

Tshig rkang bcu gnyis erroneously shows another *sa* written after that sign. Since reporting this orthographic peculiarity every time would have made the critical edition unnecessarily cumbersome, we have preferred to mention it here.

CRITICAL EDITION AND ANNOTATED TRANSLATION

ZN Ca 169,1,
SP Ca 231,
KS Nga 98a,[1]
TK Ja, 1a[2]

rDzogs pa chen po zhang zhung snyan rgyud las rgyud bu chung bcu gnyis bzhugs so / /

ZN 170,1,
SP 232,
KS 98b,
TK 1b

① [232] {98b} (1b)[3] zhang zhung smrar[4] gyi skad du na / /
ī[5] thi ku yig khri rtse u pa tan tra thad do ci / /
bod skad du / /
rdzogs pa chen po byang chub sems kyi gnad byang / /
thig le nyag gcig e ma ho / /   5

---

1. KS: rdzogs pa chen po zhang zhung snyan rgyud kyi lta ba spyi gcod kyi rtsa ba'i klad don rgyud bu chung bcu gnyis yod.

2. TK: g.yung drung tshig rkang bcu gnyis bzhugs s.ho.

3. KS and TK have a sort of *yi mgo* at this point.

4. smrar ZN, SP : smar KS, TK. See relevant note in the translation (p. 79, n. 2).

5. ī ZN, SP : i KS, TK.

(ZN 169,1) **The Twelve Little Tantras, from the Zhang Zhung Aural Transmission of the Great Perfection.**[1]

(ZN 170,1) In the language of Zhang Zhung *smrar*,[2]
İ thi ku yig khri rtse u pa tan tra thad do ci.[3]
In Tibetan, Great Perfection, the focal-point[4] of the Pure-and-Perfect-Mind.
Single Essence. *E ma ho!*[5]   5

---

1. KS: The Twelve Little Tantras, primary introduction to the general doctrine of the Zhang Zhung Aural Transmission of the Great Perfection. TK: The Twelve Everlasting Verses.

2. *smrar* or *smar* is one of the four main idioms of the Zhang Zhung language (Phug pa, Bar pa, sGo pa, i.e. Zhang Zhung sMar, and Phal pa). See the *sGra yi don sdeb snang gsal sgron me* by Zhu ston Nyi ma Grags pa (1616-1670), *Tibetan Żang Żung Dictionary*, Bonpo Association, Lahore Press, Jama Masjid, New Delhi, 1965, p. 6; cf. E. Haarh 1968, p. 9; see also the *Zhang bod kyi skad gnyis shan sbyar sgra yi rtogs brjod* (n.d.), compiled by sLob dPon Kun bzang Blo gros (present century) of g.Yung drung gling monastery, a work based on the *mDzod sgra 'grel* (op. cit.) and other sources, p. 122b2 et seq.; cf. R. A. Stein 1971, pp. 231-234. For other works on the Zhang Zhung language, see Bibliography under Chang, Hoffmann, Laufer, Orofino and Thomas. The term *smrar* (*smar*) is also considered the Zhang Zhung equivalent for the Tibetan *yag po, bzang po, legs po,* 'good', or 'well', and *phan thog po,* 'beneficial'.

3. dPon slob 'Phrin las Nyi ma: *İ thi* = *gsang ba*; *ku yig* = *bka'*; *khri rtse* = *'bras bu*; *u pa* = *man ngag*; *tan tra* = *rgyud*; *thad do ci* = *ces bya ba*, that is to say, the *Tantra* describing the secret instructions on the Fruit, quintessence of the Word (*don la bka' yi snying po 'bras bu man ngag ston pa'i rgyud ces bya ba bzhugs so*). The *Dictionary* of Nyi ma Grags pa, op. cit., has *i thi ya* = *gsang bar bya* (p. 20 last line); *khri rtse* = *'bras bu* (p. 9 line 6); *u pa* = *bka'* (p. 20, line 7); cf. S. Hummel 1974-1975, p. 503, where *u pa* = *man ngag*. For explanations on the particle *ci* and relevant references in Nyi ma Grags pa, see E. Haarh, op. cit., p. 23, "Vocabulary" p. 30; and for the closing particle *do*, ibidem, p. 21 and p. 35.

4. We understand *gnad byang* as *gnad ka*; see BGTC, vol. 2, p. 1536. On the meaning of *byang*, see J. Gyatso, "The Relic Text as Prophecy: The Semantic Drift of *Byang-bu* and its Appropriation in the Treasure Tradition", *TJ*, Rai Bahadur T. D. Densapa Commemorative Issue, n.d.

5. *E ma ho*, like *e ma* is an expression conveying wonder, joy, astonishment and surprise; cf. H. A. Jäschke 1993, p. 607.

ZN 170,2   kun tu¹ bzang po ② rang 'byung rig pa'i lha la phyag
'tshal lo //

1/² 'di skad bdag gis bstan³ pa'i dus cig⁴ na //
gnas 'og min bon nyid kyi dbyings na //

KS 99a   2/⁵ ye nyid kyi ston {99a} pa kun tu⁶ bzang po //
cir yang mtshon du⁷ dka' ste //   5

ZN 170,3,   gdod (2a) nas brjod med ③ chen por bzhugs so⁸ //
TK 2a   de'i ngang las⁹ //
thugs rje'i ston pa kun tu¹⁰ bzang po //
thugs rje¹¹ kun la snyoms¹² par bzhugs so¹³ //

---

1. tu ZN, SP : du KS, TK

2. 1/ ZN, SP, TK : om. KS

3. bstan ZN, SP : ston KS : stan TK

4. cig ZN, SP, TK : gcig KS

5. 2/ ZN, SP, TK : om. KS

6. tu ZN, SP : du KS, TK

7. du incl. ZN, SP, KS : om. TK

8. so ZN, SP, KS : swo TK

9. de'i ngang las incl. ZN, SP, TK : om. KS

10. tu ZN, SP : du KS, TK

11. rje ZN, SP, TK : rjes KS

12. snyoms ZN, SP : khyab KS

13. so ZN, SP : s.ho KS, TK

(ZN 170,2)   Homage to Kun tu bZang po, the deity of Self-Originated
Awareness![1]

1.[2] With these words I[3] expressed myself at one time[4]
in *'Og min*,[5] the Dimension of Reality.

2. The Primordial Teacher Kun tu bZang po,
difficult to be defined in whatever way,   5
(ZN 170,3)   abides from the origin in (the state of) great ineffability.
From the Condition of That,
the Compassionate Teacher Kun tu bZang po
equally extends (his) compassion towards all.

---

1. This is the deity gShen lha 'Od dkar, appearing and teaching at the level of the
Body of Perfection (*rDzogs sku*). For a description, see e.g. the *sDong po dgu 'dus lta
ba'i rgyud chen*, a text related to the cycle of the *Byang sems gab pa dgu skor*; BKSR, vol.
99, p. 98a5-98b2 (text listed in P. Kværne 1974 as K 109, 3., p. 111).

2. Three out of the four versions examined (ZN, SP, TK) maintain the numbering '1.'
for this passage (cf. critical edition, p. 80, line 2), '2.' for the following one (p. 80, line
4), '3.' for the one introducing the request for instructions by gShen Tshad med 'Od
ldan (p. 84, line 6), and then '2.' again for the passage where gShen lha 'Od dkar
answers the petition of gShen Tshad med 'Od ldan (p. 86, line 7). It seems logical to
consider paragraph '1.' as connected with the fourth of the above-mentioned paragraphs numbered '2.', while the first 'no. 2.' and 'no. 3.' would rather appear as supplementary, inasmuch as they provide details about the underlying spatio-temporal
circumstances leading to the exposition of these precepts.

3. That is to say gShen lha 'Od dkar.

4. See critical edition, p. 80, line 2. This is an unusual opening when compared with
those contained in Buddhist texts. Cf. J. Brough 1950; see also J. Silk 1989. For another example of unusual opening cf. the *sDong po dgu 'dus lta ba'i rgyud chen*, op. cit.,
p. 98a3: "'*di skad ston pas gsung pa'i dus cig na...*" (at one time when the Teacher spoke
these words).

5. gShen lha 'Od dkar is said to reside at the level of the Body of Perfection in the
divine 'Og min palace (*'og min lha'i pho brang du rdzogs sku gshen lha 'od dkar*; cf. *'Dus
pa rin po che'i rgyud zer mig*, Bonpo Foundation, New Delhi, 1965, (*po ti*), p. 505,2).

thugs nyid ma g.yos pa'i ngang las[1] //
g.yo ba ye shes[2] kyi cho 'phrul du //
ZN 170,4   sems can gzhan la ④ tshad med pa'i snying rje[3] shar ro //
tshad med pa'i snying rje des //
sems can thams cad la phyogs dang ris med par
khyab par[4] gyur[5] to[6] //[7]   5
snying rje de nyid thugs rje'i bdag nyid du
sangs rgyas pa'i rtags su //
sprul pa'i ston pa gshen lha 'od dkar //[8]
ZN 170,5   ⑤ chu zla'i dkyil 'khor ltar gsal la 'tsher ba //
sku snang la rang bzhin med pa //
mtshan dang dpe byad yongs su rdzogs pa //   10
'khor dang zhing khams dang bcas par gyur te //

Bon po cosmology parallels the Buddhist one as to the classification of existence into three spheres: the sphere of desire (*'dod khams*, Skr. *kāmadhātu*), the sphere of form (*gzugs khams*, Skr. *rūpadhātu*) and that without form (*gzugs med khams*, Skr. *arūpadhātu*). The heaven 'Og min (Skr. *Akaniṣṭha*), located in the sphere of form, is considered as a plane where one is reborn in order to purify the most subtle obscurations of consciousness (cf. T. Namdak 1992, p. 10-11). For a description of the three spheres according to the Bon po tradition, see the *Srid pa las kyi gting zlog gi rtsa rgyud kun gsal nyi zer sgron ma*, a text attributed to Dran pa Nam mkha' (eighth century) and revealed by Bra bo sGom nyag (thirteenth century; cf. S. G. Karmay 1972, p. 16, n. 3, p. 191), g.Yung drung rGyal mtshan, New Delhi, (about 1965), fol. 35,3 et seq. Cf. Y. Ishihama and Y. Fukuda 1989, pp. 156-161; M. Ishikawa 1990, p. 121; F. Edgerton 1953, vol. 2, Dictionary, p. 270; T. Rikey and A. Ruskin 1992, p. 116 et seq.

1. las ZN, SP, TK : nas KS

2. ye shes incl. ZN, SP, KS : >ye shes< TK

3. rje ZN, SP, KS : brje TK

4. khyab par incl. TK : om. ZN, SP, KS

5. gyur ZN, SP : 'gyur KS, TK

6. to ZN, SP, TK : ro KS

7. up to this point, rkyang shad ZN, SP, TK : nyis shad KS

8. tsheg ZN : ... SP : rkyang shad KS, TK

From the Condition of the immovable Mind-itself,
as the miracle of active Primordial Wisdom,
(ZN 170,4)   immeasurable loving kindness shines forth for other beings.
That immeasurable loving kindness
encompasses all sentient beings without partiality or
   inclination.   5
That very loving kindness, which is the texture of
   compassion, the token of Enlightenment,
(took the form of) the Emanated Teacher gShen lha
   'Od dkar;
(ZN 170,5)   shining clearly like the moon disk (reflected in) water,
(his) bodily appearance has no (inherent) nature;
fully perfected (in) signs and attributes,   10
(he) revealed himself with (his) retinue and (his) pure
   field.

de'i thugs rje'i[1] 'od zer las //

ZN 171,1, SP 233   thugs rje ma 'gags[2] pa'i ① [233] rtsal du //

TK 2b   rig pa 'od kyi khye'u (2b) chung zhes kyang[3] bya //

KS 99b   [4]gshen tshad med 'od ldan zhes bya ba {99b} byung
ste[5] //[6]

ye ci[7] bzhin ma'i sangs rgyas rig pa rang snang can
dang thabs cig[8] tu[9] bzhugs so[10] //[11]   5

3/[12] de'i tshe (*cir yang sprul pa'i ston pa*)[13] gshen tshad
med 'od ldan gyis //

ZN 171,2   ② ston pa la bla na med pa'i mchod pa phul te //
thugs kyi[14] mdzod bskul[15] nas zhus pa //

---

1. rje'i ZN, SP, TK : rjes'i KS

2. 'gags ZN, SP, TK : 'gag KS

3. kyang ZN, SP : dang KS, TK

4. TK has >Kha< (dbu chen) written above gshen.

5. TK has spyir (sic) yang sprul pa'i ston pa here, with >Ka< (dbu chen) written
above yang. See below, n. 13.

6. rkyang shad ZN, SP, KS : nyis shad TK

7. ci ZN, SP, KS : ji TK

8. cig ZN, SP : gcig KS, TK

9. tu ZN, SP : du KS, TK

10. so ZN, SP, KS : swo TK

11. rkyang shad ZN, SP : nyis shad KS, TK

12. 3/ ZN, SP, TK : om. KS

13. (*cir yang sprul pa'i ston pa*) ZN, SP : om. KS : (*spyir yang sprul pa'i ston pa*) TK

14. kyi ZN, SP, KS : gyi TK

15. bskul ZN, SP, KS : skul TK

From the rays of his compassion,

(ZN 171,1)   as the potential of unobstructed compassion,

gShen Tshad med 'Od ldan,

also called Rig pa 'Od kyi Khye'u chung, appeared;

(he) abides as one

with the Primordially Enlightened One, endowed with

self-seeing Awareness.[1]   5

3. At that time gShen Tshad med 'Od ldan

[*the teacher who reveals himself in all sorts of ways*]

(ZN 171,2)   made supreme offerings to the Teacher,[2] (and)

driven from the bottom of (his) heart implored:

---

1. The passage starting from "The Primordial teacher Kun tu bZang po" up to this point can be seen as an illustration of the way in which the Three Bodies (*Bon, rDzogs* and *sPrul sku*) are conceived and displayed in terms of their emptiness (*stong pa nyid*), dynamic potential (*rtsal*) and inseparability (*dbyer ba med pa*).

2. I.e., to gShen lha 'Od dkar.

ston pa thugs rje'i[1] mnga' bdag lags / /
'gro ba thugs rjes bzung slad du / /
nyon mongs 'khrul pa'i sems can rnams / /

ZN 171,3   ③ ma rig mun pas bsgribs[2] pa la / /
rang rig ye shes bstan[3] tu[4] gsol / /   5
ces[5] zhus pas / /

2/[6] ston pa nyid kyis bka' stsal[7] pa / /[8]
(kun tu[9] bzang pos tshig tu[10] rdul[11] tsam yang gsung[12]
    pa med de[13] / /
ting nge 'dzin dgongs pa'i[14] ngang nas gsungs so)[15] / /[16]

---

1. rje'i ZN, SP, TK : rjes KS

2. bsgribs ZN, SP : sgrib KS, TK

3. bstan ZN, SP, TK : bsten KS

4. tu ZN, SP : du KS, TK

5. ces ZN, SP, KS : ces, with zhabs kyu written under ca, TK

6. 2/ ZN, SP, TK : om. KS

7. rtsal ZN, SP, KS, TK : stsal ego

8. rkyang shad ZN, SP, TK : nyis shad KS

9. tu ZN, SP : du KS, TK

10. tu ZN, SP : du KS, TK

11. rdul ZN, SP, KS : bdul TK

12. gsung ZN, SP, KS : gsungs TK

13. de ZN, SP, KS : ste TK

14. pa'i ZN, SP, KS : >pa'i< (dbu chen) TK

15. so ZN, SP, TK : s.ho KS

16. rkyang shad ZN, SP : nyis shad KS, TK

"Oh Teacher, Lord of Compassion,
on account of the compassion with which (You) look upon
    living beings,
to sentient beings deluded (by) afflictions (and)

(ZN 171,3)   blinded by the darkness (of) non-awareness
please show the Primordial Wisdom of Self-Awareness!"   5
Having thus implored,

2. the Teacher himself proclaimed:
[(this) *is not in the least* (to be considered as) *a verbal*
    expression by Kun tu bZang po, (since)
it is spoken from the condition of meditative contemplation]

rang 'byung ka[1] dag ye sangs rgyas / /
TK 3a   bon dang (3a) bon can thams cad kyang[2] / /
ZN 171,4   rang gi sems yin gzhan ④ min[3] pas / /
thams cad rang 'byung nyid du ltos[4] / /

zhes[5] gsung[6] pas / /   5

'khor rnams rang rig pa'i ye shes rang las[7] shar te / /
ZN 171,5   rang 'byung gi[8] ye shes rang gis rtogs ⑤ par gyur to / /[9]

yang gsungs[10] pa / /

---

1. ka ZN, SP, KS : bka' TK

2. kyang ZN, SP, KS : dang TK

3. min ZN, SP : med KS : men TK

4. rkyang shad ZN, SP, KS : one single sentence together with ces (sic) gsung pas TK

5. zhes ZN, SP : ces KS, TK

6. gsung ZN, SP, KS : gsungs TK

7. las ZN, SP : la KS, TK

8. gi ZN, SP, TK : gis KS

9. rkyang shad ZN, SP, TK : nyis shad KS

10. gsungs ZN, SP, TK : gsung KS

"Self-originated, Primordial Enlightenment pure from the
    beginning,
the state of being and all phenomena
(ZN 171,4) are one's (own) Mind, (they) are not (something) else;
    therefore,
look at everything as (being) the Self-Originated!"

Having thus spoken (he added):   5

"Retinue, when the Primordial Wisdom of Self-Awareness
    has appeared in oneself,
(ZN 171,5) the Self-Originated Primordial Wisdom will be naturally
    perceived."

Further (he) said:

ᠠ| rang rig gnyug ma kun gyi[2] gzhi / /

(*g.yung drung tshig rkang bcu gnyis kyi mdor bstan*[3]) / /

ᠠ| rtsol bral bgrod[4] med lhun rdzogs[5] lam / /

ᠠ| ci bzhin lhun grub 'bras bu ste[6] / /

ᠠ|[7] yang dag don la lta ru med[8] / /   5

ZN 172,1,
SP 234 ᠠ| ① [234] yang dag don la sgom du med / /

KS 100a ᠠ| yang dag don la spyod[9] {100a} du med / /

---

1. Kha ZN, SP, TK : om. KS

2. gyi ZN, SP, TK : gyis KS

3. bstan ZN, SP, TK : bstan pa KS

4. bgrod ZN, SP, KS : sgrod TK

5. rdzogs ZN, SP, TK : grub KS

6. ste ZN, SP, TK : te KS

7. tsheg incl. ZN, SP : om. KS, TK

8. med incl. ZN, SP, KS : >med< (dbu chen) TK

9. spyod ZN, SP : spyad KS, TK

[*Outline of the twelve everlasting verses*][1]

Ka. "The Basis of all (is) pristine Self-Awareness.

Kha. The Path (is) spontaneously perfected, without progression (and) without effort.

Ga. The Fruit is spontaneously accomplished as it is.

Nga. There is nothing to investigate with respect to the real sense.

5

(ZN 172,1) **Ca.** There is nothing to meditate with respect to the real sense.

Cha. There is no conduct (to be adopted) with respect to the real sense.

---

1. Although in the texts this note appears after the first Little Tantra (see the critical edition, line 2), we have preferred to translate it before, in order to present the Twelve Little Tantras without interruption.

ཨེ། sems kyi dpe ni nam mkha' 'dra / /

ཧྥ། sems kyi rtags ni sems nyid yin / /

ཏྲ། sems kyi don ni bon nyid do / /

ཝ། skye[1] ba[2] med pa'i bon dbyings na[3] / /

ZN 172,2   ཀ། 'gag pa[4] med[5] pa'i ye shes ② gnas / /   5

TK 3b   ཉ། skye 'gag gnyis med (3b) thig le gcig / /

gleng[6] gzhi'i[7] le'u 'o[8] / /[9]

---

1. skye ZN, SP, KS : kye TK
2. ba ZN, SP, TK : 'gag KS
3. na ZN, SP, KS : nas TK
4. pa incl. ZN, SP, TK : >pa< (dbu chen) TK
5. med incl. ZN, SP, KS : >med< (dbu chen) TK
6. gleng ZN, SP, KS : kleng TK
7. gzhi'i ZN, SP, KS : bzhi'i TK
8. le'u 'o ZN, SP, KS : le u'o TK
9. rkyang shad ZN, SP : nyis shad KS, TK

Ja. The example for the Mind is (that it is) like the sky.

Nya. The token for the Mind is the Mind-itself.

Ta. The meaning[1] of the Mind is the Reality.

Tha. In the unborn Dimension (of) Reality,

(ZN 172,2)   **Da.** Unobstructed Primordial Wisdom abides.   5

Na. Single Essence without birth and interruption."[2]

This is the basic chapter.[3]

---

1. dPon slob 'Phrin las Nyi ma: *don* = *ngo bo*, essence.

2. dPon slob 'Phrin las Nyi ma: birth and interruption are synonyms of appearance (*snang ba*) and emptiness (*stong pa nyid*). Cf. The View which is like the Lion's Roar, *passim*, where the same principles are expressed in terms of Condition (*ngang*), Nature (*rang bzhin*) and Identity (*bdag nyid*).

3. Cf. BGTC, vol. 1, p. 427, *gleng gzhi*, (1) and (2).

byang sems thig le nyag gcig e ma ho / /[1]

ཀ[2]

(*rgyas par bstan*[3] *te*[4] *bshad*[5] *pa la*)[6] / /
sems nyid stong pa ka[7] nas[8] dag / /
sems nyid stong pa 'od du[9] gsal / /
'od gsal stong pa gdod nas dag[10] / /   5

ZN 172,3   ③ 'khor 'das gnyis kyi gzhi mar[11] gyur / /
'khor 'das gnyis su gyes pa med / /
de nyid rang bzhin med par shes / /
rtogs pas kun bzang ye sangs rgyas / /
de ma yin la der bzung nas / /   10

---

1. rkyang shad ZN, SP : nyis shad KS, TK

2. Ka ante notam ZN, SP, TK : Ka post notam KS

3. bstan ZN, SP, TK : bshad KS

4. te ZN, SP, KS : ste TK

5. bshad ZN, SP, TK : bsten KS

6. This sentence is not written as a note in TK.

7. ka ZN, SP, KS : bka' TK

8. nas ZN, SP, KS : na>s< TK

9. du inc. ZN, SP, KS : >du< (dbu chen) TK

10. dag ZN, SP, KS : yad TK

11. mar ZN, SP, KS : ma >r< (dbu chen) TK

Pure-(and-Perfect-)Mind, Single Essence. *E ma ho!*

Ka. [*The extended explanation:*]
"The Mind-itself (is) empty, (it is) pure from the beginning.
The Mind-itself, (which is) empty, shines forth as light.[1]
(This) Clear Light, (which is) empty, (is) pure from the
    beginning.   5
(ZN 172,3) (It) becomes the Basis of transmigration and the state
    transcending suffering.
There is no separation between transmigration and the
    state transcending suffering.
Know (that) That itself has no (inherent) nature!
Realizing (That) is Kun (tu) bZang (po), (the state of)
    Primordial Enlightenment;
Although (it) is not that, it is grasped as that;[2]   10

---

1. This 'light' should not be considered as light in mere physical terms, since it represents the dynamic potential (*rtsal*) of the Mind-itself to appear in different ways; this 'active' aspect of the Mind-itself, i.e. the Basis, is also symbolized by the Primordial Wisdom of Self-Awareness, which perceives itself as inseparable from the Absolute Reality. Cf. The View which is like the Lion's Roar, section Da p. 223. "The Explanation of the Twelve Little Tantras" (*rGyud bu chung bcu gnyis kyi don bstan pa*, op. cit.) states that light as such represents the dynamic potential of Primordial Wisdom (see Introduction, p. 65). Cf. Tucci 1980, pp. 63-67.

2. I.e. when existence is considered as having an inherent nature.

bzung 'dzin gnyis su spyad pa yis[1] //
ZN 172,4   ma rtogs sems can 'khor ④ bar 'khyams //
lam lnga rgyu[2] drug so so dang //
sku dang zhing khams thams cad dang //
'khor ba dang ni[3] myang 'das gnyis //   5
thams cad byang chub sems las byung //
nyon mongs dug lnga[4] nga yi sems //
dug lnga spangs pa'i pha[5] rol na //
ZN 172,5   sangs rgyas bya ba'i[6] ⑤ ming yang med //
TK 4a   dug lnga ye nas rnam[7] (4a) par dag //   10
KS 100b   ye shes lnga'i rang bzhin {100b} yin //
rang 'byung thig le nyag gcig e ma ho ///[8]

---

1. pa yis ZN, SP, KS : pa'i TK

2. rgyu ZN, SP, KS : rgyud TK

3. For the use of the topicalizer *ni* with particular reference to archaic literature see S. V. Beyer 1992, pp. 275-278.

4. lnga incl. ZN, SP, KS : >lnga< (dbu chen) TK

5. pha ZN, SP, KS : phyi TK

6. bya ba'i ZN, SP, TK : bya'i KS

7. rnam ZN, SP, KS : rnams TK

8. rkyang shad ZN, SP : nyis shad KS, TK

and by adopting the duality (of) grasping (and) grasped,

(ZN 172,4)   ignorant sentient beings wander in transmigration.

The various five paths[1] (and) six causes,[2]

Bodies[3] and all the pure fields,

both transmigration and the state transcending

suffering,   5

everything originates from the Pure-and-Perfect-Mind.

Afflictions (and) the five poisons (originate from) the

mind of the I.

On the other side of renunciation (of) the five poisons,[4]

(ZN 172,5)   not even the name 'Enlightened' exists.

The five poisons are pure from the origin.   10

(In) nature, (they) are the Five Wisdoms.[5]

Self-Originated Single Essence. *E ma ho!*

---

1. See Introduction, p. 53, n. 157.

2. dPon slob 'Phrin las Nyi ma: the six spheres of transmigration.

3. The Three Bodies of Reality (*Bon sku*), Perfection (*rDzogs sku*), and Emanation (*sPrul sku*).

4. That is to say, the side of the View of the Great Perfection, where both the five poisons (desire, aversion, stupidity, pride and jealousy) and Enlightenment are neither rejected nor accepted, in virtue of their lacking inherent nature. Since the real nature of the five poisons or passions is that of the Five Wisdoms (the latter notion being common to both Buddhist and Bon po *tantric* teachings), they cannot be considered as impure, and therefore they are not to be rejected. In the *tantric* systems the transformation and sublimation of the five poisons is used as a path of realization, which is the reason why the vehicle of *Tantra* is known as the path of transformation (*bsgyur lam*). In contemplative practices of the Great Perfection, the arising of passions, feelings, emotions and so on is observed and left just as it is, there is no question of rejection or transformation; this is also a reason why the path of the Great Perfection is called that of self-liberation (*rang grol*).

5. See section Na, p. 129.

ཁ།

sems kyi mtshan nyid gang yin pa //
yang dag nges[1] par bstan[2] par bya //
byang chub[3] sems la rgyu rkyen med //

ZN 172,6   byang chub sems la ⑥ bcos slad[4] med //

byang chub sems la gdags[5] su med[6] //   5

byang chub sems la skye shi med //
sems kyi sku ni mtshon du med //
sems kyi gsung[7] ni rang bzhin med //
sems kyi thugs ni mtshan ma[8] med //[9]

---

1. ngos ZN : nges SP, KS, TK

2. bstan ZN, SP, TK : bsten KS

3. chub ZN, SP, KS : byub TK

4. slad ZN, SP, TK : bslad KS

5. gdags ZN, SP, KS : gdang TK

6. The whole verse is an addenda in TK.

7. gsung ZN, SP, KS : gsang TK

8. mtshan ma ZN, SP, KS : dmigs su TK

9. tsheg ZN, SP, TK : om. KS

Kha

(As to) that which is the essential characteristic of the
Mind,
(it has) to be explained in a correct and certain way:
the Pure-and-Perfect-Mind is without primary and
instrumental causes.

(ZN 172,6) The Pure-and-Perfect-Mind is untainted (and) unaltered.
The Pure-and-Perfect-Mind is inexpressible.   5
The Pure-and-Perfect-Mind is without birth and death.
The Body of (the Pure-and-Perfect-)Mind is without
definitions;
the Speech of (the Pure-and-Perfect-)Mind is without
inherent nature;
the Mind of (the Pure-and-Perfect-)Mind is without
characterization;

ZN 173,1,
SP 235

sems kyi yon tan mi zad[1] pa[2] //
sems kyi phrin[3] las ① [235] lhun gyis[4] grub //
lhun grub sems la 'bad rtsol med //
rtsol ba[5] byas pas[6] sangs rgyas men[7] //
tshig gi[8] lam dang don gyi[9] lam //   5
tshig gi[10] lam gyis[11] don la sbyor //
don gyi[12] lam la bgrod[13] du med //
bgrod[14] med[15] rtsol bral lhun la[16] rdzogs //

ZN 173,2   rtsol ② bral thig le nyag gcig e ma ho //[17]

---

1. zad ZN, SP, TK : bzad KS

2. mi zad (bzad) pa ZN, SP, KS : zad med gter TK

3. phrin ZN, SP, KS : 'phrin TK

4. gyis ZN, SP, TK : gyi KS

5. bas ZN, SP, TK : ba KS

6. pa ZN, SP, TK : pas KS

7. Cf. n. 8 to the critical edition of the *lTa ba seng ge sgra bsgrags*, p. 168.

8. gi ZN, SP, TK : gis KS

9. gyi ZN, SP, KS : kyi TK

10. gi ZN, SP, TK : gis KS

11. gyis ZN, SP, TK : gyi KS

12. gyi ZN, SP, TK : gyis KS

13. bgrod ZN, SP, KS : sgrod TK

14. bgrod ZN, SP, KS : sgrod TK

15. lam la om. ZN, SP, TK : incl. KS

16. la ZN, SP, TK : par KS

17. rkyang shad ZN, SP : nyis shad KS, TK

the Qualities of (the Pure-and-Perfect-)Mind (are)
  inexhaustible;
(ZN 173,1)   the Activity of (the Pure-and-Perfect-)Mind (is) spontaneously accomplished.
There is no effort (to be undertaken) with respect to the
  spontaneously accomplished (Pure-and-Perfect-)Mind;
if effort is undertaken, (it) is not the Enlightened (state).
(With respect to) the path of words and the path of the
  (real) sense,   5
the path of words (is that which) prepares for the sense;
as to the path of the (real) sense, (that is) without
  progression.
Without progression, without effort, spontaneously
  perfected.
(ZN 173,2)   Single Essence without effort. *E ma ho!*

ག །[1]

sems nyid gdod nas ye sangs rgyas / /

TK 4b   dang po'i[2] ye shes rgyu med (4b) pas[3] / /

rgyu las skye[4] pa'i[5] ye shes min[6] / /

rang gsal ye shes nyag gcig ma / /

kun tu[7] bzang po[8] thugs nyid yin[9] / /   5

ZN 173,3   sangs rgyas sems can ③ kun la khyab / /

'das dang ma byung[10] da ltar[11] gsum / /

rtogs[12] pa snga phyi'i khyad par las / /

dus gsum gcig ste[13] khyad par med / /

---

1. Ga ZN, KS, TK : Ka SP

2. po ZN, SP, KS : po'i TK

3. pas ZN, SP, KS : pa>s< (dbu chen) TK

4. skye ZN, SP, KS : skyed TK

5. pa'i ZN, SP : pa KS, TK

6. min ZN, SP, KS : men TK

7. tu ZN, SP : du KS, TK

8. po ZN, SP : po yi KS, TK

9. yin ZN, SP, KS : kyis TK

10. byung ZN, SP, KS : byon TK

11. ltar ZN, SP, TK : ta KS

12. rtogs ZN, SP, TK : rtog KS

13. ste ZN, SP, KS : de TK

Ga

The Mind-itself (is) from the origin Primordial
　　Enlightenment.
The original Wisdom is without cause,
(it) is not Wisdom generated by causes.
(This) single Wisdom (that is) clear (to) itself
is the very Heart (of) Kun tu bZang po.[1]   5

(ZN 173,3) (It) encompasses all enlightened (and) sentient beings,
past, future and present.
(It is) beyond the distinction of before (and) after
　　realization.[2]
The three times are one, there is no differentiation.

---

1. dPon slob 'Phrin las Nyi ma: the Self-Originated Primordial Wisdom of the Basis
(*gzhi'i rang 'byung ye shes*).

2. dPon slob 'Phrin las Nyi ma: *rtogs pa* stands for realization of the state of Reality;
snga is the state preceding that realization, which is the condition of transmigratory
beings; *phyi* refers to the state that comes after realization of Reality has occurred.

KS 101a   {101a} byang chub sems la[1] rgyu med pas / /
rgyu las[2] skyes[3] pa'i[4] 'bras bu min[5] / /
rtsol bral nam mkha' lta bur gnas / /

ZN 173,4   sems ④ nyid nor bu rin po che[6] / /
gzhan nas btsal[7] bas mi rnyed de[8] / /   5
sems kyis[9] sems la[10] btsal[11] bar bya / /
btsal bas rnyed par mi 'gyur te[12] / /
ma btsal[13] bar[14] yang stor bral med / /

---

1. la ZN, SP, TK : las KS

2. las ZN, SP, KS : la TK

3. skyes ZN, SP, KS : skyed TK

4. pa'i ZN, SP : pa KS, TK

5. min ZN, SP, KS : me>n< (dbu chen) TK

6. rin po che ZN, SP, KS : rin chen ni TK

7. btsal ZN, SP : brtsal KS : rtsal TK

8. tsheg ZN, SP : om. KS, TK

9. kyis ZN, SP, TK : kyi KS

10. sems kyis sems la ZN, SP : sems kyi sems la KS : sems la sems kyis TK

11. btsal ZN, SP : brtsal KS : rtsal TK

12. te ZN, SP, KS : ste TK

13. btsal ZN, SP, KS : rtsal TK

14. bar ZN, SP : ba KS : par TK

The Pure-and-Perfect-Mind is without cause,
(it) is not an effect produced by causes;
(it) exists without effort, like the sky.
(ZN 173,4)   The precious jewel (of) the Mind-itself
is not found by looking (for it) elsewhere;   5
(it is) to be looked for in the mind by the mind.
(But) when (it is) looked for, (it) will not appear;
(and) when (it is) not looked for, (it) won't be lost either.

rgyu med 'bras bu byang chub sems //

ZN 173,5   rtsol bral nam mkha' lta bu'i ⑤ don //

rtogs shing[1] khong du[2] chud gyur[3] na //

de dag mthar phyin brtan[4] pa thob //

'bras bu kun tu bdag nyid yin //   5

dang po'i[5] sangs rgyas rgyu med pas[6] //

rgyu las byung ba'i[7] sangs rgyas min[8] //

TK 5a   (5a) gdod ma nyid nas ye sangs rgyas //

ZN 173,6   sku gsum rang 'byung ⑥ lhun gyis[9] grub //

lhun grub thig le nyag gcig e ma ho //[10]   10

---

1. shing ZN, SP, KS : cing TK

2. khong du ZN, SP, TK : khongs su KS

3. gyur ZN, SP, KS : 'gyur TK

4. brtan ZN, SP : brten KS : bstan TK

5. po'i ZN, SP, TK : po KS

6. pas ZN, SP : pa KS, TK

7. pa'i ZN, SP : ba KS : pa TK : ba'i ego

8. min ZN, SP, KS : men TK

9. gyis ZN, SP, TK : gyi KS

10. rkyang shad ZN, SP : nyis shad KS, TK

The Pure-and-Perfect-Mind, the Fruit without cause,
(ZN 173,5)   (is) the state (that exists) without effort like the sky.
Realizing (that), taking (it) to heart, (and)
bringing those[1] to ultimate stability
is the substance (of) all realizations.   5
The original Enlightenment is without cause,
(it) is not Enlightenment generated by causes;
(it is) Primordial Enlightenment from the very beginning.
(ZN 173,6)   The Three Bodies (are) self-originated (and) spontaneously accomplished.
Spontaneously accomplished Single Essence. *E ma ho!*   10

---

1. I.e. understanding it and taking it to heart.

ད།[1]
snang srid 'khor 'das thams cad kun//
thams cad byang chub sems su rdzogs //
de phyir rdzogs pa chen po yin //
rdzogs chen zab mo'i don la lta //

ZN 174,1,
SP 236 'di zhes bya bar lta ru ① [236] med //   5
bltas[2] pas mthong bar[3] mi 'gyur te[4] //
ma mthong pa nyid[5] mthong ba'i[6] mchog[7] //

---

1. nga, tsheg om. ZN, KS, TK : ga SP

2. ltas ZN, SP, TK : bltas KS

3. bar ZN, SP, KS : par TK

4. te ZN, SP, KS : ste TK

5. nyid ZN, SP, KS : ni TK

6. ba'i ZN, SP : pas KS : pa'i TK

7. mchog ZN, SP, TK : chog KS

Nga
All appearance (and) coming into being, transmigration
  (and) the state transcending suffering,
everything (is) perfected in the Pure-and-Perfect-Mind.
For that reason (it) is (called) Great Perfection.
To look at the profound state (of) the Great Perfection
(ZN 174,1) is not investigating (and thinking) "this (is it)." 5
Since by investigating (it) will not be seen,
not seeing itself (is) the best seeing.

kun tu[1] bzang po'i lta ba ni / /
'di zhes bya bar ma gsung[2] ste / /

cir[3] yang {101b} 'char zhing[4] cir yang snang / /
gang yin gang min[5] cir[6] yang min / /

byang sems ka[7] dag 'dus ma ② byas / /   5
rgya chad phyogs lhung ris[8] chad sogs[9] / /
mu bzhi gang gi[10] mthas[11] ma reg / /

---

1. tu ZN, SP : du KS, TK

2. gsung ZN, SP, KS : gsang TK

3. ci ZN, SP : cir KS, TK

4. cing ZN, SP, KS : zhing TK

5. min ZN, SP, KS : men TK

6. cir ZN, SP, KS : ci TK

7. ka ZN, SP : dka' KS : bka' TK

8. ris ZN, SP, TK : rig KS

9. sogs ZN, SP, TK : swogs KS

10. gi ZN, SP, TK : gis KS

11. mthas ZN, SP : mtha' KS, TK

As to the View of Kun tu bZang po,
(it) cannot be explained as "this (is it)";
(as) coming forth in this way or appearing in that way,
(as) being this way, not being that way (or) being nothing
at all:[1]

(ZN 174,2) the Pure-(and-Perfect-)Mind (is) pure from the beginning,
(it is) uncompounded.   5
(It is) unaffected by the extremes of the four limits,[2]
(by) any connotation, partiality or inclination;

---

1. dPon slob 'Phrin las Nyi ma: it is not transmigration, it is not the state transcending suffering, it is not found as something that can be specified (*'khor ba ma yin, 'das pa ma yin, 'di zhes ci yang ma grub*).

2. The four limits according to the *rDzogs pa chen po yang rtse klong chen gyi nges don*, op. cit., pp. 193,5-194,3: "(It is) not ascertained as being; (it is) not refuted as non-being; (it is) not acknowledged as being the two; (it is) not discarded as not being the two. (The Pure-and-Perfect-Mind) is not ascertained as being: it is not ascertained as that which is because, really and truly, nothing, not even an atom, exists. However, since (it) unobstructedly arises in various ways, (it) is not refuted as non-being. (It) is not acknowledged as being the two, since that which is appearance is emptiness (and) that which is emptiness is appearance, and there is no distinction between these two. (It) is not discarded for not being the two, because on the other side of rejecting appearance there is no emptiness, and on the other side of rejecting emptiness there is no appearance." (*de la mu bzhi ni yin par mi sgrub / min par mi 'gegs / gnyis ka yin pa khas mi len / gnyis ka min par yal bar mi 'dor ba'o / de la yin par mi sgrub ste / yang dag par bden par grub pa rdul tsham men pos* [sic] */ yin par mi sgrub / sna tshogs su ma 'gags par 'char bas / min par mi 'gegs / gnyis ka yin par khas mi len te / snang ba gang yin stong pa / stong pa gang yin snang ba / de gnyis la tha dad med pa'i phyir / gnyis ka min par yal bar mi 'dor te / snang ba spang ba'i pha rol na stong pa med de / stong pa spangs pa'i* [sic] *pha rol na snang ba med pa'i phyir ro //*).

tha dad rtag par 'dzin[1] pa dang / /
stong pa phyal[2] chad 'dzin pa[3] dang / /
TK 5b   (5b) bzung[4] 'dzin gnyis su lta ba[5] dang / /
rol pa'i snang ba[6] bkag pas chad / /
ZN 174,3   mtha' bral[7] dbu ma'i don ③ 'dzin pa / /   5
mtha' bzhi gsal ba'i dgongs pa'o / /[8]
mtha' bral chen po lta ba'i mchog / /
'di ni lta ba'i rgyal po ste / /
spyi gcod[9] kun gyi thun[10] mong[11] min[12] / /
mtha'[13] bral thig le nyag gcig e ma ho / /[14]   10

---

1. 'jin ZN, SP : 'dzin KS, TK

2. phyal ZN, SP, KS : chal TK

3. 'dzin pa ZN, SP, KS : cig pu TK

4. bzung ZN, SP, KS : bzu TK

5. ba ZN, SP, KS : pa TK

6. pa ZN, SP : ba KS, TK

7. bral ZN, SP, KS : dral TK

8. rkyang shad ZN, SP, TK : nyis shad KS

9. gcod ZN, SP, KS : bcod TK

10. thun ZN, SP, KS : mthun TK

11. mong ZN, SP : mongs KS, TK

12. min ZN, SP, KS : men TK

13. mtha' ZN, SP, KS : 'tha' TK

14. rkyang shad ZN, SP : nyis shad KS, TK

(it is) cut off (from) conceiving the various (phenomena)
    as eternal,[1]
(from) conceiving univocal[2] emptiness,[3]
(from) viewing grasping and grasped as two,[4]
(from) the appearance of manifestation.

(ZN 174,3)   (It) seizes the central point without extremes;   5
it is contemplation free (from) the four limits.
This 'great separation from extremes' (is) the best View,
(it) is the king of (all) views,
(it) is not a view customary to everyone.[5]
Single Essence without extremes. *E ma ho!*   10

---

1. dPon slob 'Phrin las Nyi ma: the view of eternalists.

2. *phyal;* cf. BGTC, vol. 2, p. 1738, *phyal dpyad.*

3. dPon slob 'Phrin las Nyi ma: the view of the nihilists.

4. dPon slob 'Phrin las Nyi ma: the view of ordinary beings.

5. Cf. The View which is like the Lion's Roar, p. 169.

ཅ|

rdzogs chen zab mo'i don la sgom[1] //
'di ④ zhes bya ba[2] sgom[3] du med //
sgom[4] pas gsal bar mi 'gyur te[5] //
ma sgom[6] par yang gsal 'grib[7] med //
kun tu[8] bzang po'i[9] dgongs pa ni //
so ma rang lugs ma bcos pa[10] //
ma bcos gnyug ma'i[11] rang sa zin //
sgom[12] du med cing yengs su med //

5

---

1. sgom ZN, SP, TK : bsgom KS

2. ba ZN, SP : bar KS, TK

3. sgom ZN, SP, TK : bsgom KS

4. sgom ZN, SP : bsgom KS : sgoms TK

5. te ZN, SP, KS : ste TK

6. sgom ZN, SP : bsgom KS : sgoms TK

7. 'grib ZN, SP, KS : grib TK

8. tu ZN, SP : du KS, TK

9. po ZN, SP : po'i KS, TK

10. ma bcos pa ZN, SP, KS : mi rtog, struck through and followed by ma bcos pa TK

11. ma ZN, SP, TK : ma'i KS

12. sgom ZN, SP, TK : bsgom KS

(ZN 174,4)   **Ca**

> Meditation referred to the profound state (of) the Great
>   Perfection
> is not meditating (and thinking) "this (is it)."
> Through meditation, (it) doesn't get clear;
> without meditation, (it is) neither cleared nor obscured.
> The contemplation of Kun tu bZang po   5
> (is) fresh, natural (and) unaltered;
> (it is) to remain in one's pristine, unaltered condition,
> without meditating and wandering.

ZN 174,5   ⑤ sgom du med pa'i sems nyid la / /
yengs su med pa'i gzer gyis[1] btab[2] / /
rang rig gsal stong 'du 'bral med / /

TK 6a   'khor 'das (6a) gnyis med mnyam par gnas / /

KS 102a   {102a} gnyug ma'i ngang[3] thag rgyun mi bcad / /   5
sgom[4] du med pa sgom[5] pa'i mchog / /

ZN 174,6   sgom[6] med ⑥ thig le nyag gcig[7] e ma ho / /[8]

---

1. gyis ZN, SP, TK : gyi KS

2. btab ZN, SP, TK : gtab KS

3. ngang ZN, SP, TK : rang KS

4. sgom ZN, SP, TK : bsgom KS

5. sgom ZN, SP, TK : bsgom KS

6. sgom ZN, SP, TK : bsgom KS

7. gcig ZN, SP, TK : cig KS

8. rkyang shad ZN, SP : nyis shad KS, TK

(ZN 174,5)   The Mind-itself, which is not (something to be) meditated
  upon,
  is hit by the nail of non-wandering.[1]
  (In) Self-Awareness, clarity (and) emptiness are neither
  separated nor unified.
  Transmigration (and) the state transcending suffering are
  not two, (they) exist in equality.
  There is no interruption (in) the continuum (of) the
  pristine Condition.   5
  The best meditation (is) without meditation.
(ZN 174,6)   Single Essence without meditation. *E ma ho!*

---

1. Cf. The View which is like the Lion's Roar, section Ta, p. 217.

ཚ|[1]

rdzogs chen zab mo'i don la spyad / /
'di zhes bya bar[2] spyad du med / /
lta sgom ma[3] dang ma bral bar / /
skye med spros[4] bral chen po la / /
'bral med spyod pa spyod pa yin / /   5
bcos pa'i spyod pa spyod pa min[5] / /

ZN 175,1,
SP 237

ma bcos dgag[6] ① [237] sgrub[7] med pa ru / /
lta spyod zung du 'brel ba[8] na / /
rol pa'i spyod pa rdzogs chen rgyan / /
ji[9] ltar spyad kyang rnam par dag / /   10
padma bzhin du skyon ma gos / /
blang dor med pa spyod pa'i mchog / /
spyod mchog thig le nyag gcig e ma ho / /[10]

---

1. cha ZN, KS, TK : *** SP

2. ba ZN, SP : bar KS, TK

3. All versions examined contain the syllable 'ma' after sgom. Both dPon slob 'Phrin las Nyi ma and dGe bshes rNam rgyal Nyi ma maintain that 'ma' is not a mistake for 'pa' (sgom pa), but a supplementary syllable (kha skong). On this cf. BGTC, vol. 1, p. 186, kha skong.

4. sprol ZN, SP : spros KS, TK

5. min ZN, SP, KS : men TK

6. dgag ZN, SP, KS : bkag TK

7. sgrub ZN, SP, TK : bsgrub KS

8. ba ZN, SP, TK : pa KS

9. ci ZN, SP, KS : ji TK

10. rkyang shad ZN, SP : nyis shad KS, TK

Cha

To conduct oneself with respect to the profound state (of)
    the Great Perfection
is not to behave (in some way, thinking) "this (is it)."
Without being separated from the View (and) Meditation,
totally spontaneous (and) undiversified,
the 'unseparated' conduct is the (real) one;   5
an artificial conduct is not (the real) one.

(ZN 175,1) When View (and) conduct (are) inseparably coordinated
    in (a way
that is) not artificial (and) devoid of forbidding and
    allowing,
(all) manifested conduct[1] (becomes) the ornament of the
    Great Perfection;
in whatever way (it) is pursued, (it is) pure;   10
like a lotus, (it) wears no stains.
Absence (of) acceptance and rejection (is) the best conduct.
Best conduct, Single Essence. *E ma ho!*

---

1. dPon slob 'Phrin las Nyi ma: *rol pa'i spyod pa = spyod pa sna tshogs.*

ཧ།

ZN 175,2 byang chub sems ni ② dpe'i mtshon //
dpe'i[1] nam mkha' 'dus[2] ma byas //
nam mkha' stong pa'i ngang nyid las //
TK 6b gzha' sprin (6b) khu rlangs sna tshogs dang //
ci yang 'char zhing[3] cir yang snang //   5
nam mkha'i ngang du gnas shing[4] thim[5] //
mtha' dbus mdog[6] dbyibs phyogs ris bral //
ZN 175,3 yang dag ③ don la mtshon du med //
KS 102b mtshon bral thig le nyag gcig {102b} e ma ho //[7]

---

1. dpe'i ZN, SP, TK : dpe ni KS
2. 'du ZN, SP : 'dus KS, TK
3. cing ZN, SP, KS, TK : zhing ego
4. shing ZN, SP, KS : cing TK
5. thim ZN, SP, TK : thims KS
6. mdog ZN, SP : mdogs KS : 'dog TK
7. rkyang shad ZN, SP : nyis shad KS, TK

Ja

(ZN 175,2) The example illustrating the Pure-and-Perfect-Mind
(is that of) the uncompounded sky:
from the condition of the empty sky,
the various rainbows, clouds, haze,
whatever comes forth and however it appears,   5
exists and dissolves in the condition of the sky.
Without partiality (and) inclination, form, colour, centre
(or) borders,
(ZN 175,3) the real sense (is) without definition.
Single Essence without definitions. *E ma ho!*

ༀ|
byang chub sems kyi gtan[1] tshigs[2] ni //
dman[3] pa'i sems kyis[4] mi shes te[5] //
gtan[6] tshigs[7] gsum gyis[8] shes par bya'o[9] //
ngang dang rang bzhin bdag nyid gsum //
ngang ni rig pa cir[10] yang gsal //   5

ZN 175,4   ④ rang bzhin rig pa cir[11] yang stong //
bdag nyid gsal stong gnyis su med //
bdag nyid chen po'i gtan[12] tshigs[13] kyis[14] //
thams cad byang[15] chub sems su shes //

---

1. gtan ZN, SP, KS : rtan TK
2. tshigs ZN, SP, TK : tshig KS
3. dman ZN, SP, KS : rman TK
4. kyis ZN, SP, TK : kyi KS
5. te ZN, SP, KS : ste TK
6. gtan ZN, SP, KS : rtan TK
7. tshigs ZN, SP, TK : tshig KS
8. gyis ZN, SP, TK : gyi KS
9. bya'o ZN, SP, KS : bya TK
10. cir ZN, SP, TK : ci KS
11. ci ZN, SP : cir KS, TK
12. gtan ZN, SP, KS : rtan TK
13. tshigs ZN, SP, TK : tshig KS
14. kyis ZN, SP, TK : gis KS
15. byang ZN, SP, KS : bya TK

Nya

As to the cause (of being)[1] of the Pure-and-Perfect-Mind:
since the inferior mind does not know (it),
(it) has to be made known by way of the three causes (of
   being).
(These are) the Condition and the Nature (and) the
   Identity.
With respect to the Condition, Awareness (is) clear in all
   sorts of ways.   5
(ZN 175,4)   (With respect to) the (Ultimate) Nature, Awareness (is)
   empty in whatsoever way;
The Identity (is the Awareness that) the clear (and) the
   empty do not exist as a duality.[2]
Through the cause (of being) of the Great Identity
everything is known as the Pure-and-Perfect-Mind.[3]

---

1. *gtan tshigs*, Skr. hetu. See M. Monier-Williams 1986, p. 1303; cf. BGTC, vol. 1, p. 1036, *gtan tshigs*, (1).

2. dPon slob 'Phrin las Nyi ma: that is to say, the Primordial Wisdom of Self-Awareness (*rang rig pa'i ye shes*) perceives the Condition (*ngang*) as clear, (i.e., as capable of appearing in all sorts of ways), and the Ultimate Nature (*rang bzhin*) as empty, without any duality between the two.

3. On *bdag nyid chen po* cf. S. G. Karmay 1988a, p. 114, n. 40.

sems nyid stong pa rtsa bral la //
sems dang sems 'byung[1] ci shar yang //
sems nyid ngang du gnas shing[2] thim[3] //

ZN 175,5   ⑤ sems nyid bzung[4] 'dzin mtha' dang bral //
mkha' la nyi ma shar ba 'dra //   5
gsal stong zung 'jug dbye ru med //

TK 6bis/a   (6bis/a) dbyer med thig le nyag gcig e ma ho //[5]

---

1. 'byung ZN, SP, KS : byung TK
2. shing ZN, SP, KS : cing TK
3. thim ZN, SP, TK : thims KS
4. bzung ZN, SP, KS : bzu TK
5. rkyang shad ZN, SP : nyis shad KS, TK

The Mind-itself (is) empty, (it is) without root; in that
   respect,
the mind and all mental creations
exist and dissolve in the Condition (of) the Mind-itself;
(ZN 175,5)   the Mind-itself (is) without limits (of) grasping (and)
   grasped.
Like the sun shining in the sky,   5
the clear (and) the empty (are) unified, there is no
   separation.
Inseparable Single Essence. *E ma ho!*

ཏྲི།

don dam bon nyid skye ba med / /
skye ba med pa'i bon dbyings nas / /
bon dang bon can thams cad kyang[1] / /

ZN 175,6   ci[2] yang 'char ⑥ zhing[3] cir yang snang / /

bon nyid ngang du gnas shing[4] thim / /   5
bon nyid don la skye 'gag med / /
bon nyid don la phyogs ris med / /
bon nyid don la brjod du med / /
brjod[5] bral thig le nyag gcig e ma ho / /[6]

ཤི།

dbyings dang ye shes mtshan nyid ni / /   10

KS 103a   dbyings {103a} ni dag pa'i rgyu yin te[7] / /

ZN 176,1,   ① [238] bon nyid dbyings la skye ba med / /[8]
SP 238

ཤི།

ye shes 'bras bu nyid du gsal / /
'od gsal ye shes 'gag pa med / /[9]

---

1. kyang ZN, SP : dang KS, TK

2. ci ZN, SP, KS : cir TK

3. zhing ZN, SP : cing KS, TK

4. shing ZN, SP, KS : cing TK

5. brjod ZN, SP, KS : sbyor TK

6. rkyang shad ZN, SP : nyis shad KS, TK

7. te ZN, SP, KS : ste TK

8. rkyang shad ZN, SP : nyis shad KS, TK

9. rkyang shad ZN, SP : nyis shad KS, TK

Ta

The Absolute Reality (is) unborn.
From the Dimension of unborn Reality,
the state of being and all phenomena,
(ZN 175,6)   whatever comes forth and however (it) appears,
exists and dissolves in the Condition (of) Reality.   5
The state (of) Reality (is) without birth (and) interruption.
The state (of) Reality (is) without partiality (and) inclination.
The state (of) Reality (is) ineffable.
Ineffable Single Essence. *E ma ho!*

Tha

The essential characteristics (of) Dimension and
   Primordial Wisdom: 10
(ZN 176,1)   the Dimension is the pure cause,
the unborn Dimension (of) Reality.

Da

Primordial Wisdom shines forth as the intrinsic effect,
the uninterrupted Primordial Wisdom (of) Clear Light.

ৰ|
skye 'gag gnyis med thig le gcig //
thig le nyag gcig bon gyi sku //
bon gyi sku la mtshon[1] du med //
mtshon med ngang las[2] ye shes shar //

ZN 176,2,
TK 6bis/b

stong nyid ② ye shes phyogs ris (6bis/b) med //   5
me long ye shes gsal sgrib[3] med //
mnyam nyid ye shes mthon[4] dman med //
sor rtogs ye shes ma 'dres gsal //
bya grub ye shes lhun gyis[5] grub //

---

1. mchon ZN, SP : mtshon KS, TK
2. las ZN, SP, KS : la TK
3. 'grib ZN, SP, KS : sgrib TK
4. mthon ZN, SP : mtho KS : mtho' TK
5. gyis ZN, SP, TK : gyi KS

Na
Single Essence without birth and interruption.
Single Essence, Body of Reality.
The Body of Reality (is) undefinable.
From the undefinable Condition, Primordial Wisdom
    shines forth
(ZN 176,2)   (as) the Wisdom of Emptiness, (which is) without
    partiality (and) inclination;   5
(as) the Mirror(-like) Wisdom, (which is) without clarity
    (and) obscuration;
(as) the Wisdom of Equality, (which has) no high (or) low;
(as) the Discriminating Wisdom, (which) shines forth
    unmixed;
(as) the Accomplishing Wisdom (that) spontaneously
    achieves.

[1]ye shes lnga ldan longs spyod rdzogs //
rgyan dang cha lugs mtshan dpe[2] ldan //

ZN 176,3   ③ 'khor dang zhing khams lhun gyis[3] grub //
rdzogs pa'i sku las[4] thugs rje[5] shar //
gang la gang 'dul sprul par[6] ston //   5
sna tshogs sprul skus[7] 'gro don mdzad //
sku gsum rang bzhin lhun la rdzogs //
sku gsum lhun rdzogs chen po las[8] //

ZN 176,4   sangs rgyas gzhan nas ④ bsgrub[9] tu[10] med //

---

1. TK has a kind of *yi mgo* at this point.
2. dpe ZN, SP : dper KS, TK
3. gyis ZN, SP, TK : gyi KS
4. las ZN, SP, KS : la TK
5. rje ZN, SP, TK : rjes KS
6. par ZN, SP, KS : pa TK
7. skus ZN, SP, TK : sku'i KS
8. la ZN, SP, KS, TK : las ego
9. bsgrub ZN, SP, KS : sgrub TK
10. tu ZN, SP : du KS, TK

The Five Wisdom Holders (are endowed with) Perfect
   Enjoyment,
with attires and ornaments, signs (and) attributes,
(ZN 176,3)   spontaneously accomplished retinues and pure fields.
From the Body of Perfection compassion shines forth,
miraculously displaying (itself to) whoever needs to be
   tamed.   5
(In) various (ways,) the Emanated Bodies perform the
   benefit (of) beings.
The nature (of) the Three Bodies (is) spontaneous
   perfection.
Apart from the great, spontaneous perfection (of) the
   Three Bodies,
(ZN 176,4)   Enlightenment cannot be achieved from elsewhere.

gsas mkhar lhun rdzogs chen po la //
bskyed[1] bya skyed[2] byed ci yang med //
bon nyid lhun rdzogs chen po la //
rdzogs bya rdzogs byed ci yang med //

KS 103b   dam {103b} tshig ye bsrung[3] chen po la //   5
bsrung[4] bya srung[5] byed ci yang med //

ZN 176,5   ye dbang sems la rdzogs ⑤ pa la //

TK 7a   dbang ni[6] thob[7] bya[8] (7a) thob byed med //

---

1. bskyed ZN, SP, KS : skyed TK
2. skyed ZN, SP, TK : bskyed KS
3. bsrung ZN, SP, KS : srungs TK
4. bsrung ZN, SP : bsrungs KS : srung TK
5. srung ZN, SP, TK : bsrungs KS
6. ni ZN, SP : gis KS : gyi TK
7. 'thob ZN, SP : thob KS, TK
8. gya ZN, SP : bya KS, TK

> In the great, spontaneous perfection (of) the gSas mkhar
> (deities),[1]
> (there is) no one (that) generates (and) nothing (to be)
> generated.[2]
> In the great, spontaneous perfection (of) Reality,
> (there is) no one (that) perfects (and) nothing (to be)
> perfected.
> In the great commitment observed from the origin,   5
> (there is) no keeper (and) nothing (to be) kept.
> In the perfected Mind, empowered from the origin,
> (there is) no empowerment (to be) obtained (and) no one
> (that) obtains (it).

(ZN 176,5)

---

1. dPon slob 'Phrin las Nyi ma: *gsas mkhar* = *lha chen po*. The five most important *gSas mkhar* deities, called *Yi dam gsas mkhar mchog lnga*, are dBal gsas rNgam pa, lHa rgod Thog pa, gTso mchog mKha' 'gying (these three, being the deities associated with the *sPyi spungs* tantric cycle are also known as the *sPyi spungs lha*), dBal chen Ge khod (the main deity of the homonymous *tantric* cycle) and 'Brug gsas Chem pa (the main deity of the *Phur pa tantric* cycle). Cf. S. G. Karmay 1975a, pp. 196-202 and P. Kværne 1974, pp. 104-109; for iconographic descriptions see P. Kværne 1995, *passim*.

2. dPon slob 'Phrin las Nyi ma: that is to say the adept has all deities perfected in him or herself, and doesn't need to go through the meditative stages of Generation (*bskyed rim*) and Perfection (*rdzogs rim*) as required in the *tantric* practices of the Seventh and Eighth Vehicles.

dngos grub rgya mtsho chen po la //
dngos grub thob[1] bya thob byed med //
'od gsal lhun rdzogs chen po la //
sa'i rim pa ci yang med //
rtsol[2] bral lhun rdzogs chen po la //   5
lam gyi rim pa ci yang med //
ZN 176,6 rang 'byung lhun rdzogs chen[3] po ⑥ la //
'bras bu'i[4] bye brag[5] ci yang med //
thams cad rdzogs pa chen po la //
theg pa'i rim pa ci yang med //   10

---

1. 'thob ZN, SP : thob KS, TK
2. rtsol ZN, SP, KS : rtso>l< (dbu chen) TK
3. chen incl. ZN, SP, KS : >chen< (dbu chen) TK
4. bu'i ZN, SP : bu yi KS : bu'i >a chung< (dbu chen) TK
5. brag ZN, SP, KS : brags TK

In the great ocean (of supernatural) accomplishments,
(there is) no (supernatural) accomplishment (to be)
    reached (and) no one (that) reaches (it).
In the great, spontaneous perfection (of) the Clear Light,
(there is) no succession of stages.
In the great, spontaneous perfection without effort,   5
(there is) no graduality of paths.

(ZN 176,6)   In the great, self-originated spontaneous perfection,
(there is) no distinction in results.
In the total Great Perfection,
(there is) no succession of vehicles.   10

med pa ma yin snying po'i don //
ngang la¹ ngang gis gnas pa ni //
nor bu chu gdangs bzhin du gsal //²
ngang gsal nyag gcig bri ba³ med //

ZN 177,1,   mtha' bral thig ① [239] le nyag gcig yin //   5

SP 239   thig le nyag gcig bon gyi sku //
thams cad bon skur rtogs pa⁴ na //
rin chen gser gling phyin pa 'dra //
phyogs ris med na lta ba yin //
mnyam nyid rtogs na sgom⁵ pa yin //   10
blang dor med na spyod pa yin //

ZN 177,2, TK 7b   re ② dogs (7b) med na 'bras bu yin //

KS 104a   bzung 'dzin med na rtogs {104a} pa yin⁶ //

---

1. >gzhi la< (dbu chen) TK
2. TK has a kind of *yi mgo* at this point.
3. bri ba ZN, SP, KS : dri ma TK
4. pa ZN, SP, KS : rtsam TK
5. sgom ZN, SP, TK : bsgom KS
6. rkyang shad ZN, SP, TK : tsheg shad KS

It is not non-existence, (that is) the essential meaning.
(What) naturally exists in the Condition
shines forth like a jewel in transparent waters.
The Condition (and) the clear (are) one, there is no
    diminishment.

(ZN 177,1) It is (one) Single Essence without demarcation.   5
Single Essence, Body of Reality.
When everything is realized as (being) the Body of Reality
it is like reaching the island of precious gold.[1]
When there is no partiality (nor) inclination, (that) is the View.
When equality is realized, (that) is Meditation.   10
When there is no acceptance (nor) rejection, (that) is the
    Conduct.

(ZN 177,2) When there is no hope (nor) apprehension, (that) is the Fruit.
When there is no grasping (nor) grasped, (that) is the
    Realization.

---

1. dPon slob 'Phrin las Nyi ma: *rin chen gser gling* or *rdo med gser gling*, an imaginary island where everything is entirely made of gold. Cf. mDo smad pa dGe 'dun Chos 'phel (1903-1951), *rGya gar gyi gnas chen khag la 'grod pa'i lam yig. Guide to Buddhist Sacred Places in India*, Maha Bodhi Society, Calcutta, 1939, pp. 29-30, where *gser gling* is the name for the Indonesian island of Sumatra (*sum tar*): (29) ... *sum tar la slebs / de ni gser gling ste bstan pa ni med /* (30) *gser gling gi shar lho phyogs su 'ja ba'am 'bru'i gling yod...//.*

sems nyid rtogs pa'i[1] rnal 'byor pa[2] //
khyung dang seng[3] ge'i bu bzhin du //
rgya gsum ral nas rtsal gsum rdzogs //
rtogs pa mngon gyur[4] sangs rgyas nyid //
ZN 177,3   bsgrub[5] pa[6] med par ③ lhun gyis[7] grub //   5
rtsol ba[8] med par rang sa zin //
sangs pa med par nyong mong[9] sangs //
rgyas pa med par ye shes rgyas //
phyin pa med par mtha' ru phyin //
sgrib g.yogs[10] med par thams cad gsal //   10
'das pa med par mya ngan 'das[11] //
ZN 177,4   myang ④ 'das thig le nyag gcig e ma ho //[12]

---

1. pa'i ZN, SP, TK : pas KS

2. pa ZN, SP, KS : ba TK

3. seng ZN, SP, TK : sing KS

4. gyur ZN, SP, KS : 'gyur TK

5. bsgrub ZN, SP, KS : sgrub>s< (dbu chen) TK

6. pa incl. ZN, SP, KS : >pa< (dbu chen) TK

7. gyis ZN, SP, TK : gyi KS

8. rtsol ba ZN, SP, KS : 'bad rtsol TK

9. mong ZN, SP : mongs KS, TK

10. g.yogs ZN, SP, TK : g.yog KS

11. The whole verse is an addenda in dbu chen in TK.

12. rkyang shad ZN, SP : tsheg shad KS : nyis shad TK

The *rnal 'byor pa*[1] who realizes the Mind-itself
(is) like the offspring of lions and eagles;
when the three seals[2] come apart,[3] the three potentialities[4]
    (are already) perfected, (and)
realization reveals itself (as) true Enlightenment.
(ZN 177,3) Spontaneous accomplishment without accomplishing.   5
Effortless remaining in one's place.[5]
Purified afflictions without purification.
Wisdom developed without development.
Perfection attained without perfecting.
Total clarity without obscuration.   10
Suffering transcended without transcendence.
(ZN 177,4) Transcending-of-suffering, Single Essence. *E ma ho!*"

---

1. dPon slob 'Phrin las Nyi ma: a practitioner (*nyams len pa*) who abides in the state of the Great Perfection.

2. dPon slob 'Phrin las Nyi ma: body, speech and mind.

3. dPon slob 'Phrin las Nyi ma: at the moment of death.

4. dPon slob 'Phrin las Nyi ma: those of body, speech and mind.

5. I.e. the state of the Great Perfection.

(rgyud kyi che ba brjod[1] pa dang //
rgyud yongs su gtad pa'o) //[2]

(yang ston pas gsungs pa) //[3]

rdzogs pa chen po byang sems thig le nyag gcig 'di //
rgyud rnams kun tu rgyal po ste //   5
lung rnams kun tu rtsa ba yin //

ZN 177,5   man ngag kun tu ⑤ snying khu yin //
brgyad khri bzhi stong mthar thug yin //

TK 8a   (8a) theg pa dgu'i[4] yang rtse yin //
kun tu[5] bzang po'i dgongs pa ste[6] //   10
dus gsum sangs rgyas thams cad kyis //
tshig tu[7] rdul[8] tsam gsung[9] pa med //
ma gsung[10] mi gsung gsung mi[11] 'gyur //

ZN 177,6   de'i ⑥ phyir yang dkon pa'o //[12]

---

1. brjod ZN, SP, KS : rjod TK

2. rkyang shad ZN, SP : nyis shad KS, TK. The whole sentence is not a note and it is written in dbu chen in TK.

3. rkyang shad ZN, SP, TK : nyis shad KS. The sentence is not a note in TK.

4. theg pa dgu'i ZN, SP, KS : theg >dgu< (dbu chen) rnams kyi TK

5. tu ZN, SP : du KS, TK

6. ste ZN, SP, TK : yin KS

7. tu ZN, SP : du KS, TK

8. rdul ZN, SP, KS : bdul TK

9. gsung ZN, SP, KS : gsungs TK

10. gsung ZN, SP, KS : gsungs TK

11. mi incl. ZN, SP, KS : >mi< (dbu chen) TK

12. rkyang shad ZN, SP, TK : nyis shad KS

[*This is the exposition of the Tantras
and their full delivery.*]

[*Further, the Teacher said:*]

"This Single Essence, Pure-(and-Perfect-)Mind, Great
    Perfection,
is the king of all *Tantras*,   5
the root of all precepts,
(ZN 177,5)   the pith of all instructions,
the finality of the eighty-four thousand (teachings),[1]
the summit of the Nine Vehicles.
Being the contemplation of Kun tu bZang po,   10
all enlightened beings (of) the three times
are not in the least able to express (it) in words.
It was inexpressible, it is inexpressible, it will be
    inexpressible.
(ZN 177,6)   For that reason, it is, indeed, valuable.

---

1. All the teachings of Bon. See D. Snellgrove 1967, p. 227 et seq. Cf. J. Hackin 1924,
p. 31.

KS 104b   {104b} ston pa ngas kyang[1] ma bshad de //
            ma bshad mi bshad[2] bshad mi 'gyur //
            de'i phyir yang dkon pa'o //[3]
            sems can blo la mi snang ste[4] //
            nam mkha' rgya mtsho'i tshul bzhin du //   5
            rgya che gting[5] zab cha phra[6] bas //
ZN 178,1,   rtogs par[7] dka' ① [240] zhing rig[8] par[9] dkon //
SP 240   tshig dang yig ger mi bzhugs[10] te[11] //
            de'i phyir yang dkon pa'o //[12]
            yid bzhin nor bu rin chen ltar //   10
            dgos 'dod 'byung ste shin tu[13] dkon //

---

1. kyang ZN, SP, KS : yang TK

2. bshad ZN, SP, KS : gshad TK

3. rkyang shad ZN, SP, TK : nyis shad KS

4. de ZN, SP : ste KS, TK

5. gting ZN, SP, KS : rting TK

6. phra ZN, SP, KS : 'phra TK

7. par ZN, SP, KS : pa TK

8. rig ZN, SP, TK : rigs KS

9. par ZN, SP : pa KS, TK

10. bzhugs ZN, SP, KS : bzhug TK

11. te ZN, SP, KS : ste TK

12. rkyang shad ZN, SP, TK : nyis shad KS

13. tu ZN, SP : du KS, TK

Even I, the Teacher, could not explain (it).
It was inexplicable, it is inexplicable, it will be inexplicable.
For that reason, it is, indeed, valuable.
It does not appear in the mind (of) sentient beings;
like the ocean or the sky,   5
(it is) vast, profound and subtle;

(ZN 178,1)   it is hard to understand and rarely known.
It is not found in words and letters;
for that reason, it is, indeed, valuable.
Like the precious Wish-fulfilling Gem   10
realizing (all) needs and wants, (it is) extremely valuable.[1]

---

1. Cf. the View which is like the Lion's Roar, p. 213.

de phyir khyed la gdams par bya //
shin tu[1] gnyan[2] cing gces[3] par zungs[4] //

ZN 178,2   rang rig ye ② shes bder gshegs kun tu thugs //
ma yengs ma brjed[5] sems kyi dkyil du zhog //

TK 8b   (8b) 'di nyid 'di'i don rnams rtogs par gyis //   5
'di ni gsang ba'i man ngag ste //
shin tu[6] gsang ba'i[7] gsang pa'o //[8]
yang gsang bla na med pa'o //[9]

ZN 178,3   nor bu chu srin khar ③ chud ltar //
shin tu[10] gsang ba dam pa'i mchog //   10

---

1. tu ZN, SP : du KS, TK

2. gnyan ZN, SP, KS : snyan TK

3. gces ZN, SP, KS : ces TK

4. zungs ZN, SP : bzung KS, TK

5. brjed ZN, SP, KS : rjed TK

6. tu ZN, SP : du KS, TK

7. bas ZN, SP, KS : pa'i TK : ba'i ego

8. rkyang shad ZN, SP, TK : nyis shad KS

9. rkyang shad ZN, SP, TK : nyis shad KS

10. tu ZN, SP : du KS, TK

On that account, (it is) transmitted to you.
Keep (it) dearly and very solemnly,
(ZN 178,2) (this) Wisdom of Self-Awareness, Heart (of) all the Well-
gone Ones.
Without being distracted, without forgetting, keep it at
the centre of (your) mind!
Understand this and its implications!   5
This is the essential instruction on the secret,
the most secret of secrets,
the unsurpassable, supreme secret.
(ZN 178,3) Like a jewel put into the mouth of a crocodile,[1]
(this) very secret, most sacred (teaching),   10

---

1. dPon slob 'Phrin las Nyi ma: if someone tries to recover a jewel from the mouth of
a crocodile, that would not only be extremely dangerous, but the jewel could be
swallowed by the crocodile and be lost forever. Cf. R. A. Stein 1977.

snod med gcam[1] bu kha khyer mkhan //
'phyar la g.yeng[2] zhing[3] dam mi srung[4] //
slob dpon gsang cing[5] rang che bsgrub //
mu stegs[6] ru tra log par lta //
de lta bu'i gang zag la //   5

ZN 178,4   rab tu gsang ba dam pa'i ④ mchog //
KS 105a   sgra[7] tshig[8] {105a} tsam yang mi brjod[9] do//[10]

---

1. gcam ZN, SP, TK : cam KS

2. g.yeng ZN, SP, KS : dbyeng TK

3. zhing ZN, SP : cing KS, TK

4. srung ZN, SP : bsrungs KS : srun TK

5. cing ZN, SP, TK : zhing KS

6. stegs ZN, SP : teg KS : rtegs TK

7. sgra ZN, SP, KS : smra TK

8. tshig ZN, SP, TK : tshigs KS

9. brjod ZN, SP, KS : rjod TK

10. rkyang shad ZN, SP, TK : nyis shad KS

with respect to individuals such as
unworthy (and) hypocrite charlatans,[1]
wandering and inattentive (people) and (those who) do
    not keep (their) commitments,
instructors (who keep it) secret and (consider it as their)
    great personal accomplishment,
heretics[2] (and) *ru tra*[3] (holding) mistaken views,   5

(ZN 178,4)   (it is to be kept) very secret (and) most sacred:
not even the words (or) sound (of it) are (to be) mentioned.

---

1. dPon slob 'Phrin las Nyi ma: who are such because they only speak about the *rDzogs pa chen po* but do not practise it.

2. *mu stegs*; cf. M. Ishikawa 1990, entry no. 293, p. 97. See also BGTC, vol. 2, p. 2102. In *rDzogs chen* textual sources the term *mu stegs pa* is specifically referred to those who follow the views of eternalism (*rtag pa'i lta ba*) and nihilism (*chad pa'i lta ba*). Cf. e.g. the *rDzogs pa chen po yang rtse klong chen gyi nges don*, op. cit., pp. 194,6-195,5, and the *Byang sems gab pa dgu bskor gyi dgongs pa bkrol ba'i 'grel bzhi rig pa'i rgya mtsho*, section 4, *lTa ba'i sgang 'grel* in *Gal mdo*, TBMC, New Delhi, 1972, pp. 472,2-474,2. For this collection see S. G. Karmay 1977, p. 143.

3. dPon slob 'Phrin las Nyi ma: *ru tra* = enemies of the doctrine; cf. the *Tibetan Żang Żung Dictionary*, op. cit., p. 8,7, where *ru tra* = *srin po*, a class of demons; see R. Nebesky-Wojkowitz 1956, *passim*. Note that crocodiles are *chu srin* in Tibetan. Cf. R. A. Stein 1985b. *Rudra* is also the archaic vedic name of Śiva. Is this to be regarded as a critique to the followers of this god? Cf. R. A. Stein 1973-1974; I. Nobumi 1985; K. Mimaki and A. Akamatsu 1985; D. Snellgrove 1987, *passim*; R. A. Stein 1995.

snod ldan[1] mi 'gyur[2] brtan[3] pa'i blo //[4]
gzhan gyis mi 'gyur [5] seng[6] ge'i bu //
dad brtson[7] shes rab snying rje ldan //
dam tshig srog 'dzin bla ma spyi bor khur //
de lta bu'i gang zag la //   5

ZN 178,5   shin tu[8] gsang zhing ⑤ bstan[9] par[10] bya //
zhes[11] gsungs[12] so[13] //[14]

sa ma ya[15] //[16]

---

1. ldan ZN, SP, TK : >?< KS

2. mi 'gyur ZN, SP, KS : 'gyur med TK

3. brtan ZN, SP, KS : stan TK

4. rkyang shad ZN, SP : nyis shad KS, TK

5. ma incl. ZN, SP, KS : incl. but struck through TK

6. sang ZN : seng SP, TK : sangs KS

7. dad brtson ZN, SP : *** KS : rtson TK

8. tu ZN, SP : du KS, TK

9. bstan ZN, SP, TK : bsten KS

10. par inc. ZN, SP, KS : >par< (dbu chen) TK

11. zhes ZN, SP : *** KS : ces TK

12. gsungs ZN, SP, TK : gsung KS

13. so ZN, SP, TK : s.ho KS

14. rkyang shad ZN, SP : nyis shad KS, TK

15. sa ma ya ZN, SP : sā mā yā KS : swa mā yā TK

16. rkyang shad ZN, SP : nyis shad KS, TK

As for worthy individuals (who are) stable (and) steady in
    mind,
(who are) not influenced by others, (who are like) the
    offspring of the lion,
endowed with faith, diligence, superior knowledge (and)
    loving kindness,
(who) keep (their) commitments (as they would protect
    their own) life, (and who) carry (their) teacher on the
    crown (of their) head,
to such kind of individuals,   5

(ZN 178,5) even (if it is) very secret, it is to be taught."
Thus it was spoken.

Promise.

de nas tshad med 'od ldan las sogs[1] 'khor rnams kyis / /

TK 9a   (9a) e ma ho / /[2]

zhes[3] mgrin[4] gcig tu[5] bstod[6] pa[7] / /
ston pa kun tu[8] bzang po thugs rje'i mnga' bdag / /[9]
gang la gang 'dul ston pa / /   5
ZN 178,6   rang ⑥ rig mchog gi[10] ston pa e ma ngo mtshar che'o / /[11]

---

1. sogs ZN, SP, TK : swogs KS

2. rkyang shad ZN, SP, TK : tsheg shad KS

3. zhes ZN, SP, KS : zhes >ngag< (dbu chen) kyis TK

4. mgrin ZN, SP, KS : 'grin TK

5. tu ZN, SP : du KS, TK

6. bstod ZN, SP, KS : stod TK

7. pa ZN, SP, KS : pas TK

8. tu ZN, SP : du KS, TK

9. ... ZN, SP : rkyang shad KS, TK

10. gi ZN, SP, KS : gyi TK

11. rkyang shad ZN, SP, TK : nyis shad KS

Then, Tshad med 'Od ldan (and) the rest of the entourage
thus praised with one voice:

"E ma ho!

How really wonderful is the Teacher Kun tu bZang po,
the Lord of compassion,
(who) teaches whoever (needs to be) tamed,   5
(ZN 178,6)   the best Teacher of Self-Awareness!

rdzogs pa chen po byang sems thig le nyag gcig / /[1]
rgyud thams cad kyi rgyal po / /[2]
lung thams cad kyi rtsa ba / /
man ngag thams cad kyi nying khu / /
bon gyi sgo mo brgyad[3] khri bzhi stong gi[4] yang
    snying / /   5

ZN 179,1,
SP 241

① [241] theg pa rim pa dgu'i yang rtse / /
gsas mkhar gsum brgya drug cu'i[5] yang bcud / /
'das pa'i gshen rab thams cad kyi[6] gshegs pa'i lam / /
ma 'ongs[7] pa'i[8] gshen rab[9] thams cad 'byung ba'i[10] yum / /

ZN 179,2,
KS 105b

da lta'i[11] gshen[12] {105b} rab[13] thams cad ② kyi[14]
    dgongs pa / /   10

---

1. ... ZN, SP : rkyang shad KS, TK

2. rkyang shad ZN, SP : nyis shad KS

3. brgyad ZN, SP, KS : rgya TK

4. gi ZN, SP, TK : gis KS

5. cu'i ZN, SP : bcu'i KS, TK

6. kyi incl. ZN, SP, KS : om. TK

7. 'ongs ZN, SP : 'ong KS : byon TK

8. pa'i ZN, SP, TK : ba'i KS

9. rab ZN, SP, KS : rabs TK

10. pa'i ZN, SP, TK : ba'i KS

11. lta'i ZN, SP, KS : ltar kyi TK

12. gshen ZN, SP, TK : *** KS

13. rab ZN, SP, KS : rabs TK

14. kyi ZN, SP, TK : kyis KS

The Single Essence, Pure-(and-Perfect-)Mind, Great
Perfection,
(is) the king of all *Tantras,*
the root of all precepts,
the pith of all instructions,
the innermost essence of the eighty-four thousand gates
of Bon,[1]   5
(ZN 179,1)   the summit of the Nine Vehicles,
the essence of the three hundred and sixty gSas mkhar
(deities);[2]
the path of all the gShen rab who have gone in the past,
the mother (from whom) all the gShen rab of the future
will be generated,
(ZN 179,2)   the contemplation of all the gShen rab of the present
(time),   10

---

1. dPon slob 'Phrin las Nyi ma: all the teachings of Bon.

2. A description of the three hundred and sixty *gSas mkhar* deities is found in the
gSas mkhar rin po che spyi spungs gsang ba bsen thub, one of the three basic *tantras* of the
sPyi spungs cycle discovered by Gyer mi Nyi 'od in 1108 (see S. G. Karmay 1977, p.
10), T. Namdak, TBMC, New Delhi, 1972, pp. 233-391; BKSR, vol. 112, chapter eight,
p. 44b6 et seq.

ma rig pa'i mun pa sel ba'i[1] sgron me / /
dgos 'dod thams cad 'byung ba'i[2] nor bu / /
rdzogs pa chen po byang sems thig le nyag gcig / /[3]
e ma ngo mtshar che'o / /[4]

zhes mgrin[5] gcig tu[6] bstod do / /[7]   5

TK 9b   ston pa kun tu[8] (9b) bzang po nyid kyang / /
ZN 179,3   ③ 'khor 'das kyi bon thams cad
           mnyam pa chen po'i ngang la gcig tu[9] bsdus te[10] / /
           thugs nyid ma g.yos pa'i ngang la bzhugs so[11] / /[12]

---

1. ba'i ZN, SP, KS : pa'i TK
2. ba'i ZN, SP, KS : pa'i TK
3. ... ZN, SP, KS : rkyang shad TK
4. rkyang shad ZN, SP : nyis shad KS : ... TK
5. mgrin ZN, SP, KS : 'drin TK
6. tu ZN, SP : du KS, TK
7. rkyang shad ZN, SP, TK : nyis shad KS
8. tu ZN, SP : du KS, TK
9. tu ZN, SP : du KS, TK
10. te ZN, SP, KS : ste TK
11. so ZN, SP : s.ho KS : swo TK
12. rkyang shad ZN, SP, TK : nyis shad KS

the lamp that dispels the darkness of non-awareness,
the Jewel fulfilling all wishes and wants.
Single Essence, Pure-(and-Perfect-)Mind, Great Perfection.
How really wonderful!"

So they praised with one voice.   5

The Teacher Kun tu bZang po himself and
(ZN 179,3)   all phenomena of transmigration and the state transcending suffering,
being reunited as one in the Condition of great equality,
abide in the Condition of the immovable Mind-itself.

tshad med 'od ldan la[1] sogs[2] te[3] 'khor rnams kyang[4] / /
rang rig pa'i ye shes rang la shar te[5] / /

rang 'byung gi[6] ye shes ④ rtogs nas[7] / /
thams cad kun tu[8] bzang po'i ngang la gnas par gyur to[9] / /

rdzogs pa chen po byang chub sems kyi gnad byang
    las[10] / /   5
rgyud bu chung bcu gnyis man ngag gi[11] rtsa bar
    bstan[12] pa / /
thig le nyag gcig rdzogs so[13] / /[14]

---

1. las ZN, SP : la KS, TK

2. sogs ZN, SP, TK : swogs KS

3. te ZN, SP, KS : ste TK

4. kyang ZN, SP, KS : dang TK

5. te ZN, SP, KS : ste TK

6. gi ZN, SP, TK : gis KS

7. nas ZN, SP, KS : te TK

8. tu ZN, SP : du KS : 'du TK

9. to ZN, SP : ro KS, TK

10. las ZN, SP, KS : la TK

11. gi ZN, SP, TK : gis KS

12. bstan ZN, SP : bsten KS : stan TK

13. so ZN, SP, KS : s.ho TK

14. rkyang shad ZN, SP : nyis shad KS, TK

After the Primordial Wisdom of Self-Awareness arose in
themselves,
(ZN 179,4) (and) after having realized the Self-Originated Primordial
Wisdom,
Tshad med 'Od ldan (and) the rest of the retinue
all established themselves in the Condition of Kun tu
bZang po.

From the focal-point of the Pure-and-Perfect-Mind, Great
Perfection,   5
the Twelve Little *Tantras*, taught as the root of the essential
instructions,
Single Essence, are (hereby) completed.

ZN 179,5   bder gshegs dgongs rgyud dgu'i ⑤ thugs kyi bcud[1] //
gang zag nyi shu rtsa bzhi'i nyams kyis[2] man ngag dril[3] //
sprul pa'i sku yis[4] las can gshen la bstan[5] //
dus mthar mi nub 'gro don byed par shog //

ces gsungs so[6] //[7]

5

---

1. thugs kyi bcud ZN, SP : man ngag KS : thugs >kyi< (dbu chen) bcud TK

2. kyi ZN, SP : kyis KS, TK

3. man ngag dril ZN, SP, KS : man ngag gi bcud dril TK

4. sku yis ZN, SP, TK : sku'i KS

5. bstan ZN, SP, TK : bsten KS

6. so ZN, SP, KS : swo TK

7. rkyang shad ZN, SP, TK : nyis shad KS

(ZN 179,5) May (this) quintessence of the mind-transmission (of) the
Nine Well-Gone Ones,[1]
(this) *summa* (of) the essential instructions (which comes)
through the experience of the Twenty-four individuals,[2]
(and which is) taught by emanations to the lucky gShens,[3]
unceasingly create the benefit for living beings till the end
of time.

Thus it was spoken.   5

---

1. I.e. the lineage starting from the Primordial Teacher Kun tu bZang po and ending
with gSang ba 'Dus pa. See section Ka of the *rDzogs pa chen po zhang zhung snyan
rgyud kyi brgyud pa'i bla ma rnam thar*, op. cit., pp. 5,4-13,4.

2. The uninterrupted lineage of twenty-four human beings who transmitted the teaching of the *rDzogs pa chen po* in Zhang Zhung. See section Ka of the *rDzogs pa chen po
zhang zhung snyan rgyud kyi brgyud pa'i bla ma rnam thar*, op. cit., pp. 21,2- 26,1.

3. This term is traditionally associated with a category of officiating 'priests', some
of whom played an influential role as spiritual protectors of the king (*sku gshen*)
during the period of the ancient Tibetan monarchy. Cf. P. Kværne 1995, p. 25.

KS 106a   sprul pa'i {106a} sku nyid [1] nam mkha' la gzha'[2] yal ba ltar[3] gshegs so[4] / /[5]

ZN 179,6   ⑥ Gyer spungs nyid [6] dgongs pa [7] mkha' ltar grol lo / /[8]

TK 10a   (10a) rim gyis rgyud nas dar ba'o / /

sarba manga lam / /

bkra shis[9] / /   5

---

1. dang incl. KS : kyang incl. TK : om. ZN, SP
2. gzha' ZN, SP, KS : bzha' TK
3. ltar ZN, SP, TK : bzhin du KS
4. so ZN, SP, KS : s.ho TK
5. rkyang shad ZN, SP, TK : nyis shad KS
6. kyang incl. TK : om. ZN, SP, KS
7. >nam< (dbu chen) TK : om. ZN, SP, KS
8. rkyang shad ZN, SP : nyis shad KS, TK
9. After grol lo, the concluding words of the four versions examined are as follows:
ZN and SP: rim gyis rgyud nas dar ba'o / sarba manga lam / bkra shis / /
KS: de nas rim par rgyud nas da lta bdag ngo sho tshul rgyal to / rig pa ma rig pas gsal gdab shing bris pa dge legs 'phel / dge ba 'gro ba bsngo / bkra shis bde leg [sic] phun tshog [sic] nas / don gnyis mtha' ru phyin par shog / /
TK: swa mā yā / 'gro don rgyas par shog / bkra shis 'phel / 'di bris dge ba'i rtsa ba ci mchis pa / bdag gi drin can pha mas brtse byas / mkha' khyab tshad sems can thams cad kyi don du bsngo / rdzogs pa'i sangs rgyas thob par gyur cig / bkra shis s.ho / ho / ho / /

The emanation itself[1] departed like a rainbow vanishing
in the sky.

(ZN 179,6)   Gyer spungs[2] was released (in) heavenly contemplation.

Gradually (this teaching) became diffused through
transmission.

May everything be auspicious!

Fortune![3]   5

---

1. dPon slob 'Phrin las Nyi ma: Ta pi Hri tsa; cf. Introduction, p. 49, n. 137.

2. Gyer spungs sNang bzher sLod po. See Introduction, pp. 28-29.

3. Cf. n. 9 to the critical edition, p. 160. KS: "Then, through rows of consecutive transmission, (this teaching) has remained victorious up to my present time. Not know-
ing (the state of) Awareness, may the good virtues (derived from) writing (about it)
and clearly remembering (it) increase. Merits are dedicated to (all) beings. May the
two benefits [for oneself and others] be perfectly achieved in complete happiness!"

TK: "Promise. May the welfare of living beings expand! May fortune increase! Whatever meritorious cause may exist in having written this, (I) dedicate to the benefit of
all sentient beings, (who are) infinite (as) the sky, and have been kind (to me like) my
gracious parents. May perfect Enlightenment be attained! Fortune! *Ho! Ho!*" (Sound
of a powerful laugh).

Part Three:

THE VIEW WHICH IS LIKE
THE LION'S ROAR

NOTE TO THE CRITICAL EDITION OF THE
LTA BA SENG GE SGRA BSGRAGS

The text chosen as the basis for this critical edition is the *gter ma* entitled *lTa ba seng ge sgra bsgrags* contained in the collection *rDzogs pa chen po zab lam gnad kyi gdams pa bsgrags pa skor gsum ma bu cha lag dang bcas pa*—a reproduction of a *dbu med* manuscript preserved at the monastery of bSam gling, Dolpo, and published by Patshang Lama Sonam Gyaltsen, TBMC, 1973 (pp. 619-630; no folio numbering; no marginal title; p. 619, 1 line (title); p. 620, 6 lines; pp. 621-629, 7 lines; p. 630, 8 lines; *dbu med* script).[1]

The text has been collated with the homonymous ones contained in:

* the *g.Yung drung bon gyi bka' dang bka' rten*,[2] and in the first and second reprint of the Bon po *bKa' 'gyur* (ff. 1-10, pp. 373-391; marginal title: *Seng ge*; first folio, 1 line recto, (title), five lines, verso; second folio, 5 lines, recto, 6 lines, verso; remaining folios, 6 lines; *dbu med* script);[3] and with

---

1. The text is indexed as K 111,9 = 2 (*Sen-ge sgra-sgrags lta-ba'i lun*) in P. Kværne 1974, p. 112, and as no. 40 in S. G. Karmay 1977, pp. 101. My thanks to E. Gene Smith for having offered me the relevant volume (and quite a few others) as a gift.

2. See n. 2 in Note to the critical edition of the *rGyud bu chung bcu gnyis*, p. 73. I am grateful to the library of the TBMC and to P. Kværne for having provided me with the relevant volume.

3. The versions of the texts here used for collation contained in the first and second reprint of the Canon (*mDzod sde* section, vol. 3/Nga and vol. 109 respectively), bear exactly the same folio and page numbering of the *g.Yung drung bon gyi bka' dang bka'*

♦ the *Seng ge sgra sgrags* [sic] *lta ba'i lung,* from the *rDzogs chen bsgrags pa skor gsum* cycle of the Snellgrove collection preserved at the British Library, Oriental and India Office Collections (section marked with key-letter Na, ff. 1-8, no page numbering; marginal title: *sGra sgrags;* first folio, 1 line, recto (title), 8 lines, verso; ff. 2-8 recto, 9 lines; folio 8 verso, 8 lines; *dbu med* script).[1]

---

rten (vol. 2, ff. 1-10, pp. 373-391). No contextual differences have been remarked between the three versions. My thanks to S. Meinheit of the Library of Congress for the reproduction of the text of the first reprint, and to the library of the Shang Shung Institute, Italy, for that of the second.

1. I am grateful to U. Pagel for having provided me with the relevant microfilm and photostatic copy.

LEGENDA

GK = *rDzogs chen bsgrags pa skor gsum*
KG = *g.Yung drung bon gyi bka' dang bka' rten,* TBMC version, and
          versions contained in the first and second Sichuan reprints
          of the Bonpo *bKa' 'gyur*
TL = *Seng ge sgra bsgrags lTa ba'i lung,* text preserved at the British
          Library

①   = line starting point in GK
[373]   = page starting point in KG
(1a/b) = folio recto/verso starting point in TL

We would like to remark here the constant occurrence in TL of the
'a rjes 'jug after the demonstrative pronoun *'di ('di')* and the term *bde*
(bde'), as well as the use of *gyi* and *gyis* instead of *kyi* and *kyis.*[1]
GK has a *gter shad* (॥) separation mark after each verse.

---

1. Cf. Y. Nagano 1995, pp. 133-141.

CRITICAL EDITION AND ANNOTATED TRANSLATION

<table>
<tr><td>GK 619,1,
KG 373,
TL Na 1a[1]</td><td>lTa ba seng ge sgra bsgrags bzhugs s.ho[2] / /</td></tr>
<tr><td>GK 620,1,
KG 374,
TL 1b</td><td>① [374] (1b) kun tu[3] bzang po gshen lha 'od dkar
la phyag 'tshal lo / /[4]</td></tr>
</table>

<table>
<tr><td></td><td>ston pa thugs rje che mnga' bas / /
thugs kyi dkyil nas bcud phyung nas / /</td><td></td></tr>
<tr><td>GK 620,2</td><td>byin gyis brlabs kyis ② bshad pa'i lung / /
seng ge sgra bsgrags lta ba'i lung / /
lung[5] 'di[6] kun gyi thun mong[7] men[8] / /</td><td>5</td></tr>
</table>

---

1. seng ge sgra sgrags lta ba'i lung bzhugs s.ho

2. s.ho GK : om. KG

3. du GK : tu KG, TL

4. rkyang shad GK, KG : nyis shad TL

5. lung incl. GK, KG : om. TL

6. 'di GK, KG : 'di' TL

7. mongs GK : mong KG, TL

8. men GK, KG, TL. dPon slob 'Phrin las Nyi ma: *men* is the old form for *ma yin*. Cf.
E. Haarh 1968, p. 24: "The negative copula is *ma-min, min* or *men*." See also A. Wayman
1988.

(GK 619,1)   **The View which is like the Lion's Roar.**

(GK 620,1)   Homage to Kun tu bZang po gShen lha 'Od dkar![1]

The greatly Compassionate Teacher
(GK 620,2)   has expounded (these) precepts of the View which is like
        the Lion's Roar as a blessing,
bringing (them) forth from the centre of (his) Heart.   5
These precepts are not customary to everyone.

---

1. dPon slob 'Phrin las Nyi ma: The term *gShen* implies the meaning of *g.yo ba med pa*, immovable, and *'gag pa med pa*, unobstructed.

dper na seng ges[1] sgra bsgrags[2] na //
sder chags thams cad[3] rang bzhin bra[4]
de bzhin lta ba 'di[5] rtogs na //

GK 620,3   ③ 'khor ba'i dngos po rang grol 'gyur //
de phyir seng ge sgra bsgrags[6] pa'i //   5
lta ba'i lung chen 'di[7] nyid bstan[8] //[9]

---

1. ges GK, KG : ge'i TL

2. bsgrags GK, KG : sgrags TL

3. >?< GK : thams cad KG, TL

4. See note 2 to the translation, p. 171.

5. 'di GK, KG : 'di' TL

6. bsgrags GK, KG : sgrags TL

7. 'di GK, KG : 'di' TL

8. bstan GK, KG : stan TL

9. The last two verses are treated as a single sentence in TL.

For example, when the lion roars,
all clawed animals[1] (feel) naturally lost.[2]
Similarly, when this View is realized,

(GK 620,3) the substantiality[3] of transmigration will be self-released.
That is why these great precepts[4] of the View which is   5
like the Lion's Roar are taught.

---

1. dPon slob 'Phrin las Nyi ma: *sder chags* refers here to animals with claws, like tigers, leopards, birds, dogs and cats, as well as to all other carnivores and animals of prey (*gcan gzan*).

2. dPon slob 'Phrin las Nyi ma: they feel lost because they know that in terms of ferociousness and ability in catching a prey, the lion surpasses them all; *bra* is an old term for *sems stor ba*; cf. BGTC, vol. 2, p. 1897.

3. dPon slob 'Phrin las Nyi ma: *dngos po* is here intended as the outer sphere (*phyi'i yul*), i.e. the external appearances which sentient beings perceive as endowed with inherent nature.

4. dPon slob 'Phrin las Nyi ma interprets *lung chen* as *lung rtsa ba chen po*, very fundamental precepts.

ཀ།[1]

rang bzhin ma rtogs sems can la //
rang bzhin dngos po'i 'dug tshul bstan //

GK 620,4   ④ rang bzhin nyid ni ma bcos ste[2] //
de nyid de ltar snang ba[3] yin //
des[4] na de don rtogs pa dka' //   5
de phyir de don bstan[5] par bya //
rang bzhin gcig tu ma nges ste[6] //
ji ltar btags[7] pas de ltar snang //

---

1. TL has no key-letters as section headings.

2. ste GK, TL : te KG

3. pa GK : ba KG, TL

4. de na GK, KG : des na TL

5. bstan GK, KG : stan TL

6. ste GK, TL : te KG

7. btags GK, KG : rtags TL

Ka

Sentient beings (who do) not realize the (Ultimate) Nature,
are taught the real way (in which) the (Ultimate) Nature
exists.[1]

(GK 620,4)   The (Ultimate) Nature is (by) itself unaltered.
(That) That itself is like that,[2] is the appearance.[3]
Now, the meaning of that is difficult to understand;   5
that is why the meaning of that has to be explained.
Since the (Ultimate) Nature is not determined[4] as (being) one,
(it) appears according to the way in which (it) is defined.[5]

---

1. dPon slob 'Phrin las Nyi ma: that is to say the way in which the Primordial Wisdom of Self-Awareness (*rang rig pa'i ye shes*) perceives the Basis of all.

2. dPon slob 'Phrin las Nyi ma: that the Ultimate Nature is unaltered.

3. dPon slob 'Phrin las Nyi ma: the perception by the Primordial Wisdom of Self-Awareness.

4. Cf. H. A. Jäschke 1993, p. 128, and BGTC, vol. 1, p. 655, *nges pa*, (1).

5. *ji ltar btags pas de ltar snang*. Cf. a very similar expression found in the *lTa ba'i rim pa bshad pa* attributed to sKa ba dPal brtsegs (late eighth/early ninth centuries): *mnyam nyid rang bzhin ma nges pas / ji ltar bltas pa der snang phyir / (bsTan 'gyur* Derge edition, vol. Co (204), fol. 237b1). See also D. S. Ruegg 1981, p. 209; cf. S. G. Karmay 1988a, p. 149, n. 62.

GK 620,5   cir[1] ⑤ bltas cir bsam[2] cir bsgrub[3] cing[4] //
KG 375   ji[5] ltar chags [375] pa de ltar snang //
       de ni de yi[6] ngang la gnas //
       ngang ni thams cad kun gyi gzhi[7] //
       rgya mtsho bzhin du ye gnas pas //   5
GK 620,6   bon rnams thams cad 'byung ba'i[8] ⑥ gzhi //[9]
       gnyis su med pa'i[10] de nyid la //
       bdag nyid chen po zhes su bya //
TL 2a   (2a) ma spros pa ru kun la khyab //
       bsdus pa med par gcig tu gsal //   10
       ma btsal[11] lhun gyis grub pa yin //
GK 621,1   dus gsum gcig ① ste khyad par med //

---

1. ci GK, KG : cir TL
2. bsam GK, KG : sams TL
3. bsgrub GK : bsgrubs KG : sgrub TL
4. cing GK, TL : shing KG
5. ji GK, KG : ci TL
6. de yi GK, KG : de'i TL
7. gzhi GK, KG : bzhi TL
8. pa'i GK : ba'i KG, TL
9. rkyang shad GK, KG : nyis shad TL
10. pa'i GK, KG : pa TL
11. btsal GK, KG : rtsal TL

(GK 620,5)   In whatever way (it) arises and according to the way in
which (it) is
investigated, reflected upon (and) accomplished, so it
appears.[1]
As to that,[2] it exists in the Condition of That.[3]
The Condition (is) the Basis of all (and) every thing.
Since it exists (from) the beginning, like the ocean,   5
(GK 620,6)   (it is) the Basis from where all phenomena originate.
As to the fact that there is no duality,[4]
(that) is called the Great Identity.
Without diversifying, (it) encompasses everything;
without contracting, (it) shines forth as one;   10
without seeking, (it) is spontaneously accomplished;[5]
(GK 621,1)   The three times are one, there is no differentiation.

---

1. dPon slob 'Phrin las Nyi ma: this is a reference to the eight lower Vehicles and to
the principles that inspire them.

2. dPon slob 'Phrin las Nyi ma: as to the fact that there exist different ways of viewing or defining the Nature.

3. The Basis of all; see following passage.

4. dPon slob 'Phrin las Nyi ma: there is no duality between the Basis of all and all
phenomena.

5. dPon slob 'Phrin las Nyi ma: *lhun gyis grub pa* = *'byung rung ma 'gag pa*, capable of
arising without obstruction.

ཁ།
des na khyad par nga yis byas / /
nga med pa'i sngon rol na / /
srid pa gsum gyi ming yang med / /
'byung ba[1] lnga'i ming yang med / /
sems can sangs rgyas ming yang med / /   5
thams cad kun bas[2] nga sngar 'byung / /
thams cad nga yis byas pa yin[3] / /
nga yi[4] rang bzhin rnam par dag / /[5]

---

1. pa GK : ba KG, TL

2. bas GK, KG : pas TL

3. >nga ... yin< (dbu chen) GK : incl. KG, TL

4. nga yi GK, KG : nga'i TL

5. rkyang shad GK : om. KG, TL

Kha

Now, (as to) the difference, (it is) I[1] (who) made (it).
In former times when I did not exist,
not even the name of the three existence[2] existed;
not even the name of the five elements existed;
not even the name of enlightened and sentient beings
    existed.   5
Before anything whatsoever, I appeared.
(It is) I (that) created everything.
My Nature (is) pure.

---

1. dPon slob 'Phrin las Nyi ma: *Kun tu bZang po* of the Basis (*gzhi'i kun tu bzang po*), the inexpressible *Kun tu bZang po* (*gdags su med pa'i kun tu bzang po*), the Self-Originated Primordial Wisdom of the Basis (*gzhi'i rang 'byung ye shes*).

2. dPon slob 'Phrin las Nyi ma: the three existences of subterranean beings (*klu*) below the earth (*sa 'og*), of humans (*mi*) on the surface (*sa steng*), and of gods (*lha*) above the earth (*sa bla*).

gdod nas rang bzhin ka¹ dag pas² //
ye sangs rgyas pa kho³ na yin //
ye sangs rgyas pa'i gzhung⁴ 'di⁵ la //
GK 621,2   blta⁶ ② ru⁷ med cing bsrung du med //
KG 376   btsal du med cing sgom [376] du med //   5
sems can don yang bya ru med //
de lta bu'i don rtogs na //
seng ge sgra bsgrags⁸ lta ba rtogs //⁹

---

1. ka GK, KG : rka TL

2. TL has: gdod nas rka [sic] dag rang bzhin pas.

3. kho GK, KG : kha TL

4. gzhung GK, KG : bzhung TL

5. 'di GK, KG : 'di' TL

6. blta GK, KG : lta TL

7. ru GK, TL : rgyu KG

8. bsgrags GK, KG : sgrags TL

9. rkyang shad GK, TL : nyis shad KG

Since (it) is the primordial Nature pure from the beginning,
(it) is Primordial Enlightenment itself.
With respect to this doctrine of Primordial Enlightenment,

(GK 621,2)   there is nothing to be investigated[1] and nothing to be
protected;
there is nothing to be sought and nothing to be meditated
upon;   5
there is also nothing to be done (for) the benefit (of)
sentient beings.[2]
When (one) realizes the meaning in that way,
(one) realizes the View which is like the Lion's Roar.

---

1. dPon slob 'Phrin las Nyi ma always intends *lta ru med pa* as *lta rgyu med pa*, whenever the expression occurs in both the *lTa ba seng ge sgra bsgrags* and the *rGyud bu chung bcu gnyis*. In this case, the reading of KG supports his interpretation; see relevant n. 7 in the critical edition, p. 178.

2. See below, p. 199, n. 1.

ག།[1]
rtogs par byed pa'i thabs dag ni //

GK 621,3   'di[2] ③ yin gzhan gyis rtogs mi 'gyur //

ji ltar gnas pa'i don bstan[3] pa //

ngang dang rang bzhin bdag nyid chen por gnas //

snang ba[4] stong pa gnyis su med par gnas //   5

snang ba[5] nyid kyi[6] gnas lugs ni //

---

1. tsheg shad GK : ' ' KG : ga ego
2. 'di GK, KG : 'di' TL
3. bstan GK, KG : stan TL
4. pa GK : ba KG, TL
5. pa GK : ba KG, TL
6. kyi GK, KG : gyi TL

Ga

As to the correct method that brings about realization,

(GK 621,3)   (it) is this; through other (methods), realization will not
occur.

The explanation of how (it) exists:

(it) exists as the Condition, the (Ultimate) Nature, and the
Great Identity;

(it) exists as non-duality (of) appearance and emptiness.   5

As for the way of being of appearance itself,

GK 621,4   rtog pa 'dun[1] ④ pa 'di[2] kho[3] na / /
           rgyu rkyen yod pa 'di[4] kho[5] na / /
           rtsol sgrub yod pa 'di[6] kho[7] na / /[8]
           'pho 'gyur yod pa 'di[9] kho na / /
           'gag[10] sgrub yod pa 'di[11] kho[12] na / /   5
           de kho[13] na nyid ni stong par gnas / /
           brtags[14] na[15] ngo bo yongs[16] kyis[17] med / /

---

1. 'dun GK, KG : 'thun TL
2. 'di GK, KG : 'di' TL
3. kho GK, KG : kha TL
4. 'di GK, KG : 'di' TL
5. kho GK, KG : kha TL
6. 'di' TL : 'di ego
7. kha TL : kho ego
8. The whole verse is omitted in GK and KG.
9. 'di GK, KG : 'di' TL
10. dgag GK, KG : 'gag TL
11. 'di GK, KG : 'di' TL
12. kho GK, KG : kha TL
13. kho GK, KG : kha TL
14. brtags GK, KG : rtags TL
15. rtags na rep. TL
16. yongs GK, KG : yong TL
17. kyi GK, KG : kyis TL

(GK 621,4)   (it is) precisely (that of) desires (and) thoughts,
(it is) precisely (that of) primary (and) instrumental causes,
(it is) precisely (that of) effort (and) achievement,
(it is) precisely (that of) transformation (and) change,
(it is) precisely (that of) hindrance (and)
    accomplishment.   5
As for that (which is) precisely so, (it) exists in emptiness;
when examined, (it is found that) there is no essence
    whatsoever.

GK 621,5, (2b) de la rgyu rkyen ⑤ ga la 'ong[1] / /
TL 2b rtsol sgrub 'pho 'gyur ga[2] la 'ong / /
des na de dang de gnyis gcig[3] / /
'dug pa dus dang rang bzhin gcig[4] / /
dbyings chen gcig[5] na thams cad gnas /   5
de nyid shin tu[6] rtogs pa dka'[7] / /
GK 621,6 rtogs pa dka'[8] phyir ⑥ lung 'dir blta'o[9] / /[10]

---

1. yangs GK : yongs KG : 'ong TL
2. gang GK, KG : ga TL
3. gcig GK, KG : cig TL
4. gcig GK, KG : cig TL
5. gcig GK, KG : cig TL
6. du GK : tu KG, TL
7. dka' GK, KG : rka TL
8. dka' GK, KG : rka TL
9. blta'o GK, KG : lta'o TL
10. rkyang shad GK, KG : nyis shad TL

(GK 621,5)   In that respect, where do primary (and) instrumental
            causes take place?
            Where do effort (and) achievement, transformation (and)
            change take place?
            Thus, that[1] and that,[2] the two, (are) one;
            existence,[3] time[4] and the (Ultimate) Nature (are) one;
            everything abides in the single great Dimension.[5]   5
            That itself[6] (is) very difficult to understand;
(GK 621,6)   because (it is) difficult to understand, (it is) contemplated
            in (the form of) these precepts.

---

1. dPon slob 'Phrin las Nyi ma: appearance.

2. dPon slob 'Phrin las Nyi ma: emptiness.

3. dPon slob 'Phrin las Nyi ma: all phenomena of transmigration and the state transcending suffering.

4. dPon slob 'Phrin las Nyi ma: past, present and future.

5. dPon slob 'Phrin las Nyi ma: the Dimension of the Self-Originated Primordial Wisdom of the Basis. Cf. Introduction, p. 59 et seq.

6. dPon slob 'Phrin las Nyi ma: the Way of Being of the Basis.

yod par mos pa drangs pa'i[1] phyir // .
thams cad yod par bstan[2] par bya //
med pa'i zhen pa bzlog[3] pa'i phyir //
thams cad yod[4] par bstan[5] par bya //
kho na nyid kyi[6] don rtogs phyir[7] //   5
GK 621a7,   ⑦ [377] thams cad yod par bstan[8] par bya //
KG 377   de las bzlog[9] ste[10] de don bstan[11] //

---

1. pa'i GK, KG : ba'i TL

2. bstan GK, KG : stan TL

3. bzlog GK, KG : zlog TL

4. TL has yod corrected into med. Cf. note 1 to the translation, p. 187.

5. bstan GK, KG : stan TL

6. kyi GK, KG : gyi TL

7. phyir GK, KG : sbyar TL

8. bstan GK, KG : stan TL

9. bzlog GK, KG : zlog TL

10. de GK, KG : ste TL

11. bstan GK, KG : stan TL

In order to guide those who delight in existence,
(it) has to be taught that (it) exists (as) everything;[1]
in order to refute those who are attached to non-existence,
(it) has to be taught that (it) exists (as) everything;
in order to understand the meaning of That (which is)
    precisely so,   5
(GK 621,7)   (it) has to be taught that (it) exists (as) everything;
having been dissuaded from those,[2] (one) is shown the
    meaning (of) That.

---

1. According to dPon slob 'Phrin las Nyi ma, the term *thams cad* is here specifically referred to the Basis (*gzhi*), its dynamic potential (*rtsal*) and manifestation (*rol pa*).

2. dPon slob 'Phrin las Nyi ma: when the two views of existence and non-existence are overcome.

des na bon rnams thams[1] cad la / /
dgag sgrub med ces bya ba yin / /
spong len med ces bya ba yin / /
gzung[2] 'dzin med ces bya ba yin / /
GK 622,1   ① de ltar rang gi gzhung[3] bsgrub[4] na / /   5
gzhan gzhung[5] khegs[6] par gdon[7] mi za / /

---

1. thams incl. GK, TL : >thams< KG
2. gzung GK, KG : bzung TL
3. gzhung GK, KG : bzhung TL
4. bsgrub GK, KG : grub TL
5. gzhung GK, KG : bzhung TL
6. khyegs GK, TL : khegs KG
7. gdon GK, KG : bdon TL

Thus, with respect to all phenomena,
(it) is said (that) there is no obstruction (nor) achievement;
(it) is said (that) there is no acceptance (nor) rejection;
(it) is said (that) there is no grasping (nor) grasped.

(GK 622,1)   When (this) doctrine is accordingly made one's own,   5
there is no doubt that other doctrines will be disproved.

ཀ

khyad par bla med don bstan[1] na / /
brda[2] dang man ngag gnyis kyis[3] bstan[4] / /
'khor 'das gnyis kyi[5] bar shed na / /
bar pa byed pa'i brda[6] gcig[7] bdog / /
de bzhin sems can[8] sangs rgyas ② kyang[9] / /
dbyings dang ye shes de las rtsogs[10] / /
des na brda yis[11] shes par bya / /

GK 622,2 (left margin, beside line 5)

5 (right margin, beside line 5)

---

1. bstan GK, KG : stan TL

2. brda GK, KG : bda' TL

3. kyis GK, KG : gyis TL

4. bstan GK, KG : stan TL

5. kyi GK, KG : gyi TL

6. brda GK, KG : bda' TL

7. gcig GK, KG : cig TL

8. ? GK : sems can KG, TL

9. kyang GK, KG : dang TL

10. rtsogs GK : sogs KG : bsogs TL

11. brda'i GK, KG : bda' yis TL : brda yis ego

Nga

In particular, when the supreme meaning is taught,
(it is) taught through symbols and instructions.
In between transmigration (and) the state transcending
    suffering,
there is one symbol that acts (as) mediator;[1]

(GK 622,2) (it is) the same with enlightened, sentient beings,   5
Dimension and Primordial Wisdom and so on.
Consequently, (it) is made known through the symbol.

---

1. dPon slob 'Phrin las Nyi ma: the symbol is the Awareness of the individual about the Ultimate Nature of all phenomena.

lta ba lta ru med pa la[1] //
rang bzhin lta ba'i grogs po la //
gcig dang du ma las 'das cing[2] //
dbyibs[3] dang kha dog lta ru[4] med //
bzang ngan che chung lta rgyu med[5] //   5
ye nas rang bzhin ka dag yin //
GK 622,3   ③ de las rang bzhin med pa gcig //
kun tu[6] bzang po ngas ma bshad //

---

1. med pa la GK, KG : nges par bcad TL

2. cing GK, TL : shing KG

3. dbyib GK : dbyibs KG, TL

4. ru GK, KG : rgyu TL

5. The whole verse is omitted in GK and KG.

6. du GK : tu KG, TL

For what concerns the View (that is) without investigation,
(the Ultimate) Nature, (which is) the companion of the View,
(is) beyond the one and many;
(it) cannot be looked upon (as having) colour or form;
(it) cannot be looked upon (as being) good (or) bad, big
    (or) small.   5
(It) is the primordial Nature, pure from the beginning.

(GK 622,3)   (That there is an Ultimate) Nature (which is) not that one,
I, Kun tu bZang po, have not proclaimed.

TL 3a   (3a) gang gis de rtogs kun bzang yin //
            de las logs na kun bzang med //
            thams cad gzhi[1] mnyam rang bzhin pas //
            de la de ltar rtogs par gyis //
            byang chub sems la rang bzhin med //   5
GK 622,4,   byang chub ④ sems [378] la phyogs ris med //
KG 378   byang chub sems la gzugs[2] med de[3] //
            byang chub sems la bltar[4] yang med //

---

1. gzhi GK, KG : zhi TL
2. gzugs GK, KG : bzugs TL
3. de GK, KG : ste TL
4. bltar GK, KG : ltar TL

Whoever realizes that, is Kun (tu) bZang (po).

In turning away from that, Kun (tu) bZang (po) does not
exist.

Everything is the (Ultimate) Nature (of) the equal Basis.

Understand it to be like that!

The Pure-and-Perfect-Mind has no (inherent) nature.   5

(GK 622,4)   The Pure-and-Perfect-Mind has no partiality (and)
inclinations.

The Pure-and-Perfect-Mind has no form; and because of that,
the Pure-and-Perfect-Mind is not (something that can be)
investigated.

de ltar gang du ma grub pas //
phyogs ris med de[1] phyal par[2] gnas //
thams cad byang chub sems su gcig //
bon rnams thams cad sems su gcig[3] //

GK 622,5   bon rnams khyad par ⑤ chen por cig //   5
gcig pu 'di[4] zhes mtshon du med //
mtshon du med pa'i don 'di ni //
kun tu[5] bzang po nyid kyis[6] bshad //
des na ma btsal[7] lhun gyis grub //
lhun grub phyogs su lhung ba[8] med //   10
de ni lta ba'i dam tshig yin //

---

1. de GK, KG : ste TL

2. par GK, KG : bar TL

3. The whole verse is omitted in TL.

4. 'di GK, KG : 'di' TL

5. du GK : tu KG, TL

6. kyi GK : kyis KG, TL

7. btsal GK, KG : rtsal TL

8. pa GK : ba KG, TL

Likewise, (it) cannot be accomplished in any way.
Being without partiality (and) inclinations, (it) exists in
    equality.
Everything (is) one in the Pure-and-Perfect-Mind.
All phenomena (are) one in the Mind.

(GK 622,5)   Phenomena (are) one in the Great Difference.   5
This so-called 'singleness' is (itself) without definitions.
(It is) this meaning of being without definitions
(that) Kun tu bZang po himself has proclaimed.
Therefore, without seeking, (it is) spontaneously
    accomplished.
(Being) spontaneously accomplished, (it) doesn't fall into
    partiality;   10
that is the commitment of the View.

GK 622,6   rtsol ⑥ dang sgrub pa'i mtha'[1] dang bral / /
dkar dmar dngos[2] por[3] bsgom[4] du med / /
de ltar rtogs na thams cad yo[5] / /
ye sangs rgyas pa kho[6] nar 'dug / /
de phyir 'gro don bya ru med / /   5
med kyang[7] med par thabs[8] kyis bstan[9] / /
GK 622,7   rim pas legs par ma ⑦ bstan[10] na / /
bdag don med la gzhan don brlag[11] / /
gnyis kas[12] bon gyi don mi 'gyur / /
de phyir de ltar bstan[13] par bya / /   10

---

1. mtha' GK, KG : mtha TL

2. dngos GK, KG : mngos TL

3. po GK, KG : por TL

4. bsgom GK, KG : sgom TL

5. yo GK, KG : yod TL

6. kho GK, KG : kha TL

7. yang GK, TL : kyang KG

8. thabs GK, KG : thab TL

9. bstan GK, KG : stan TL

10. bstan GK, KG : stan TL

11. brlag GK, KG : rlag TL

12. kas GK, KG : ka TL

13. bstan GK, KG : stan TL

(It is) without limits of effort and achievement.

(It) cannot be meditated (upon) as a substance (that is) white (or) red.

(GK 622,6)   When it is understood in that way, everything altogether exists precisely in Primordial Enlightenment.

For that reason there is nothing to be done (for) the benefit (of) beings.[1]   5

Even so, (the fact that) there is nothing (to be done for the benefit of beings) is to be taught by (appropriate) means;

(GK 622,7)   if (it is) not duly taught by degrees,

there is no benefit (for) oneself, the benefit (of) others is lost, (and)

the two will not come (to) the state of Reality;

that is why (it) has to be taught in that way.   10

---

1. dPon slob 'Phrin las Nyi ma: Given that everything finds itself in the condition of Primordial Enlightenment, there is no reason for trying to accomplish the benefit of beings; on the contrary, by abiding in that state, the benefit of beings will actually be achieved.

༃།
thams cad rang bzhin ka dag la / /
gnyis su 'dzin pa 'khrul pa ste / /
mig¹ btsir zla ba gnyis snang 'dra / /

GK 623,1,   gnyis su ① snang yang gcig [379] nyid yin / /
KG 379   gcig las de na ga la yod / /   5
de bzhin thams cad gcig gi ngang / /

TL 3b   (3b) gnyis su lta ba'i theg dman² rnams / /
'bras bu thob par ngas ma bshad / /

---

1. mig GK, KG : dmig TL
2. dman GK, KG : rman TL

Ca

As to the (Ultimate) Nature (of) everything, (which is)
    pure from the beginning,
to conceive (it) as dual is a delusion;
(it is) like seeing two moons when pressing the eyes.

(GK 623,1)   Although (it) appears as two, (it is) just one;
If that (doesn't come) out of the one, how (come it) is
    there?   5
Accordingly, everything (is) the Condition of One.
(That) lower vehicles viewing (things) as two
attain the Fruit, I have not proclaimed.

nga yis gnyis su ma bstan[1] te //
khyed kyi blo la gnyis snang bas[2] //
GK 623,2   des na ② blo yi[3] rnam[4] pa yin //
blo[5] de bden par khyod ma 'dzin //
gyi[6] ling mig[7] la nyin mtshan med //   5
nga la[8] ye nas[9] gnyis su med //
gzhi de mnyam[10] pa'i rang bzhin las //
blo[11] yis so sor phye ba yang //
mnyam[12] pa gcig las ma g.yos so //[13]

---

1. bstan GK, KG : stan TL

2. pas GK : bas KG, TL

3. blo yi GK, KG : glo'i TL

4. rnam GK, KG : gnam TL

5. blo GK, KG : glo TL

6. gyi GK, KG : khyi TL

7. mig GK, KG : dmig TL

8. la GK, KG : yang TL

9. ye nas rep. GK

10. mnyam GK, KG : gnyam TL

11. blo GK, KG : glo TL

12. mnyam GK, KG : gnyam TL

13. rkyang shad GK, KG : nyis shad TL

I have not taught duality;
(it) appears (as) duality to your mind;
(GK 623,2)   consequently, (that) is the manner (of perceiving) of the mind.
Do not consider that mind as truthful.
In the eyes (of) a fine horse,[1] day and night do not exist;   5
In me, there is no duality from the beginning.
Out of the equal Nature (of) that Basis,
the mind has created distinctions; nonetheless,
(it) has never moved from (that) single equality.

---

1. According to dPon slob 'Phrin las Nyi ma, the metaphor refers to the View of *Kun tu bZang po*, which is undifferentiated, as is the sight of good and thoroughbred horses. For *gyi ling*, see B. Laufer 1916, p. 508; dGe bshes Chos kyi Grags pa's *brDa dang ming tshig gsal ba*, Mi rigs dPe skrun khang, Beijing, 1981, p. 125, where *gyi ling* = *rta mchog*, and reference is made to the good horses of Amdo, of which twelve different breeds are said to exist; cf. *A mdo'i kha skad tshig mdzod*, edited by Hwa Khan and Klu 'bum rGyal, Kan su'u Mi rigs dPe skrun khang, Lanzhou, 1993, p. 92 and BGTC, vol. 1, p. 382.

क|

GK 623,3   mnyam[1] ③ pa nyid kyi[2] don de la / /
glang chen ma bskyod[3] rnal mar zhog[4] / /
mthar ni nam mkha'i rgya yis thob / /
dper na gser gling rdo med ltar / /
theg pa gzhan[5] gyi skyon dag dang[6] / /   5
spang ba[7] med par ngang gis[8] zhi[9] / /
theg pa gzhan[10] gyi yon tan kyang[11] / /
GK 623,4   'bad ④ pa med par lhun gyis grub / /
des na mnyam pa'i rgyal po thob / /

---

1. mnyam GK, KG : gnyam TL

2. kyi GK, KG : gyi TL

3. bskyod GK, KG : skyod TL

4. zhog GK, KG : bzhag TL

5. gzhan GK, KG : bzhan TL

6. dang GK, KG : kyang TL

7. pa GK, KG, TL : ba ego

8. gi GK, KG : gis ego.

9. ngang gi zhi GK, KG : rang bzhin zhi TL

10. gzhan GK, KG : bzhan TL

11. kyang GK, KG : yang TL

Cha

(GK 623,3) With respect to that state of equality,
remain calmly unshaken (like an) elephant.
In the end, find (it) through the token of the sky.[1]
(In that way,) as for example (in) the golden island
    without stones,
the shortcomings of other vehicles are purified and   5
are naturally abated without being discarded;
also the virtues of other vehicles

(GK 623,4) will be spontaneously accomplished without effort;
therefore, (one) becomes the king of equality.

---

1. dPon slob 'Phrin las Nyi ma: that is to say, let your mind be empty and clear as the sky.

de ltar rtogs pa'i gang zag de //
ye sangs rgyas pa kho[1] nar[2] yin //
bde[3] ba chen po'i klong dkyil na //
rnam rtog mi mnga' cir yang gsal //

gzhi ni rang bzhin bcos su [380] med pa la //   5
⑤ rnam rtog blo[4] yis ji ltar brtags[5] par snang //
ji ltar snang yang de don bcos su med //
ma bcos ye nas snying po byang chub sems //
byang chub sems ni 'gyur med g.yung drung yin //

---

1. kho GK, KG : kha TL
2. nar GK, KG : na TL
3. bde GK, KG : bde' TL
4. blo GK, KG : klo TL
5. brtags GK, KG : btags TL

The individual who realizes (that it is) in that way
is in the very (state of) Primordial Enlightenment.
Within the Expanse of great bliss
there is no conceptuality, everything shines forth in all
    sorts of ways.
As to the Basis, which is the (Ultimate) unaltered Nature,   5
(GK 623,5)   (it) appears in whatever way (it is) considered by the
    conceptual mind.
But no matter how (it) may appear, the state of That
    (remains) unaltered.
(It is) the Pure-and-Perfect-Mind, the unaltered, primor-
    dial quintessence.
The Pure-and-Perfect-Mind is immutable (and) everlasting.

ཤ།

TL 4a   sems nyid mi 'gyur g.yung drung (4a) don rtogs na //
GK 623,6   skye 'chi¹ 'pho 'gyur ye ⑥ nas g.yung drung don //
g.yung drung don dang skye 'chi gnyis su med //
sems ni 'pho 'gyur med de² rtag par gnas //
'pho 'gyur nyid ni ye nas rtag par gnas³ //   5
des na thams cad rtag pa⁴ chen por gnas //
sems can 'pho 'gyur ye nas g.yung drung don //
GK 623,7   ⑦ g.yung drung don ni ye nas sems nyid⁵ yin //

---

1. shi GK, KG : 'chi TL

2. de GK, KG : ste TL

3. The whole verse is omitted in TL.

4. brtag pa GK : rtag pa KG, TL

5. sems can and >sems nyid< GK : sems nyid KG : sems can TL

Ja

When the state of the everlasting, immutable Mind-itself
   is realized,

(GK 623,6)   birth (and) death (and) transformations (and) changes
   (are) from the origin the Everlasting State.

The Everlasting State and birth (and) death do not exist as
   a duality.

The Mind, being without transformations (and) changes,
   exists as eternity;

transformations (and) changes (themselves) exist in
   eternity from the origin;   5

hence, everything exists as great eternity.

Transformations (and) changes (of) sentient beings (are)
   from the origin the Everlasting State.

(GK 623,7)   The Everlasting State is from the origin the Mind-itself.

gnyis su med pa ye nas g.yung drung don / /
bon nyid g.yung drung rgya mtsho lta bu la / /
brgyad khri bzhi stong chu bran 'bab pa 'dra / /
de yi[1] don la nges par rtogs 'dod na / /
dang por[2] chags par byed pa'i yid thul[3] la / /   5
GK 624,1   dgon[4] ① pa'i gnas su yun ring[5] bsdad[6] par bya / /
bag chags ngan pa'i g.yo 'khrug[7] bzlog[8] par bya / /
des na mi g.yo[9] g.yung drung don la bzhag / /

---

1. yis GK : yi KG, TL
2. por GK, KG : po TL
3. thul GK, KG : btul TL
4. dgon GK, KG : sgon TL
5. ring GK, KG : rings TL
6. bsdad GK, KG : 'dug TL
7. 'khrug GK, KG : 'khrul TL
8. bzlog GK, KG : zlog TL
9. g.yo GK, KG : 'gyur TL

(It is) the primordial, Everlasting State without duality.
Reality (is) everlasting, (it is) like the ocean; in that respect
the eighty-four thousand (afflictions)[1] are like converging
    streams.
If (one) wishes to realize with certainty the state of That,
at first, in order to tame the mind that creates
    attachment,   5

(GK 624,1)   (one) should reside (for a) long time in a place of
    seclusion (and)
repulse the tumult of bad imprints,
so as to abide without distraction in the Everlasting State.

---

1. dPon slob 'Phrin las Nyi ma: the eighty-four thousand kinds of afflictions, which are counteracted by the eighty-four thousand teachings of Bon. Cf. The Twelve Little Tantras, p. 141, n. 1.

३१

g.yung drung don ni yid bzhin nor bu 'dra / /
dper na yid bzhin nor bu[1] rin chen de / /

GK 624,2   sngon gyi las ② dang sbyin pa gtong[2] ba[3] yi[4] / /
KG 381   gang zag skal [381] ldan 'ga'[5] la yod pa las[6] / /
kun dang kun la de ni ga la yod[7] / /   5
de bzhin de la[8] de dang de 'dra'o / /[9]

---

1. 'dra / / dper na yid bzhin nor bu incl. GK, TL : >'dra / / dper na yid bzhin nor bu<
(dbu chen) KG

2. thongs GK, KG, TL : gtong ego

3. pa GK, KG, TL : ba ego

4. yi GK, KG : de'i TL

5. 'ga' GK, KG : 'ga TL

6. la GK, KG : las TL

7. yod GK, KG : 'ong TL

8. la GK, KG : yang TL

9. rkyang shad GK, KG : nyis shad TL

Nya

The Everlasting State is like the Wish-fulfilling Gem.
For example, the precious Wish-fulfilling Gem

(GK 624,2)   —except for being possessed by a few lucky individuals
in virtue of their generosity and previous meritorious
    actions—
in respect with all the others, where is it?   5
Hence, in that respect, That and that are alike.[1]

---

1. The Everlasting State is difficult to perceive as much as the Wish-fulfilling Gem is difficult to obtain.

sems ni u[1] du 'bar ba'i me tog 'dra / /
u du 'bar ba'i me tog yang[2] / /

GK 624,3   gser gyi ③ grang[3] ma las[4] skyes nas / /
ri rgyal lhun po'i sbubs byung[5] ste / /
ston pa re re byon dus su / /   5
sum bcu rtsa gsum gnas su 'khrungs[6] / /
de ltar 'khrungs[7] pa[8] dka'[9] ba bzhin / /
sems nyid g.yung drung don 'di[10] yang / /

TL 4b   (4b) de bzhin rtogs pa dka'[11] ba yin / /

GK 624,4   ④ ye nas sems nyid ma bcos pa / /   10
rnam par rtog pa'i ra ba nas / /
mi rtog sems nyid 'khrungs[12] pa dka'[13] / /

---

1. u GK, KG : ud TL
2. yang GK, TL : kyang KG
3. grang GK, KG : drang TL
4. la GK, KG : las TL
5. phyung GK, KG : byung TL
6. 'khrungs GK, KG : 'khrung TL
7. 'khrungs GK, KG : 'khrung TL
8. pa GK, KG : ba TL
9. dka' GK, KG : rka TL
10. 'di GK, KG : 'di' TL
11. dka' GK, KG : rka TL
12. 'khrungs GK, KG : 'khrul TL
13. dka' GK, KG : rka TL

The Mind-itself is like the *Udumbara* flower.
Also the *Udumbara* flower,
(GK 624,3)   which stems out of (cold) gold dust[1]
produced (in) the trunk[2] of Mount Meru,
at the time when each master appeared,   5
blossomed (only) in the place (of) the Thirty-three (gods).[3]
Similarly, as (it is) difficult (for it) to blossom,
so (it) is difficult (for) this Everlasting State, the Mind-
itself, to be perceived.
(GK 624,4)   The Mind-itself (is) unaltered from the origin.   10
(It is) difficult (for) the non-conceptual Mind-itself to arise
from the enclosure of conceptuality.

---

1. *gser gyi grang ma;* cf. BGTC. vol. 1, p. 393, *grang gser:* "*Phye mar btul ba'i gser 'byug dus me la brten mi dgos pa zhig.*"

2. *sbubs;* cf. BGTC, vol. 2, p. 2018, *sbubs ma.*

3. Skr. *Trāyastriṁśa,* the heaven situated at the top of Mount Meru in the sphere of desire (*'dod khams*), inhabited by the thirty-three gods; see the MVy, Sasaki, Tokyo, 1916-1926, entry no. 3079, and also He Wenxuan and Hou Cunqi, *Bod rgya shan sbyar gyi shes bya'i rnam grangs kun btus tshig mdzod,* mTsho sngon Mi rigs dPe skrun khang, Xining, 1987, pp. 786-787. Cf. P. Kværne 1990b, p. 208.

༿།

sems nyid de don rtogs 'dod na / /
rnam par rtog pa'i rjes mi 'breng / /
mtshan ma 'khrul pa'i rjes mi gcod / /

GK 624,5   sems ⑤ la rtsol ba gzhug[1] mi bya / /
gza' gtad med pa'i dgongs pa la / /   5
byung tshor rnam rtog med par bzhag / /
mi dmigs thig le chen po la / /
ma bcos don gyis gsal gdab bya / /
des na de don rnyed par 'gyur / /

GK 624,6   lam nor ⑥ lam stor lam nyes kyis[2] / /   10
de don rnyed par mi 'gyur te[3] / /
byis pas[4] 'ja'[5] mtshon 'ded[6] pa 'dra / /
glang chen smig[7] sgyu snyeg pa 'dra / /

KG 382   lam ni nye[8] [382] lam bde[9] rdzogs yin / /

---

1. bzhug GK : gzhug KG, TL

2. kyi GK : kyis KG, TL

3. ste GK : te KG, TL

4. pa GK, TL : pas KG

5. 'ja' GK, KG : gzha TL

6. 'ded GK, KG : ded TL

7. smig GK, KG : smigs TL

8. nye GK, KG : nyid TL

9. bde GK, KG : der TL

Ta

If one wishes to realize the state of That, the Mind-itself,

(one) does not pursue conceptuality;

(one) does not follow the delusion (of) characterization.

(GK 624,5)   With respect to the Mind, no effort is to be undertaken.

With respect to the contemplation which is not

conceived,[1]   5

(one) remains without concepts (and without following)

feelings.

The unimagined great *Thig le*

is to be clearly hit by the unaltered state.[2]

In that way, the state of That will be found.

(GK 624,6)   Through mistaken,[3] astrayed[4] and wrong[5] paths   10

the state of That will not be found.

(Followers of those paths) are like children chasing a

rainbow,

like elephants pursuing a mirage.

The (real) path is the direct path (of) perfection and bliss.

---

1. dPon slob 'Phrin las Nyi ma: *gza' gtad med pa = dmigs su med pa*.

2. dPon slob 'Phrin las Nyi ma: by remaining in the state of contemplation (*dgongs pa*), the Ultimate Nature of the individual spontaneously appears in the external space in the form of spheres (*thig le*). These spheres are absolutely not created through the mind's imagination. Visions of such kind can be experienced by consummate meditators in daytime and at night as well, since they do not depend on secondary sources such as sunlight etc. That is why it is said that the *thig le* is unconstrued and that it can only appear by remaining in the state of contemplation.

3. dPon slob 'Phrin las Nyi ma: the mistaken views of the lower eight Vehicles.

4. dPon slob 'Phrin las Nyi ma: the views of heretics.

5. dPon slob 'Phrin las Nyi ma: mistaken views applied to the teachings of the Great Perfection. These consist in the inclusion of the views of the eight lower Vehicles into the View of Great Perfection; wrong interpretations of the instructions; and mistaken

ཐ།

sems nyid[1] mi 'gyur g.yung drung yin //
'khrul pa sna tshogs cir[2] yang snang //

GK 624,7   ⑦ snang ba[3] nyid na g.yung drung don //
sbrul dang thag pa ji[4] bzhin no //
thag pa med par sbrul mi 'khrul //   5
sbrul du snang ba[5] thag pa yin //
'khrul pa nyid ni g.yung drung yin //
'di don rtogs pa'i dpe[6] bstan[7] na //

GK 625,1   rgyal bu stor ba khungs ① chod 'dra //
des na de dang de 'dra bas //   10

---

views that can be naturally overcome. Cf. the *'Od gsal rdzogs pa chen po'i lam gyi rim pa'i khrid yid kun tu bzang po'i snying tig* by Shar rdza bKra' shis rGyal mtshan, in T. Namdak 1993, Tibetan Text, p. 21,1 et seq.

1. nyid GK, KG : ni TL

2. cir GK, KG : jir TL

3. pa GK : ba KG, TL

4. ji GK, KG : ci TL

5. pa GK : ba KG, TL

6. dpe GK, KG : dpes TL

7. bstan GK, KG : stan TL

Tha

The Mind-itself is immutable (and) everlasting.

Various delusions appear in all sorts of ways.

(GK 624,7)   In appearance itself is the Everlasting State.

It is like (when there is) a rope and (the rope is mistaken

for) a snake.

Without rope, there is no delusion (of) a snake;   5

(what) appears as a snake is the rope.

Delusion itself is the Everlasting.

To show an example for understanding the meaning (of) this,

(GK 625,1)   it is like (when) the son (of a) king has been lost (and

then) found.[1]

Thus, that[2] and that[3] resemble each other.   10

---

1. dPon slob 'Phrin las Nyi ma: perceiving the Mind-itself is a cause of great joy, just like finding the lost son of a king. For an account of the lost prince, cf. N. Namkhai 1995, p. 10.

2. dPon slob 'Phrin las Nyi ma: the snake.

3. dPon slob 'Phrin las Nyi ma: delusion.

dngos su de nyid de yin med[1] //
de don 'dod pa'i gang zag gis //
yid kyis[2] kun gzhi la bltas[3] na //
gnyis su med pa'i don rtogs[4] na //

TL 5a   (5a) bde[5] ba chen po'i don zhes bya //[6]   5
GK 625,2 ngang dang rang bzhin bdag ② nyid don //
chen po zhes kyang de la bya //
ngang ni kun gzhi ma bcos pa //
rang bzhin de las ma g.yos pa[7] //
gnyis su med par shes pa ni //   10
de la bdag nyid chen po[8] bya //

---

1. med GK, KG : mod TL
2. kyi GK : kyis KG, TL
3. bltas GK, KG : ltas TL
4. rtogs GK, KG : 'thong TL
5. bde GK, KG : bde' TL
6. rkyang shad GK, KG : nyis shad TL
7. pas GK, KG : pa TL
8. pos GK, TL : po KG

(But) in reality, is that[1] That itself?[2] (It) is not.
For someone who aspires to the state of That,
to realize the meaning of non-duality[3] after having
intellectually reflected upon the Basis (of) all,
(is what) is called the state of great bliss.   5
(GK 625,2) The meaning of Condition, (Ultimate) Nature and
        Identity,
which is also called Great:
the Condition (is) the Basis (of) all (which is) unaltered;
the (Ultimate) Nature doesn't move from that
        (Condition);
as to the knowledge of (their) non-duality,   10
that is called the Great Identity.

---

1. I.e. the delusion.

2. I.e. the Everlasting State.

3. dPon slob 'Phrin las Nyi ma: the non-duality of the mind with the Mind-itself.

ༀ
sems nyid ngang gyis[1] ma bcos te[2] //
rtsol ba kun dang bral bar gnas[3] //

GK 625,3   ③ yongs kyis[4] 'od gsal de la bya //
de lta bu yi[5] g.yung drung sems //
rang gis[6] rig na brjod[7] mi 'tshal //   5
mtha'[8] dang dbus med kun tu[9] bzang po yin //
phyi nang med pas ye shes zang thal yin //

GK 625,4   skyon yon med pas lhun ④ gyis grub pa yin //
KG 383   bgrod du med pas [383] rtsol[10] ba'i sems dang bral //   10
gzung[11] du med pas chags pa kun dang bral //
mtha'[12] dbus med pas phyogs ris yongs dang bral ///[13]

---

1. nyid GK, KG : gyis TL
2. te GK, KG : ste TL
3. byas GK, TL : gnas KG
4. kyi GK, KG : kyis TL
5. yis GK : yi KG, TL
6. gi GK : gis KG, TL
7. brjod GK, KG : rjod TL
8. mtha' GK, KG : mtha TL
9. du GK : tu KG, TL
10. rtsal GK, TL : rtsol KG
11. gzung GK, KG : bzung TL
12. mtha' GK, KG : mtha TL
13. rkyang shad GK, KG : nyis shad TL

Da
Since the Mind-itself is naturally unaltered,
(it) exists without any effort;
(GK 625,3)   it is generally called Clear Light.[1]
The Everlasting Mind, which (is in) that way,
being spontaneously aware, doesn't seek to express (what
    it is aware of).   5
(Being) without borders and centre, (it) is the All-Good.
Having no outside (nor) inside, it is transparent Primor-
    dial Wisdom.
(GK 625,4)   Having no defects (nor) virtues, (it) is spontaneously
    accomplished.
Being without progression, (it is) without the intention of
    effort.
Being unprejudiced, (it is) without any attachment.   10
Having no extremes (nor) middle, (it is) without any
    partiality (and) inclination.

---

1. Cf. Introduction, p. 61.

ན།

bon gyi rang bzhin sems las med pa la[1] //

GK 625,5   yul sems ⑤ gnyis su mthong[2] ba[3] 'khrul[4] pa yin //[5]

btsal[6] bas ye nas 'khrul pa[7] ji ltar snang //

ji srid sems kyi[8] rang bzhin snang zhing srid //

sems nyid[9] byang chub sems las ma gtogs[10] pa //   5

bon kun gzhan[11] nas btsal bas gang nas rnyed //

GK 625,6   ⑥ rnyed pa kun tu[12] bzang po ngas ma gsungs //

mnyam nyid ngo bo dag la de mi snang //

nan tar spyod[13] dang rang nyid rig pa'i sems //

---

1. las GK, KG : la TL

2. mthong GK, KG : 'thong TL

3. pa GK : ba KG, TL

4. 'phrul GK : 'khrul KG, TL

5. rkyang shad GK, KG : nyis shad TL

6. btsal GK, KG : rtsal TL

7. par GK, KG : pa TL

8. kyi GK, KG : gyi TL

9. kyi GK, KG : nyid TL

10. rtogs GK, TL : gtogs KG

11. gzhan GK, KG : bzhan TL

12. du GK : tu KG, TL

13. dpyod GK : spyod KG, TL

Na

With respect to (the fact that) the (Ultimate) Nature of
    phenomena doesn't exist outside the Mind,

(GK 625,5)   it is delusive to see the mind (and its) objects as two.

By pursuing (that), as delusion manifests itself from the
    beginning (and) as it comes into being,

thus, the disposition of the mind manifests itself (and)
    comes into being.

Except for the Pure-and-Perfect-Mind, the Mind-itself,   5

if all phenomena are sought from somewhere else,
    whence shall (they) be found?

(GK 625,6)   (That they can be) found (elsewhere), I, Kun tu bZang po,
    did not proclaim.

To the actual essence (of) equality, that doesn't appear.

Earnest practice and the mind that is aware (of) itself,

TL 5b   snang (5b) ba^1 thams cad rang gi sems snang yin //
           snang ba^2 nyid tsam de na^3 dmigs su med //
GK 625,7   des na mi snang ba^4 nyid mthar ⑦ phyin yin //
           mi snang ba^5 nyid sna tshogs snang zhing 'byung //
           des na sems^6 nyid snang ba^7 mthar phyin yin //   5
           sna tshogs snang bas^8 chad lta spangs //
           snang tsam nyid na mi dmigs pas //
           des ni rtag pa'i mtha'^{9} spangs so //^{10}
           de ltar de don rtogs pa na //
GK 626,1   rtag ① chad gnyis med bon gyi sku //   10
           snang stong dag^{11} la dgag sgrub med //^{12}

---

1. pa GK : ba KG, TL

2. pa GK : ba KG, TL

3. na GK, KG : nas TL

4. pa GK : ba KG, TL

5. pa GK : ba KG, TL

6. sems GK, KG : de TL

7. pa GK : ba KG. TL

8. pas GK : bas KG, TL

9. mtha' GK, KG : mtha TL

10. rkyang shad GK, KG : nyis shad TL

11. For the numeral particle *dag*, see M. Hahn 1978, p. 145: "This concept of collectivity comprises the ideas of both singularity and plurality..."

12. rkyang shad GK, KG : nyis shad TL

all appearances are a display (of) one's (own) Mind.
Appearance, being nothing else but appearance, cannot
   be conceived.[1]

(GK 625,7) Therefore, non-appearance itself is the finality.
Non-appearance arises and manifests itself (in) various
   ways.
Therefore, the Mind-itself is the finality (of) appearance. 5
Since it manifests itself (in) various ways, (it) eludes the
   nihilistic view.
Since appearance, being nothing else but appearance,
   cannot be conceived,
(it) eludes the extreme (view) of eternalism (as well).
Realizing the state of That in such way,

(GK 626,1) (is to realize) the Body of Reality (which is) without
   duality (of) eternalism (and) nihilism, (where) 10
appearance is not obstructed, (and) emptiness is not
   produced.

---

1. dPon slob 'Phrin las Nyi ma: appearance represents the spontaneously accomplished Way of Being of the Mind-itself.

ঝ|

bon nyid g.yung drung sems las ma gtogs[1] pa //

KG 384   de las [384] lhag pa'i bon gcig[2] ga na yod //

bon nyid byang chub sems su ma shes na //

bag chags 'byung 'jug rjes su brtags[3] pas 'khrul //

GK 626,2   ② srid pa ma lus snang ba'i[4] rgyu med de[5] //   5

rnam rtog 'khrul pa'i[6] dbang gyis[7] sems nyid srid par
    'byung //

srid dgu[8] nges[9] pa'i rtsa ba gcig pu ba //

sna tshogs bag chags dngos por mthong[10] ba[11] dang[12] //

yod med rtag chad bzung bas[338] gtan du phung //

---

1. >gtogs< GK : gtogs KG : rtogs TL

2. gcig GK, KG : cig TL

3. brtags GK, KG : rtags TL

4. pa'i GK : ba'i KG, TL

5. de GK, KG : ste TL

6. pa'i om. GK, KG : pa'i incl. TL

7. gyis om. GK, KG : gyis incl. TL

8. dgu GK, KG : rgyu TL

9. nges GK, KG : nyes TL

10. mthong GK, KG : 'thong TL

11. pa GK : ba KG, TL

12. dang GK, KG : yang TL

13. pas GK, TL : bas KG

Pa

Except for the Reality, the Everlasting Mind,
beyond that, where does a single phenomenon exist?
When Reality is not known as (being) the Pure-and-
Perfect-Mind,
by conceptualizing according to (the notions that) arise
(from and) follow (one's) imprints, (one) is deluded.
(GK 626,2)   All existence[1] has no cause for appearing;[2]   5
(it is) through the power of delusive conceptuality (that)
the Mind-itself arises as existence.[3]
The real root (of) the many existences (is) one.
(In) taking imprints (of) all sorts for real, and
(in) adhering (to) existence (and) non-existence,
eternalism, (and) nihilism (one) is always doomed.[4]

---

1. dPon slob 'Phrin las Nyi ma: all phenomena of transmigration and the state transcending suffering.

2. dPon slob 'Phrin las Nyi ma: because in itself it is devoid of inherent nature.

3. dPon slob 'Phrin las Nyi ma: as transmigration.

4. Cf. BGTC, vol. 2. p. 1781, *'phung ba*, (1).

ব্|

GK 626,3   rang rig rnal chen ③ ye nas bya med la / /
snang dang[1] mi snang dpyod las 'das par bzhag / /
de ltar rig pa'i sems byung na / /
ye nas sang rgyas yin par gnas / /
sangs rgyas yin pa'i don de la / /   5
la las 'khrul pa nyid du mthong / /

GK 626,4,   (6a) la las sangs rgyas nyid ④ du mthong / /
TL 6a   mthong lugs mi mthun[2] so sor snang / /
snang tsam nyid na mnyam pa'i ngang / /
ye nas rol pa chen po yin / /   10
mi gnas gnas pa'i[3] yul med pas / /
ma rtogs[4] bon gyi dbyings las byung / /

---

1. dang GK, KG : yang TL
2. mthun GK, KG : 'thun TL
3. pa'i GK, KG : pa TL
4. rtogs GK, TL : rtog KG

Pha

(GK 626,3)   Calm Self-Awareness,[1] which is devoid of action from the
origin,

remains beyond the judgement (of what) appears[2] (or)
doesn't appear.

Once the Mind of such Awareness arises,

(it) remains (and) exists (as) Primordial Enlightenment.

As to that state that exists (as) Enlightenment,   5

some see it just as delusion,

(GK 626,4)   some see it just as Enlightenment.

The ways of seeing (it) differ; (it) appears in distinct ways.

Appearance, being nothing else but appearance, (is) the
Condition of equality;

(it) is the primordial Great Play.   10

(It) does not have a place where it exists (or where it) does
not exist:

(it) has come forth from the Dimension of unconceived
Reality.

---

1. dPon slob 'Phrin las Nyi ma: the Primordial Wisdom of Self-Awareness.

2. dPon slob 'Phrin las Nyi ma: thoughts, sensations, visions, sounds. See below, p. 233.

ༀ།

snang ba med pas chags pa spangs[1] / /

GK 626,5   ⑤ mthong[2] tshor rjes su mi 'jug bden pa'i[3] lam / /

mu med bral ba'i dbyings nyid la / /

snang med rig[4] pa rang grol ba'o[5] / /[6]

dmigs su med pas rang grol gsal / /   5

kha spub[7] spyi tshugs gar 'dres[8] kyang / /

KG 385   [385] ye shes dbyings las g.yos pa med / /

---

1. yang GK, KG : spangs TL

2. mthong GK, KG : 'thong TL

3. pa'i GK, KG : pa TL

4. >rig< GK : incl. KG, TL

5. ba'o GK, KG : pa'o TL

6. rkyang shad GK, KG : nyid shad TL

7. spub GK, KG : sbub TL

8. 'dres GK, KG : 'gres TL

Ba

Since appearance is non-existent,[1] attachment is (to be) given up.

(GK 626,5) The true path (is that of) not going after perceptions.

As to the Dimension itself, which is without limits,

(it) is self-released Awareness devoid of appearances.

Without being conceived, (it) shines forth (in a) self-released (way):   5

no matter how (it) is mixed, turned over or upside down,

Primordial Wisdom does not move from the Dimension.

---

1. dPon slob 'Phrin las Nyi ma: it doesn't have inherent nature.

GK 626,6   ⑥ ye shes nyid kyis[1] mi rnyed pas / /
ye ni mthong[2] spyad de la med / /
snang med mthong[3] bas[4] ye shes nyid / /
nyid la gsal rtogs[5] dpe[6] dang bral / /
snang med srid pa sus mthong[7] ba[8] / /   5
des ni sems kyi[9] srid pa mthong[10] / /

---

1. kyis GK, KG : gyis TL

2. mthong GK, KG : 'thong TL

3. mthong GK, KG : 'thong TL

4. pas GK : bas KG : ba TL

5. rtogs GK, KG : rtog TL

6. dpe GK, KG : dpe' TL

7. mthong GK, KG : 'thong TL

8. pa GK : ba KG, TL

9. kyi GK, KG : gyi TL

10. mthong GK, KG : 'thong TL

(GK 626,6)   Primordial Wisdom doesn't find itself:
(it is) 'Primordial', (since it) is without (any) assumed
    (way of) seeing;
(it is) 'Wisdom', just because (it) sees without appearances;
as to the 'itself', (it means that it) clearly perceives (itself)
    beyond examples.
Whoever sees the existence (of that which is) without
    appearances,   5
that (person) sees the existence of the Mind.

ཨ།

GK 626,7   snang ba¹ rang² sa³ 'khrul ⑦ pa yin / /
sna tshogs mthong⁴ ba⁵ bag chags rgyu / /
sems la 'gog pa'i bag chags yin / /
'khrul pa sna tshogs sems yin na⁶ / /
'khor ba⁷ rgyu 'bras gang nas 'ong⁸ / /   5
sems ni cir yang snang ba⁹ yin / /
de ltar smar¹⁰ ba sus rtogs pa

GK 627,1   de yis ① 'khrul pa'i phyi bzhin 'brengs / /

---

1. pa GK : ba KG, TL
2. rangs GK, KG, TL : rang ego
3. sa GK, KG : pa TL
4. mthong GK, KG : 'thong TL
5. pa GK : ba KG, TL
6. na incl. GK, KG : om. TL
7. ba GK, KG : ba'i TL
8. 'ong GK, KG : 'ongs TL
9. pa GK : ba KG, TL
10. smar GK, KG : smra TL

Ma

(GK 626,7) Appearance is (in) itself delusion.

The various (ways of) seeing (are) the cause (of) the
   imprints.

Imprints are that which (creates) obstruction with respect
   to the Mind.

If the various delusions are the Mind,

where do the causes (and) effects (of) transmigration
   come from?   5

As to the Mind, it appears in whatsoever way.

Whoever realizes (that which is) thus proclaimed,

(GK 627,1) that (person) goes after delusions.[1]

---

1. dPon slob 'Phrin las Nyi ma: that is to say, delusion is not rejected since it is perceived in its Ultimate Nature.

TL 6b

snang ba[1] ma grub zer ba nyid //
chad pa'i dngos por brtags[2] pa yin //
snang ba'i[3] rgyu la dpyad pas (6b) phung //
snang ba[4] med par ye gsal la //
kun bzang bshad[5] pa mi mdzad do //   5

---

1. pa GK : ba KG, TL
2. brtgas GK, KG : btags TL
3. pa'i GK : ba'i KG, TL
4. pa GK : ba KG, TL
5. bshad GK, KG : spyad TL

To just say (that) appearance is not produced,
is to conceive (it) as the substance of nihilism,
(and) to fail in recognizing the cause of appearance
    (itself).
(That) from the origin (it) shines forth as devoid (of)
    appearance
is not what Kun (tu) bZang (po) (himself) has
    proclaimed.   5

ཚོ།

GK 627,2   rig pa'i ye shes su ② snang ba[1] / /
dus gsum gshen rab[2] de dang 'brel / /
snying rje sna tshogs su snang ba[3] / /
khams[4] gsum sems can de dang 'brel / /
gnyis su med pa bon gyi[5] sku / /   5
de lta bu'i don nyid la / /
g.yeng ba[6] lnga dang bral ba ni / /
de nyid sangs rgyas kho[7] na yin / /
GK 627,3   rig pa rang las gsal shar ③ na / /
KG 386   nyin [386] dang mtshan du ga la yod / /   10

---

1. pa GK : ba KG, TL
2. rab GK, KG : rabs TL
3. pa GK : ba KG : bas TL
4. khams GK, KG : 'khams TL
5. gyis GK : gyi KG, TL
6. pa GK : ba KG, TL
7. kho GK, KG : kha TL

Tsa

(GK 627,2)   Appearance as the Primordial Wisdom of Awareness
is linked with the gShen rab (of) the three times.
Appearance as the various (forms of) loving kindness
is linked with sentient beings (of) the three spheres.
The Body of Reality (is) without duality.   5
As to the state which is like that, (and which is)
without the five diversions,[1]
that is precisely (the state of) Enlightenment.
(GK 627,3)   When Awareness clearly arises from itself,
where is day and where is night?[2]   10

---

1. dPon slob 'Phrin las Nyi ma: attachments related to the five senses.

2. dPon slob 'Phrin las Nyi ma: a reference to the practice of *thod rgal*. Cf. Introduction, p. 68, n. 212.

ye bdal khyab par gdod[1] gnas pas //
che chung gnyis su ga la yod //
stobs kyi[2] rgyal po thabs rig pas //
thub dang ma thub gnyis su med //
byang chub kyi[3] ni[4] snying po de //   5
sems kyi[5] snying por ye gnas pas //

GK 627,4   bde[6] ④ dang mi bde[7] gnyis su med //
ka[8] dag ye shes rang snang bas[9] //
rgyu 'bras tha dad ye nas med[10] //
bon rnams sgyu ma'i rang bzhin la //   10
bdag sems 'khrul pa'i[11] 'dzin chags med //
rnam rtog mi mnga' cir yang gsal //

---

1. gdod GK, KG : bdod TL

2. kyi GK, KG : gyi TL

3. kyi GK, KG : gyi TL

4. For the use of the topicalizer *ni* with particular reference to archaic literature see S. V. Beyer 1992, pp. 275-278.

5. kyi GK, KG : gyi TL

6. bde GK, KG : bde' TL

7. bde GK, KG : bde' TL

8. ka GK, KG : rka TL

9. pas GK : bas KG, TL

10. >med< GK : incl. KG, TL

11. pa'i GK, KG : yang TL

Since it exists from the origin as (that which is) primordi-
    ally encompassing,
where's the difference between big (and) small?
When one observes the means (of) a mighty king,
possible and impossible do not exist.
That quintessence, the Pure-and-Perfect,   5
existing (from) the origin as the quintessence of the mind,
(GK 627,4)   is without both joy and sorrow.
Since the Primordial Wisdom pure from the beginning
    appears (by) itself,
it is from the origin without distinctions (of) cause (and)
    effect.
With respect to the mirage-like nature (of) phenomena,   10
(it) doesn't have the delusive grasping (and) attachment
    (of) the mind (of the) self;
(being) without conceptuality, (it) clearly shines forth in
    all sorts of ways.

ཚྀ།

bon nyid bde[1] ba chen po[2] la / /

GK 627,5 bsgom[3] na byis ⑤ pa'i spyod yul lags / /

ma bsgom[4] tsam na bsgom pa yin / /

bdag sems ye nas lhun grub la[5] / /

mtshan ma can gyis bslad[6] du med / /   5

ye nas ma bsgrubs[7] ye grub dkyil 'khor[8] la / /

gang zag rnams kyis[9] sgrub tu[10] med / /

sgrub med btsal[11] med snying po 'di[12] / /

GK 627,6,
TL 7a ⑥ de ni ye (7a) nas de ltar gnas / /

---

1. bde GK, KG : bde' TL

2. chen po rep., first chen po struck through TL

3. bsgom GK, KG : sgom TL

4. bsgom GK, KG : sgom TL

5. pa GK, KG : la TL

6. bslad GK, KG : slad TL

7. bsgrubs GK, KG : sgrub TL

8. dkyil 'khor om. GK, KG : incl. TL

9. kyi GK : kyis KG : gyis TL

10. du GK, TL : tu KG

11. btsal GK, KG : rtsal TL

12. 'di GK, KG : 'di' TL

Tsha

To meditate on the Reality (which is) the great bliss

(GK 627,5)   is a childish activity;

when there is no meditation, (that is when it) is meditated.

One's Mind, (which is) spontaneously accomplished from
the origin,

is not tainted by that which is characterized.   5

The primordially unaccomplished Circle, (being) accomplished from the origin,

cannot be accomplished by individuals.

This quintessence, unaccomplished (and) unsought for,

(GK 627,6)   exists in that way[1] from the origin.

---

1. dPon slob 'Phrin las Nyi ma: it is unproduced and unobtainable through effort.

sus rtogs de ni dngos grub mchog / /
dngos grub gzhan[1] nas blang du med / /
med pa de[2] nyid[3] dngos grub yin / /
dngos grub mchog ni de don yin / /
mtshan ma'i dngos grub dngos[4] grub men / /   5

GK 627,7   de phyir dngos[5] ⑦ grub dam pa long[6] / /
KG 387   dngos [387] grub dam pa mi len pa / /
khyi[7] rgan[8] ha seng[9] khyer ba[10] 'dra[11] / /

---

1. gzhan GK, KG : bzhan TL

2. da GK : de KG, TL

3. nyid GK, KG : nid TL

4. dngos GK, KG : mngos TL

5. dngas GK : dngos KG, TL

6. long GK, TL : longs KG

7. kyi GK, TL : khyi KG

8. rgan GK, KG : rkan TL

9. seng GK, KG : pheng TL

10. khyer ba GK, KG : byed byed TL

11. 'dra GK, KG : bdra TL

Whoever realizes (that, obtains) the best accomplishment;
(the real) accomplishment is not received from elsewhere.
The very absence (of being received from elsewhere) is
    the accomplishment;
the best accomplishment is the state (of) That;
characterized accomplishment is not accomplishment.   5

(GK 627,7)   Therefore, take (that) sacred accomplishment!
Not to take the sacred accomplishment
is like carrying around an old, frail dog.

ཙྪ|
thams cad mnyam pa'i rgyal po la //
mi mnyam gnyis 'dzin 'khrul pa ste //
'khrul pa de la spyad mi bya[1] //
mnyam pa nyid du ye nas kyang[2] //
blo dngos[3] bzhi la so sor snang //   5

GK 628,1   ① so sor snang yang gcig las med //
khyad par chen po'i gzhung[4] 'di[5] la //
thams cad mnyam pa[6] nyid du[7] gnas //

---

1. gnas kyang GK, KG : bya TL
2. The whole verse is omitted in GK and KG.
3. dngos GK, KG : ngos TL
4. gzhung GK, KG : bzhung TL
5. 'di GK, KG : 'di' TL
6. pa incl. GK, KG : om. TL
7. la GK, KG : du TL

Dza
For the king who is total equality,
to conceive (in a) dual (and) non-equal (way) is a delusion.
As to that delusion, (it) must not be acted upon.
Although (it exists) from the origin as equality itself,
to the mind, (it) truly appears in four distinct ways.[1]   5

(GK 628,1)   (It) appears in distinct ways, but it doesn't exist otherwise
than as one.
According to this doctrine of the Great Difference,
everything exists as equality itself:

---

1. dPon slob 'Phrin las Nyi ma: a reference to the Four Vehicles of the Cause (*rgyu'i theg pa bzhi*).

'khor 'das gnyis med mnyam pa'i ngang / /
snang stong gnyis med mnyam pa'i ngang / /
rtag chad gnyis med mnyam pa'i ngang / /
mun snang gnyis med mnyam pa'i ngang / /
GK 628,2 ② dgra zin[1] gnyis med mnyam pa'i ngang / /   5
yod med gnyis med mnyam pa'i ngang / /
thams cad gnyis med mnyam pa'i ngang / /
shin tu[2] mkhas pa'i rtogs pa las / /
kun gyis[3] rtogs par mi 'gyur ro / /[4]

---

1. zin GK, TL : zun KG
2. du GK, TL : tu KG
3. gyi GK : gyis KG, TL
4. rkyang shad GK, KG : nyis shad TL

transmigration (and) the state transcending suffering are
    not two, (they are) the Condition of equality;
appearance (and) emptiness are not two, (they are) the
    Condition of equality;
eternalism (and) nihilism are not two, (they are) the
    Condition of equality;
darkness (and) light are not two, (they are) the Condition
    of equality;
(GK 628,2)   friend (and) foe are not two, (they are) the Condition of
    equality;   5
existence (and) non-existence are not two, (they are) the
    Condition of equality;
everything is not two, (it is) the Condition of equality.
Except for being realized by the very wise ones,
(it) will not be realized by all.

ཐ།

thams cad gnyis med gcig pu yin //
thams cad gnyis med gcig pu bas //

GK 628,3   mchod pa'i yul[1] yang ③ gzhan[2] na med //
rang bzhin ka[3] dag kho na bas //
de las ma gtogs[4] gzhan pa med //   5
des na de don rtogs pa dka' //
de la gtan[4] tshigs ma bstan[5] na //
mun nag nang gi mdzub[6] yug[7] yin //

---

1. yul GK, KG : lha TL

2. gzhan GK, KG : bzhan TL

3. ka GK, KG : dka' TL

4. rtogs GK, TL : gtogs KG

5. gtan GK, KG : btan TL

6. bstan GK, KG : stan TL

7. 'dzub GK, KG, TL : mdzub ego

8. yugs GK, KG, TL : yug ego

Wa

Everything is not two, (it) is one;

since everything is not two (because it) is one,

(GK 628,3) also the object of worship is not somewhere else.

The (Ultimate) Nature is precisely primordial purity;

besides that, there is nothing else;   5

for that reason, the state (of) That is difficult to understand.

When in that respect the cause (of being) is not pointed out,

(it) is (like) feeling one's way in darkness.

KG 388   de phyir gtan¹ tshigs [388] bshad cing bstan² //
GK 628,4,   ④ gnyis su med las (7b) gnyis 'dod pa //
TL 7b   de ni nyes par gol ba yin //
phyi nang gnyis med gcig gi ngang //
rtag chad las sogs gcig gi³ ngang //   5

---

1. gtan GK, KG : btan TL
2. bstan GK, KG : stan TL
3. gis GK : gi KG, TL

(GK 628,4) That is why the cause (of being) is related and pointed out.
To acknowledge duality rather than non-duality,
that is a noxious mistake.
Outside (and) inside[1] are not two, (they are) the
　　Condition of One;
eternalism (and) nihilism and so on (are not two),
　　(they are) the Condition of One.　　　　　　　　5

---

1. dPon slob 'Phrin las Nyi ma: *phyi* and *nang* refer to objects without consciousness and sentient beings endowed with a mind (*sems med pa'i yul/ sems dang yod pa'i sems can*); to the external container and the internal content (*phyi'i snod dang nang gi bcud*), such as the world and living beings, body and mind.

ཨ།
snang ba¹ nyid ni stong pa yin / /
stong pa nyid ni snang ba² yin / /
de gnyis gcig pa yin pa'i phyir / /

GK 628,5   de phyir sangs rgyas sems can ⑤ yin / /
sems can sangs rgyas ci phyir men / /   5
dmyal³ ba'i gnas ni bon gyi⁴ dbyings / /
de phyir bon dbyings dmyal ba'i gnas / /
rag sha⁵ a ba glang⁶ mgo⁷ can / /
de ni kun bzang gshen lha yin / /

GK 628,6   de phyir kun bzang gshen⁸ ⑥ lha yang / /   10
rag sha⁹ a ba¹⁰ glang¹¹ mgo¹² yin / /

---

1. pa GK : ba KG, TL
2. pa GK : ba KG, TL
3. dmyal GK, KG : gnyal TL
4. gyis GK : gyi KG, TL
5. rag sha GK, TL : ragsha KG
6. glang GK, KG : klang TL
7. mgo GK, KG : gho TL
8. byen GK : gshen KG, TL
9. rag sha GK, TL : ragsha KG
10. ba' GK : ba KG, TL
11. glang GK, KG : klang TL
12. mgo GK, KG : gho TL

Zha

Appearance is emptiness.

Emptiness is appearance.

Since those two are one,

(GK 628,5)   then, enlightened beings are sentient beings.

(So) why should sentient beings not be enlightened

beings?   5

(If) hell (is) the Dimension of Reality,

then, the Dimension of Reality (is) hell.

(If) Rag sha A ba Glang mgo can[1]

is Kun bzang gShen lha,

(GK 628,6)   then, also Kun bzang gShen lha   10

is Rag sha A ba Glang mgo can.

---

1. dPon slob 'Phrin las Nyi ma: gShin rje; the Lord of Death, which in his external form (*phyi sgrub*) is depicted as bull-headed (*glang mgo can*); see R. Nebesky-Wojkowitz 1956, pp. 82 et seq.

sdug bsngal 'di[1] nyid bde[2] ba yin / /
bde[3] ba de nyid de yin mod / /
de phyir thams cad gcig pa yin / /
zhen pa'i[4] blo[5] la so sor snang / /
kun bzang ngang du yongs kyis[6] gcig / /
GK 628,7   zhag mig[7] can la mun ⑦ par[8] snang[9] / /
chu bur[10] mig[11] la nam mkhar[12] snang / /
gyi ling mig[13] la mun snang med / /
des na thams cad gnyis med yin / /

5

---

1. 'di GK, KG : 'di' TL

2. bde GK, KG : bde' TL

3. bde GK, KG : bde' TL

4. pa'i GK, KG : pa TL

5. blo GK, KG : klo TL

6. kyi GK, KG : kyis TL

7. mig GK, KG : dmig TL

8. pa GK, KG, TL : par ego

9. snang GK, KG : na TL

10. chu bur GK, KG : chu'i TL

11. mig GK, KG : dmig TL

12. nam mkhar GK, KG : mun par TL

13. mig GK, KG : dmig TL

(If) this very suffering is joy, (and)
that very joy is certainly that,[1]
then, everything is the same.
To the biased mind (they)[2] appear differently.
In the Condition (of) Kun (tu) bZang (po), (they are)
absolutely one.   5
(GK 628,7)   To those with nocturnal[3] eyes, (it) appears as darkness;
to (those with) eyeballs,[4] (it) appears as light.
In the eyes (of) a fine horse, darkness (and) light do not exist.
Thus, everything is non-dual.

---

1. I.e., suffering.

2. I.e., joy and suffering.

3. Cf. BGTC, vol. 2, p. 2369, *zhag*, (3), and p. 2370, *zhag po* (2). dPon slob 'Phrin las Nyi ma: *zhag mig can* is a rhetoric name for *'ug pa*, the owl.

4. Cf. BGTC, vol. 1, p. 805, *chu bur mig*.

ཟ།

rang 'byung dbyings kyi thig ler ni / /
sna tshogs 'khor ba'i bon rnams gcig / /
thams cad yongs rdzogs kun gzhi'i ngang / /
GK 629,1,   yul dang ① dbang po'i [389] dbye ba med / /
KG 389   thig le kun bsdus kun la khyab / /   5
thams cad ma lus bde[1] ba'i klong / /
sdug bsngal bya ba'i ming yang med / /
thams cad ma lus ye sangs rgyas / /
ji ltar mtshan med mi g.yo ba / /
nam mkha'i rang bzhin rgyu rkyen med / /   10
GK 629,2,   ② (8a) gnyen po rtog pa'i mthus[2] mi g.yo / /
TL 8a

---

1. bde GK, KG : bde' TL

2. mthus GK, KG : 'thus TL

Za

With respect to the Essence which is the self-originated
    Dimension,
the various phenomena of transmigration (are) one.
(In) the Condition of the Basis (of) all, (where) everything
    is totally perfected,

(GK 629,1)   there is no separation of senses and (sense-) objects.
The Essence unites everything, it is all-encompassing;   5
(it is) the blissful Expanse (encompassing) everything
    without exception,
(where) not even the name of suffering exists; (where)
everything, without exception, (is) Primordial Enlightenment.
Like the unmoving (and) uncharacterized
nature of the sky, (which is) without primary (and)
    instrumental causes,   10

(GK 629,2)   (the Essence is) not moved by the power of conflictual
    conceptuality.

de phyir[1] bde[2] chen byang chub sems //
bon sku kun gzhi bde[3] ba'i ngang //
mi 'gyur mi shigs[4] g.yung drung sku //
sems dang ye shes tha dad med //
rang blo[5] bde[6] ba'i ye shes 'gyur //   5

GK 629,3   ye nas gnas pa'i[7] ③ bon gyi sku
khyab par gnas pa thig le'i klong //
snang srid zhi ba'i mya ngan 'das///[8]

---

1. phyir GK, KG : bzhin TL
2. bde GK, KG : bde' TL
3. bde GK, KG : bde' TL
4. shigs GK, TL : shig KG
5. blo GK, KG : klo TL
6. bde GK, KG : bde' TL
7. pa'i GK, KG : pas TL
8. rkyang shad GK, TL : nyis shad KG

For that reason (it is called) the Pure-and-Perfect-Mind,
   Great Bliss,
the Body (of) Reality, the Basis (of) all, the Condition of
   bliss,
the Immutable, Unwavering, Everlasting Body.
There is no distinction (between) Primordial Wisdom and
   the mind;
one's mind becomes blissful Primordial Wisdom,   5

(GK 629,3) the Body of Reality existing from the origin,
the Expanse of the Essence existing in (an all-)pervading
   (way),
the transcending-of-suffering where appearance (and)
   coming-into-being are pacified.

ༀ|
seng ge sgra bsgrags[1] lung 'di[2] la //
don gyi yan lag gnyis su bshad //
lta ba seng ge sgra bsgrags[3] dang //
man ngag seng ge sgra bsgrags[4] gnyis //

GK 629,4 lta ba seng ge sgra bsgrags[5] ④ ni //   5
phyi dang nang med thams cad kun //
ma bcos gdod[6] nas ka[7] dag nyid //
rang bzhin nyid nas[8] ye sangs rgyas //
thig le chen po bon gyi sku //
nam mkha' lta bur mtshon dang bral //   10
'di ni seng ge sgra bsgrags[9] lta ba'i mchog //

---

1. bsgrags GK, KG : sgrags TL

2. 'di GK, KG : 'di' TL

3. bsgrags GK, KG : sgrags TL

4. bsgrags GK, KG : sgrags TL

5. bsgrags GK, KG : sgrags TL

6. nyid GK, KG : gdod TL

7. ka GK, KG : rka TL

8. nas GK, KG : gyis TL

9. bsgrags GK, KG : sgrags TL

'A

As to these precepts (of) the Lion's Roar,
they are expounded in two principal parts:
(that of) the View which is like the Lion's Roar, and
(that of) the essential instructions which are like the
    Lion's Roar.

(GK 629,4)   The View which is like the Lion's Roar: 5
without outside (nor) inside, (it is) everything altogether;
(it is) unaltered, primordially pure from the origin.
(Being) the (Ultimate) Nature itself, (it is) Primordial
    Enlightenment;
(it is) the great Essence, the Body of Reality;
(it is) without defining marks, like the sky.   10
This is the excellent View which is like the Lion's Roar.

GK 629,5 mi 'gyur mi ⑤ gnas ji ltar ma yin cing //
KG 390 ji [390] ltar yang ni[1] mi 'jog pa yin no //[2]
chags med mtshon[3] bral rtog pa med //
gnyis med spros bral mi rtog ma bcos pa //
gsal la ma nor ma g.yos dngos po med //   5
cir yang spyad med cir yang brtag tu[4] med[5] //
GK 629,6 cir yang mi dmigs cir ⑥ yang 'dzin pa med //
ye nas rang bzhin snying po gcig gi ngang //
TL 8b ji bzhin ma bcos (8b) thams cad[6] de bzhin pas //
bsgom[7] du med cing bstan[8] du med pa yin //   10
'di[9] ni seng ge sgra bsgrags[10] lta ba'i mchog //

---

1. ni om. GK, KG : incl. TL

2. rkyang shad GK, KG : nyis shad TL

3. mtshon GK, KG : mtshan TL

4. rtag du TL : brtag tu ego

5. The whole verse is omitted in GK and KG.

6. cad incl. GK, TL : >cad< KG

7. bsgom GK, KG : sgom TL

8. bstan GK, KG : stan TL

9. 'di GK, KG : 'di' TL

10. bsgrags GK, KG : sgrags TL

(GK 629,5)   (It is) immutable, unlocated, (it) is not in any way
whatsoever,
and (it) is not fixed in any way at all.
(It is) unbegotten, without definition, without
conceptuality.
(It is) non-dual, without diversification, non-conceptual,
unaltered.
(It is) clear and infallible, immovable, insubstantial.   5
(It is) not (to be) acted (upon) in any way (and) not (to be)
examined in any way.

(GK 629,6)   (It is) not (to be) conceived in any way (and) not (to be)
grasped in any way.
(It is) the primordial Nature, the quintessence, the Condition of One;
how (that is) unaltered, so is everything.
(It is) not (to be) meditated (upon), (it) is without
description.   10
This is the best View which is like the Lion's Roar.

man ngag seng ge sgra bsgrags[1] la //

GK 629,7   blta ru med pa'i ⑦ lta ba la //

mi lta de bzhin ngang gnas pa[2] //

de ni man ngag sgra bsgrags[3] yin //

'gyur med g.yung drung lta ba la //   5

mi dmigs ma bcos ngang gnas[4] pa //

de yang man ngag sgra bsgrags[5] yin //

lta ba ma g.yos spros dang bral //

GK 630,1   ma yengs mi rtog ① ngang gnas pa //

de yang man ngag sgra bsgrags[6] yin //   10

bsgom[7] du ci yang med pa la //

yengs pa med par ngang[8] gnas pa //

de yang man ngag sgra bsgrags[9] yin //

---

1. bsgrags GK, KG : sgrags TL
2. pa GK, KG : pas TL
3. bsgrags GK, KG : sgrags TL
4. gnas GK, KG : rang gnas TL
5. bsgrags GK, KG : sgrags TL
6. bsgrags GK, KG : sgrags TL
7. bsgom GK, KG : sgom TL
8. ngang GK, KG : rang TL
9. bsgrags GK, KG : sgrags TL

The essential instructions which are like the Lion's Roar.
(GK 629,7)   With respect to the View which cannot be investigated,
just without investigating, (one) remains (in that) Condition.
That is the resounding Roar of the instructions.
With respect to the View (which is) immutable (and)
    everlasting,   5
(one) remains (in that) Condition without correction and
    without (working with the) imagination.
That also is the resounding Roar of the instructions.
(With respect to) the View (which is) unmoving
    (and) without diversification,
(GK 630,1)   (one) remains (in that) Condition undistracted (and)
    without conceptualization.
That also is the resounding Roar of the instructions.   10
With respect to (the fact that it) is not (something) to be
    meditated (upon) in whatever way,
(one) remains undistractedly (in that) Condition.
That also is the resounding Roar of the instructions.

des na lung 'di[1] khyad par che / /
'khor ba dong nas sprug[2] 'dod na / /

GK 630,2   lung gi rgyal po ② 'di[3] la ltos / /
seng ge sgra bsgrags[4] lta ba'i lung zhes bya ba rdzogs
s.ho[5] / /[6]
zab rgya rgya / /   5
gab rgya rgya / /

KG 391   [391] rgya rgya / /
rgya rgya / /
dge'o[7] / /[8]

---

1. 'di GK, KG : 'di' TL

2. sprug GK, KG : sprugs TL

3. 'di GK, KG : 'di' TL

4. bsgrags GK, KG : sgrags TL

5. s.ho GK, TL : so KG

6. rkyang shad GK, KG : nyis shad TL

7. zab…dge'o incl. GK, KG : om. TL

8. rkyang shad GK : nyis shad KG. TL has the following colophon: sprul sku lha rje
gzhod ston gyis lho brag khom 'thing [sic] nas bdan [sic] drangs / la stod byar pa
'bum khri dang / bla ma rgya ston jo lde la sgrags [sic] te / rim kyis rgyud nas da lta
spa'i bla dpe'o /

Thus, these precepts (are) particularly great.
If (you) wish to escape from the abyss (of) transmigration,
(GK 630,2)   contemplate this king of precepts!
The so-called precepts of the View which is like the
    Lion's Roar are (hereby) completed.
Deeply sealed, sealed.   5
Secretely sealed, sealed.
Sealed, sealed.
Sealed, sealed.
Happiness.[1]

---

1. TL: "The incarnation Divine Lord gZhod ston extracted (it) from Khom mthing lHo brag. (He) expounded (it) to Byar pa 'Bum khri (of) La stod, and to the teacher rGya ston Jo lde. Through consecutive transmission, it is now the book (of) the teacher(s) of sPa." Byar pa 'Bum khri and rGya ston Jo lde are said to be direct disciples of gZhod ston dNgos grub Grags pa, the revealer of this text; cf. S. G. Karmay 1972, pp. 154-156. As it is traditionally acknowledged, the different kinds of Bonpo teachings were entrusted to four important Tibetan families which therefore became associated with particular aspects of the doctrine: the Bru family was entrusted with the teachings related to the *Srid pa'i mdzod phug* (for which cf. Introduction, p. 53, n. 157); the rMe'u with those related to the *Khams brgyad* (for which see Introduction, p. 52, n. 153); cf. Introduction, p. 26. The sPa became the holders of the *tantric* teachings, while the Zhu family was entrusted with the preservation of the *rDzogs chen* doctrines. Cf. S. G. Karmay 1972, p. 6 et seq.; P. Kværne 1990b, p. 209

BIBLIOGRAPHY

Tibetan Sources and Works in the Tibetan Language
(*Arranged by title according to the Tibetan alphabet*)

bKa' 'gyur brten 'gyur gyi sde can sgrigs tshul bstan pa'i me ro spar ba'i rlung g.yab bon gyi pad mo rgyas byed nyi 'od, by the sMan ri abbot Nyi ma bsTan 'dzin (1813-1875); *SPS*, vol. 37, part 2, New Delhi, 1965.

Khro bo dbang chen ngo mtshar rgyas pa'i rnam bshad gsal ba'i sgron ma, by sKyabs ston Rin chen 'Od zer (b. 1353); *sPyi spungs khro bo dbang chen gyi 'grel pa dang dbal phur spyi don nyi shu rtsa lnga'i 'grel pa*, Yongzin Sangyay Tenzin, TBMC, New Delhi, 1973, pp. 31-392.

'Khor lo bzhi sbrags, rDzogs pa chen po zhang zhung snyan rgyud, section Zha, pp. 449-464, *History and Doctrines of Bonpo Nispanna Yoga*, *SPS*, vol. 73, New Delhi, 1968.

Gangs can mkhas grub rim byon ming mdzod, compiled by Ko zhul Grags pa 'Byung gnas and rGyal ba Blo bzang mKhas grub, Kan su'u Mi rigs dPe skrun khang, Lanzhou, 1992.

rGya gar gyi gnas chen khag la 'grod pa'i lam yig. Guide to Buddhist Sacred Places in India, by mDo smad pa dGe 'dun Chos 'phel (1903-1951), Maha Bodhi Society, Calcutta, 1939.

rGyal ba'i bka' dang bka' rten rmad 'byung dgos 'dod yid bzhin gter gyi bang mdzod la dkar chags [sic] *blo'i tha ram bkrol byed 'phrul gyi lde mig*, compiled by g.Yung drung Tshul khrims dBang grags in 1880, Bod lJongs Shin hwa Par 'debs bZo grwa, Bod gsar ton yig <93>, no. 019, n.d., 1391 pp.

rGyal gśen ya ṅal gyi gduṅ rabs un chen tshaṅs pa'i sgra dbyaṅs, by Yang sgom Mi 'gyur rGyal mtshan, *The History of the Ya-ṅal Lineage of Lamas of Dol-po and Other Hagiographical Materials from the Klu-brag Monastery of Dol-po*, Khedup Gyatso, New Delhi, 1978, pp. 1-135.

sGra yi don sdeb snang gsal sgron me, by Zhu ston Nyi ma Grags pa (1616-1670), *Tibetan Zang Zung Dictionary;* Bonpo Association, Lahore Press, Jama Masjid, New Delhi, 1965, pp. 1-22.

rNying ma dang bon gyi rnam zhag, by sPyan snga ba Blo gros rGyal mtshan (1390-1448), *Collected Works of sPyan snga ba Blo gros rGyal mtshan,* Ngawang Gelek Demo, New Delhi, 1982, vol. 5, pp. 459-466.

lTa ba'i sgang 'grel, Byang sems gab pa dgu bskor gyi dgongs pa bkrol ba'i 'grel bzhi rig pa'i rgya mtsho, section 4; a detailed commentary of the *Byang chub sems gab pa dgu bskor,* attributed to Dran pa Nam mkha' (eighth century), and discovered by Khu tsha Zla 'od 'bar (eleventh century) at sPa gro phug gcal in Bhutan; *Gal mdo,* TBMC, New Delhi, 1972, pp. 470-497.

lTa ba'i rim pa bshad pa, by sKa ba dPal brtsegs (late eighth/early ninth centuries), Derge bsTan 'gyur, vol. Co (204), fols. 236b5-238a7.

lTa ba la shan sgron ma, sTeng lha yul du bsgrags pa'i skor, rDzogs chen bsgrags pa skor gsum, translated into Tibetan from the Zhang Zhung language by sNya chen Li shu sTag ring (eighth century), and discovered by gZhod ston dNgos grub Grags pa, an incarnation of sNya chen Li shu sTag ring, at Khom mthing lHo brag; *rDzogs pa chen po zab lam gnad kyi gdams pa bsgrags pa skor gsum ma bu cha lag dan bcas pa,* Patshang Lama Sonam Gyaltsen, TBMC, New Delhi, 1973, pp. 278-282; BKSR, vol. 100, pp. 491-502.

lTa ba seng ge sgra bsgrags, 'Og klu yul du bsgrags pa'i skor, rDzogs chen bsgrags pa skor gsum, translated into Tibetan from the Zhang Zhung language by sNya chen Li shu sTag ring (eighth century), and discovered by gZhod ston dNgos grub Grags pa, an incarnation of sNya chen Li shu sTag ring, at Khom mthing lHo brag; *rDzogs pa chen po zab lam gnad kyi gdams pa bsgrags pa skor gsum ma bu cha lag dan bcas pa,* Patshang Lama Sonam Gyaltsen, TBMC, New Delhi, 1973, pp. 619-630; BKSR, vol. 109, pp. 373-392.

lTa ba seng ge sgra bsgrags kyi 'grel pa, rDzogs chen bsgrags pa skor gsum, rDzogs pa chen po zab lam gnad kyi gdams pa bsgrags pa skor gsum ma bu cha lag dan bcas pa, Patshang Lama Sonam Gyaltsen, TBMC, New Delhi, 1973, pp. 805-838.

bsTan pa'i rnam bshad dar rgyas gsal ba'i sgron ma, by sPa ston bsTan rgyal bZang po, *Sources for a History of Bon,* edited by T. Namdak, TBMC, Dolanji, 1972, pp. 498-769.

Dam pa'i chos kyi 'khor lo bsgyur ba rnams kyi byung ba gsal bar byed pa mkhas pa'i dga' ston, (abbr. *Chos byung mkhas pa'i dga' ston*), by dPa' bo gTsug lag Phreng ba (1504-1566), edited by rDo rje rGyal po, Mi rigs dPe skrun khang, Beijing, 1986, 2 vols.

bDen pa bon gyi mdzod sgo sgra 'grel 'phrul gyi lde mig, (*mDzod sgra 'grel*), a commentary to the *Srid pa'i mdzod phug* (for which see below, p. 278) attributed to Dran pa Nam mkha' (eighth century), and discovered by rMa ston Jo lcam (alias rMa lCam me, twelfth century); *mDzod phug: Basic Verses and Commentary,* the Yung Drung Bon Students' Committee, Benares, 1993.

'Dul ba gling grags, Sources for a History of Bon, TBMC, Dolanji, 1972, pp. 114-140.

'Dus pa rin po che'i rgyud zer mig Bonpo Foundation, New Delhi, 1965, (*po ti*), 2 vols.

sDong po dgu 'dus lta ba'i rgyud chen, a text related to the cycle of the *Byang sems gab pa dgu skor*, Bonpo Foundation, New Delhi, 1967; BKSR, vol. 99, pp. 97-146.

brDa dag ming tshig gsal ba, by dGe bshes Chos kyi Grags pa, Mi rigs dPe skrun khang, Beijing, 1981.

sPyi rgyud ye khri mtha' sel gyi lo rgyus chen mo, a text related to the cycle of the *Ye khri mtha' sel* attributed to Dran pa Nam mkha' (eighth century); 'orally transmitted' to Lung bon lHa gnyan by the son of Dran pa Nam mkha', Tshe dbang Rig 'dzin; TBMC, Dolanji, n. d., pp. 759-815; the whole cycle is contained in vol. 101 of the BKSR.

Bar do'i ngo sprod kyi gdams pa, rDzogs pa chen po yang rtse klong chen; discovered by gZhod ston dNgos grub Grags pa, an incarnation of sNya chen Li shu sTag ring, at Khom mthing lHo brag; *Bla med rdzogs pa chen po yan rtse klon chen gyi khrid gźun cha lag dan bcas pa'i gsun pod*, Sherab Wangyal, TBMC, New Delhi, 1973, 2 vols., vol. 1, pp. 667-725.

Bod kyi skung yig gi rnam gzhag chung ngu, by Nor brang O rgyan, *Bod rig pa'i ched rtsom gces bsdus*, Bod ljongs Mi dmangs dPe skrun khang, Xining, 1987, pp. 413-483.

Bod rgya tshig mdzod chen mo, (BGTC), Zhang Yisun main editor, Mi rigs dPe skrun khang, Beijing, 1993, 2 vols.

Bod rgya shan sbyar gyi shes bya'i rnam grangs kun btus tshig mdzod, compiled by He Wenxuan and Hou Cunqi, mTsho sngon Mi rigs dPe skrun khang, Xining, 1987.

Byang chub sems gab pa dgu skor, discovered by gShen chen Klu dga' (996-1035) in 1017 at 'Bri mtshams mtha' dkar; TBMC, New Delhi, 1967, (*po ti*), fols. 1-87; BKSR, vol. 99, pp. 10-96.

Bla med kyi theg pa'i don gtan la phab pa'i mdo, 'Dus pa rin po che dri ma med pa gzi brjid rab tu 'bar ba'i mdo (gZi brjid), 'orally trasmitted' by sTang chen dMu tsha Gyer med (eighth century) to sPrul sku Blo ldan sNying po (b. 1360); Bonpo Foundation, New Delhi, 1967, vol. Nga, chapter 16, pp. 245-318; BKSR, vol. 4, pp. 111-144.

sBas pa'i rgum chung, The Small Collection of Hidden Precepts: A Study of an Ancient Manuscript on Dzogchen from Tun-Huang; Shang Shung Edizioni, Arcidosso, 1984.

Man ngag 'khor ba dong sprugs, 'Og klu yul du bsgrags pa'i skor, rDzogs chen bsgrags pa skor gsum, translated into Tibetan from the Zhang Zhung language by sNya chen Li shu sTag ring (eighth century), and discovered by gZhod ston dNgos grub Grags pa, an incarnation of sNya chen Li shu sTag ring, at Khom mthing lHo brag; *rDzogs pa chen po zab lam gnad kyi gdams pa bsgrags pa skor gsum ma bu cha lag dan bcas pa*, Patshang Lama Sonam Gyaltsen, TBMC, New Delhi, 1973, pp. 667-707; BKSR, vol. 109, pp. 441-507.

rDzogs pa chen po snying thig gi lo rgyus chen mo, by Zhang ston bKra shis rDo rje (1097-1167), in *sNying thig ya bzhi*, by Klong chen Rab 'byams pa (1318-1363), *Bi ma snying thig*, vol. 7, part III, text no. 1, Trulku Tsewang, Jamyang and L. Tashi, New Delhi, 1971.

rDzogs pa chen po zhang zhung snyan rgyud kyi brgyud pa'i bla ma'i rnam thar, by sPa ston bsTan rgyal bZang po, *rDzogs pa chen po zhang zhung snyan rgyud, History and Doctrines of Bonpo Niṣpanna Yoga, SPS*, vol. 73, New Delhi, 1968, section Ka, pp. 1-31.

rDzogs pa chen po zhang zhung snyan rgyud kyi spyi don gsal ba'i sgron ma, composed by a Tshe dbang Rig 'dzin; BKSR, vol. 110, pp. 328-380.

rDzogs pa chen po zhang zhung snyan rgyud kyi bon ma nub pa'i gtan tshigs, *rDzogs pa chen po zhang zhung snyan rgyud, History and Doctrines of Bonpo Niṣpanna Yoga, SPS*, vol. 73, New Delhi, 1968, section Pa, pp. 259-267.

rDzogs pa chen po zhang zhung snyan rgyud kyi gsung pod, published in India during the 1980s through the support and sponsorship of Khyung po rTse drug mKhan po brTson 'grus rGyal mtshan, alias rTse drug Rinpoche (1914-1985), 1 vol.

rDzogs pa chen po zhang zhung snyan rgyud las rgyud bu chung bcu gnyis, *rDzogs pa chen po zhang zhung snyan rgyud, History and Doctrines of Bonpo Niṣpanna Yoga, SPS*, vol. 73, New Delhi, 1968, section Ca, pp. 169-179.

rDzogs pa chen po zhang zhung snyan rgyud las rgyud bu chung bcu gnyis kyi don bstan pa, *rDzogs pa chen po zhang zhung snyan rgyud, History and Doctrines of Bonpo Niṣpanna Yoga, SPS*, vol. 73, New Delhi, 1968, section Cha, pp. 181-192.

rDzogs pa chen po yang rtse klong chen gyi nges don, *rDzogs pa chen po yang rtse klong chen*, discovered by gZhod ston dNgos grub Grags pa, an incarnation of sNya chen Li shu sTag ring, at Khom mthing lHo brag; *Bla med rdzogs pa chen po yaṅ rtse kloṅ chen gyi khrid gźuṅ cha lag daṅ bcas pa'i gsuṅ pod*, Sherab Wangyal, TBMC, New Delhi, 1973, 2 vols., vol. 1, pp. 167-257.

Zhang bod kyi skad gnyis shan sbyar sgra yi rtogs brjod, compiled by sLob dPon Kun bzang Blo gros of g.Yung drung gling monastery, (present century, n.d.).

Zhang bod kyi lo rgyus ti se'i 'od, by Namkhai Norbu, Krung go'i Bod kyi Shes rig dPe skrun khang, Beijing, 1996.

Zab dang rgya che g.yung drung bon gyi bka' 'gyur dkar chag nyi ma 'bum gyi 'od zer, compiled by Rig 'dzin Kun grol Grags pa (b. 1700) in 1751; Krung go'i Bod gyi Shes rig dPe skrun khang, Xining, 1993.

'Od gsal rdzogs pa chen po'i lam gyi rim pa khrid yig kun tu bzang po'i snying tig, by Shar rdza bKra shis rGyal mtshan (1859-1934), *Heart Drops of Dharmakaya: Dzogchen Practice of the Bön Tradition*, Snow Lion Publications, Ithaca, New York, 1993, Tibetan Text.

Yig gzugs du ma'i ma phyi gzhon nu mdzas pa'i lang tsho, by Cha-Phur Namkha Gyal tsen (Bya 'Phur Nam mKha' rGyal mtshan, 1969-1995), Mu khri bTsan po'i Rig gzhung zhib 'jug khang, Bonpo Monastic Centre, Dolanji, 1994.

Yid dang kun gzhi'i dka' ba'i gnas rgya cher 'grel pa legs par bshad pa'i rgya mtsho, by Tsong kha pa Blo bzang Grags pa (1357-1419). This text has been translated and annotated by G. Sparham (1993).

g.Yung drung bon gyi bka' 'gyur glog par ma'i dkar chag, by g.Yung drung bsTan pa'i rGyal mtshan, alias Bla ma A g.Yung (1922-1998); Si khron Zhing chen Mi rigs Zhib 'jug su'o, Bod kyi Rig gnas Zhib 'jug khang, 1985.

g.Yung drung bon gyi bka' 'gyur, Bon sgo, Bon Cultural Centre, Dolanji, 1987, no. 1, pp. 24-34.

g.Yung drung bon gyi bka' dang bka' rten; contains the whole cycle of the Three Proclamations of the Great Perfection (*rDzogs chen bsgrags pa skor gsum*); published in India during the 1980s through the support and sponsorship of Khyung po rTse drug mKhan po brTson 'grus rGyal mtshan, alias rTse drug Rinpoche (1914-1985), 2 vols.

g.Yung drung yang rtse gsang ba'i rgyud, Collected Tantras of Bon, T. Namdak, TBMC, New Delhi, 1972, 3 vols., vol. 3, pp. 90-99; BKRS, vol. 106, pp. 223-301.

g.Yung drung gsang ba dbang gi rgyud, rGyud drug, Bar mi yul du bsgrags pa'i skor, rDzogs chen bsgrags pa skor gsum; discovered by gZhod ston dNgos grub Grags pa, an incarnation of sNya chen Li shu sTag ring, at Khom mthing lHo brag; *rDzogs pa chen po zab lam gnad kyi gdams pa bsgrags pa skor gsum ma bu cha lag dan bcas pa*, Patshang Lama Sonam Gyaltsen, TBMC, New Delhi, 1973, pp. 397-423; BKSR, vol. 109, pp. 3-97.

Lung rig rin po che'i mdzod blo gsal snying gi nor, by Shar rdza bKra shis rGyal mtshan (1859-1934); *Lung rig rin po che'i mdzod*, Toden Tsering, TBMC, New Delhi, 1972, pp. 1-552.

Shes rab kyi pha rol tu phyin pa khams brgyad stong phrag brgya pa, discovered by gShen chen Klu dga' (996-1035) at 'Bri mtshams mtha' dkar in 1017; TBMC, New Delhi, 1975, 16 vols.; BKSR, vols. 42-57.

Sangs rgyas kyi bstan rtsis ngo mtshar nor bu'i phreng, compiled in 1842 by the sMan ri abbot Nyi ma bsTan 'dzin (1813-1875); edited by sLob dpon bsTan 'dzin rNam dag in 1961 and published in *sGra yi don sdeb snang gsal sgron me, Tibetan Žang Žung Dictionary*, Bonpo Association, Lahore Press, Jama Masjid, New Delhi, 1965, pp. 23-40.

Sangs rgyas bstan pa spyi yi 'byung khung yid bzhin nor bu 'dod pa 'jo ba'i gter mdzod by Rig 'dzin Kun grol Grags pa (b. 1700), *Three Sources for a History of Bon*, TBMC, Dolanji, 1974, pp. 197-552.

Sangs rgyas g.yung drung bon gyi bstan pa'i 'byung ba brjod pa'i legs bshad bskal pa bzang po'i mgrin rgyan, (*g.Yung drung bon gyi bstan 'byung*), by dPal ldan Tshul khrims (1902-1973), TBMC, Dolanji, 1972, 2 vols.

Sems dang ye shes kyi dri lan, in *Miscellaneous Writings (gsun thor bu) of Kun-mKhyen Klong-chen-pa Dri-med-'Od-zer*. Reproduced from xylographic prints from the A-'dzom 'Brug pa Chos-sgar blocks by Sanje Dorje, vol. 1, Delhi, 1973, pp. 377,2-393.

Sems don sde bcu'i skor, discovered by gZhod ston dNgos grub Grags pa, an incarnation of sNya chen Li shu sTag ring, at Khom mthing lHo brag; *rDzogs pa chen po zab lam gnad kyi gdams pa bsgrags pa skor gsum ma bu cha lag dań bcas pa*, Patshang Lama Sonam Gyaltsen, TBMC, New Delhi, 1973, pp. 469-496; BKSR, vol. 109, pp. 123-166.

Srid pa'i mdzod phug, a cosmological and metaphysical work said to have been translated from the Zhang Zhung language into Tibetan at the time of King Gri gum; its discovery is attributed to three different *gter ston*; T. Namdak, New Delhi, 1966, pp. 2-125.

Srid pa las kyi gting zlog gi rtsa rgyud kun gsal nyi zer sgron ma, a text attributed to Dran pa Nam mkha' (eighth century) and revealed by Bra bo sGom nyag (thirteenth century); g.Yung drung rGyal mtshan, New Delhi, (about 1965), (*po ti*), fols. 1-158.

gSang mchog ma rgyud thugs rje nyi ma'i rgyud: *gZhi ye sangs rgyas pa'i rgyud, Lam mngon sangs rgyas pa'i rgyud, 'Bras bu rdzogs sangs rgyas pa'i rgyud*, discovered by sPrul sku Gu ru rNon rtse, alias A ya Bonpo lHa 'bum (b. 1136) at Dung phor bkra shis rta nag in gTsang; *Ma rgyud sangs rgyas rgyud gsum rtsa 'grel*, TBMC, New Delhi, 1971, pp. 3-205. BKSR, vol. 32, pp. 1-39, 115-170, 250-261.

gSas mkhar rin po che spyi spungs gsang ba bsen thub, one of the three basic *tantras* of the *sPyi spungs* cycle; discovered by Gyer mi Nyi 'od in 1108 at Dangs ra khyung rdzong; T. Namdak, TBMC, New Delhi, 1972, pp. 233-391; BKSR, vol. 112.

A mdo'i kha skad tshig mdzod, edited by Hwa Khan and Klu 'bum rGyal, Kan su'u Mi rigs dPe skrun khang, Lanzhou, 1993.

Works in Western Languages

ACHARD, J.-L.

1992   *Le Pic des Visions: Étude sur deux techniques contemplatives de la Grande Perfection dans les traditions rNying-ma-pa et Bon-po*. Diplôme de l'École Pratique des Hautes Études, Paris.

1995   *Les testaments de Vajradhara et des porteurs-de-science*, Les Deux Océans, Paris.

1998   *L'Essence Perlée du Secret: Recherches philologiques et historiques sur l'origine de la Grande Perfection dans la Tradition rNyingmapa*. École Pratique des Hautes Études, Paris.

APP, U.

1993   " 'Dun': A Chinese Concept as a Key to 'Mysticism' in East and West", *The Eastern Buddhist*, vol. XXVI, no. 2, The Eastern Buddhist Society, Otani University, Kyoto, pp. 31-72.

ARIS, M.

1989   *Hidden Treasures and Secret Lives: A Study of Pemalingpa (1450-1521) and the Sixth Dalai Lama (1683-1706)*, Kegan Paul International, London.

BACOT, J.
1912   "L'écriture cursive tibétaine", *JA*, vol. 19, pp. 5-78.

BALDICK, J.
1989   *Mystical Islam: An Introduction to Sufism*, I. B. Tauris & Co. Ltd., London.
1990   "Mazdaism ('Zoroastrianism')", *The World's Religions: The Religions of Asia*, edited by F. Hardy, Routledge, London, pp. 20-36.

BECHERT, H. (ed.)
1991   *The Dating of the Historical Buddha*, Part 1, Vandenhoeck & Ruprecht in Göttingen.

BECKWITH, C. I.
1989   "The Location and Population of Tibet According to Early Islamic Sources", *AOH*, vol. XLIII, Budapest, pp. 163-170.

BELLEZZA, J. V.
1997   *Divine Dyads: Ancient Civilization in Tibet*, LTWA, Dharamsala, India.

BEYER, S. V.
1992   *The Classical Tibetan Language*, SUNY *Series in Buddhist Studies*, Matthew Kapstein ed., State University of New York Press, Albany.

BIANCHI, U.
1990   "Aspects de continuité dans l'histoire religieuse de l'Iran: le cas de Zurvan", *Proceedings of the First European Conference of Iranian Studies, Turin, 1987*, Part 1, *Old and Middle Iranian Studies*, G. Gnoli and A. Panaino eds., IsMEO, Rome, pp. 19-28.

BLONDEAU, A.-M.
1971   "Le Lha-'dre bKa'-thań", *Études tibétaines dédiées à la mémoire de Marcelle Lalou*, edited by A. Macdonald, Adrien Maisonneuve, Paris, pp. 33-126.
1980   "Analysis of the Biographies of Padmasambhava according to the Tibetan Tradition: Classification of the Sources", *Tibetan Studies in Honour of Hugh Richardson, Proceedings of the International Seminar on Tibetan Studies, Oxford 1979*, M. Aris and Aung San Suu Kyi eds., Aris & Phillips Ltd., Warminster, pp. 45-52.
1984   "Le «Découvreur» du Maṇi bKa'-'Bum était-il Bon-po?", *Tibetan Studies Commemorating the 200th Anniversary of the Birth of Alexander Csoma de Kőrös*, L. Ligeti ed., Akadémiai Kiadó, Budapest, pp. 77-123.
1985   "mKhyen-brce'i dbań-po: *La Biographie de Padmasambhava sélon la tradition de bsGrags-pa Bon, et ses sources*", *Orientalia Iosephi Tucci Memoriae Dicata*, G. Gnoli and L. Lanciotti eds., IsMEO, Rome, LVI, 3, pp. 111-158.
1987   "Une polémique sur l'autenticité des *Bka'-thań* au 17ème siècle", *Silver on Lapis: Tibetan Literary Culture and History*, C. Beckwith ed., Tibet Society, Bloomington, pp. 125-160.

1988   "La controverse soulevée par l'inclusion de rituels bon-po dans le *Rin-chen gter-mjod*. Note préliminaire", *Proceedings of the Fourth Seminar of the International Association for Tibetan Studies, Schloss Hohenkammer — Munich, 1985*, Kommission für Zentralasiatische Studien, Bayerische Akademie der Wissenschaften, München, pp. 55-67.

BRAUEN, M.

1978   "A Bon-po death ceremony", *Tibetan Studies Presented at the Seminar of Young Tibetologists, Zurich, 1977*, M. Brauen and P. Kværne eds., Völkerkunde-museum der Universität Zürich, pp. 53-63.

BROIDO, M. M.

1980   "The Term *dngos po'i gnas lugs* as Used in Padma dKar-po's gZhung 'grel", *Tibetan Studies in Honour of Hugh Richardson, Proceedings of the International Seminar on Tibetan Studies, Oxford 1979*, M. Aris and Aung San Suu Kyi eds., Aris & Phillips Ltd., Warminster, pp. 59-66.

BROUGH, J.

1950   "Thus Have I Heard...", *BSOAS*, vol. XIII, Part 2, pp. 416-426.

BURLEIGH, H. S.

1968   *St. Augustine: Of True Religion*, translated by H. S. Burleigh with an intro-duction by L. O. Mink, Henry Regnery Company, Chicago. Original Latin text of *De Vera Religione* to be found in *Aurelii Augustini Opera*, Pars IV, I, Corpus Christianorum, *Series Latina*, vol. XXXII, Turnholti, Typographi Brepols Editores Pontificii, 1962.

CECH, K.

1992   "A Religious Geography of Tibet According to the Bon Tradition", *Proceedings of the Fifth Seminar of the International Association for Tibetan Studies, Narita 1989*, Naritasan Shinshoji, vol. 1, pp. 387-392.

CHANDRA, L.

1980   "*Oḍḍiyāna*: a New Interpretation", *Tibetan Studies in Honour of Hugh Richardson, Proceedings of the International Seminar on Tibetan Studies, Oxford 1979*, M. Aris and Aung San Suu Kyi eds., Aris & Phillips Ltd., Warminster, pp. 73-78.

1990   *Tibetan-Sanskrit Dictionary*, Rinsen Book Co., Kyoto.

CHANG, K.

1960   "On Zhang Zhung", *BIHP, Academia Sinica*, Extra Volume No. 4, pp. 137-154.

CHOU YI-LIANG

1945   "Tantrism in China", *HJAS*, vol. VIII, pp. 241-332.

CLARK, J. M.

1957   *Meister Eckhart: An Introduction to the Study of his Works with an Anthology of his Sermons*, Thomas Nelson and Sons Ltd., London.

COLEMAN, G.

1993   *A Handbook of Tibetan Culture*, Rider, London.

CSÖMA DE KŐRÖS, A.

1834   *A Grammar of the Tibetan Language in English*, Calcutta (reprinted by Akadémiai Kiadó, Budapest, 1984).

DARGYAY, E.

1977   *The Rise of Esoteric Buddhism in Tibet*, Motilal Banarsidass, New Delhi.

1985   "A rNying-ma Text: the Kun Byed rGyal po'i mDo", *Soundings in Tibetan Civilization*, New Delhi, pp. 283-293.

DAS, S. C.

1881   "The Bon (Pon) Religion", *JASB*, pp. 187-205.

DAVIDSON, R. M.

1981   "The *Litany of Names of Mañjuśrī*", *Tantric and Taoist Studies in Honour of R. A. Stein*, M. Strickmann ed., vol. 1, Mélanges chinois et bouddhiques, vol. XX, Institut Belge des Hautes Études Chinoises, Bruxelles, pp. 1-69.

DEMIÉVILLE, P.

1952   *Le Concile de Lhasa: Une controverse sur le quiétisme entre Bouddhistes de l'Inde et de la Chine au VIIIème siècle de l'ère chrétienne*, Bibliothèque de l'Institut des Hautes Études Chinoises, vol. VII, Presses Universitaires de France, Paris.

1970   "Récents travaux sur Touen-houang", *TP*, vol. 56, pp. 1-95.

1973   "Deux documents de Touen-huang sur le Dhyāna chinois", *Choix d'Études Bouddhiques* (1929-1970), Brill, Leiden, pp. 1-27.

1979   "L'introduction au Tibet du Bouddhisme sinisé d'après les manuscrits de Touen-houang. Analyse de récents travaux japonais", *Contributions aux études sur Touen-Houang*, Librairie Droz, Genève-Paris, pp. 1-16.

DIETZ, S.

1988   "Remarks on four Cosmological Texts from Tun-huang (Pelliot tibétaines Nos. 958, 959 and 967)", *Proceedings of the Fourth Seminar of the International Association for Tibetan Studies, Schloss Hohenkammer — Munich, 1985*, Kommission für Zentralasiatische Studien, Bayerische Akademie der Wissenschaften, München, pp. 111-117.

DREYFUS, G. and LINDTNER, C.

1989   "The *Yogācāra* Philosophy of Dignāga and Dharmakīrti", *SCEAR*, vol. 2, pp. 27-52.

DUMOULIN, H.

1963   *A History of Zen Buddhism*, translated by Paul Peachey, Faber and Faber, London.

DUDJOM RINPOCHE and JIGDREL YESHE DORJE

1991   *The Nyingma School of Tibetan Buddhism: Its Fundamentals and History*, translated and edited by G. Dorje with the collaboration of M. Kapstein, Wisdom Publications, Boston.

EDGERTON, F.

1953   *Buddhist Hybrid Sanskrit Grammar and Dictionary*, Motilal Banarsidass, New Delhi, vol. I "Grammar", vol. II, "Dictionary".

EHRHARD, F.-K.

1992   "The 'Vision' of rDzogs-chen: A Text and its Histories", *Proceedings of the Fifth Seminar of the International Association for Tibetan Studies, Narita 1989*, Naritasan Shinshoji, vol. 1, pp. 47-58.

ELIADE, M.

1958   *Patterns in Comparative Religion*, translated by Rosemary Sheed, Sheed and Ward, London. Reprinted by Sheed and Ward, London, 1993.

1985   *"Homo Faber and Homo Religiosus"*, *Orientalia Iosephi Tucci Memoriae Dicata*, G. Gnoli and L. Lanciotti eds., IsMEO, Rome, LVI, 3, pp. 287-299.

FABER, F.

1985   "A Tibetan Dunhuang Treatise on Simultaneous Enlightenment: The *dMyigs su med pa tshul gcig pa'i gzhung"*, *AO*, vol. XLVI, Copenhagen, pp. 47-77.

1989   "Vimalamitra: One or Two?", *SCEAR*, vol. 2, pp. 19-26.

FAURE, B.

1986   *Le Traité de Bodhidharma*, Éditions Le Mail, Paris.

1991   *The Rhetoric of Immediacy: A Cultural Critique of Chan/Zen Buddhism*, Princeton University Press, Princeton, New Jersey.

FILLIOZAT, J.

1970   *Les Philosophies de l'Inde*, Presses Universitaires de France, Paris.

FILORAMO, G.

1990   *A History of Gnosticism*, translated by A. Alcock, B. Blackwell, Oxford.

GERMANO, D.

1992   *Poetic Thought, the Intelligent Universe, and the Mystery of the Self: The Tantric Synthesis of rDzogs chen in Fourteenth Century Tibet*, Ph. D. dissertation, University of Wisconsin, Madison.

1995   "Architecture and Absence in the Secret Tantric History of the Great Perfection (*rdzogs chen*)", *JIABS*, vol. 17, no. 2, pp. 203-335.

GNOLI, G.
1990   "Appunti sull'idea di Iran", *Proceedings of the First European Conference of Iranian Studies, Turin, 1987*, Part 1, *Old and Middle Iranian Studies*, G. Gnoli and A. Panaino eds., IsMEO, Rome, pp. 145-158.

GÓMEZ, L. O.
1983   "Indian Materials on the Doctrine of Sudden Enlightenment", *Early Ch'an in China and Tibet*, edited by W. Lai and L. R. Lancaster, Berkeley Buddhist Series, No. 5, pp. 393-434.

GUENTHER, H. V.
1963   "Indian Buddhist Thought in Tibetan Perspective: Infinite Transcendence Versus Finiteness", *HR* vol. 3 no. 1, pp. 83-105.
1983   "'Meditation' Trends in Early Tibet", *Early Ch'an in China and Tibet*, W. Lai and L. R. Lancaster eds., Berkeley Buddhist Series, no. 5, pp. 351-366.

GYATSO, J.
1980   "The Teachings of Thang-stong Rgyal-po", *Tibetan Studies in Honour of Hugh Richardson, Proceedings of the International Seminar on Tibetan Studies, Oxford 1979*, M. Aris and Aung San Suu Kyi eds., Aris & Phillips Ltd., Warminster, pp. 111-119.
1986   "Signs, Memory and History: A Tantric Buddhist Theory of Scriptural Transmission", *JIABS*, vol. 9, no. 2, pp. 7-35.
1993   "The Logic of Legitimation in the Tibetan Treasure Tradition", *HR*, vol. 33, no. 2, pp. 97-134.
1994   "Guru Chos-dbang's *gTer 'Byung Chen mo*: An early survey of the Treasure tradition and its strategies in discussing Bon Treasure", *Proceedings of the Sixth Seminar of the International Association for Tibetan Studies, Fagernes 1992*, The Institute for Comparative Research in Human Culture, Oslo, vol. 1, pp. 275-287.
1996   "Drawn from the Tibetan Treasury: The Gter-ma Literature", *Tibetan Literature: Studies in Genre*. Essays in Honor of Geshe Lhun dup Sopa, I. Cabezón and R. R. Jackson eds., Snow Lion, Ithaca, New York, pp. 147-169.
n.d.   "The Relic Text as Prophecy: The Semantic Drift of *Byang-bu* and its Appropriation in the Treasure Tradition", *TJ*, Rai Bahadur T. D. Densapa Commemorative Issue.

HAARH, E.
1968   "The Zhang-Zhung Language: A Grammar and Dictionary of the Unexplored Language of the Tibetan Bonpos", *AJ*, vol. XL, no. 1, Aarhus Universitet, Copenhagen, pp. 7-68.

1969   *The Yar-luṅ Dynasty: A Study with Particular Regard to the Contribution of Myths and Legends to the History of Ancient Tibet and the Origin and Nature of its Kings*, Gad's Forlag, Copenhagen.

HACKIN, J.
1924   *Formulaire Sanscrit-Tibétain du Xème Siècle*, Mission Pelliot en Asie Centrale, Tome II, Librairie Orientaliste Paul Geuthner, Paris.

HAHN, M.
1978   "On the Function and Origin of the Particle Dag", *Tibetan Studies Presented at the Seminar of Young Tibetologists, Zurich, 1977*, M. Brauen and P. Kværne eds., Völkerkundemuseum der Universität Zürich, pp. 137-147.

HAKEDA, Y.-S.
1967   *The Awakening of Faith Attributed to Aśvaghosha*, Columbia University Press, New York & London.

HANSON-BARBER, A.-W.
1984   *The Life and Teachings of Vairocana*, Ph. D. dissertation, University of Wisconsin, Madison.

HARTMANN, F.
1960   *Personal Christianity: The Doctrines of Jacob Boehme*, F. Ungar, New York.

HOFFMANN, H.
1950   *Quellen zur Geshichte der Tibetische Bon-Religion*, Akademie der Wissenschaften und der Literatur in Mainz, F. S. Verlag, Wiesbaden.
1972   "Several Źaṅ-źuṅ Etymologies", *OE*, vol. 19, nos. 1-2, pp. 193-201.

HUMMEL, S.
1974-5 "Materialen zu einem Wörterbuch der Źaṅ-źuṅ-sprache", *MS*, vol. 31, pp. 448-520.

HURVITZ, L.
1992-3 "'Being' and 'Non-Being' in Ancient India and China", *SCEAR* vol. 5/6, pp. 97-121.

IMAEDA, Y.
1975   "Documents tibétains de Touen-Houang concernant le concile du Tibet", *JA*, vol. 263, pp. 125-146.

ISHIHAMA Y. and FUKUDA, Y.
1989   *A New Critical Edition of the Mahāvyutpatti, Sanskrit-Tibetan-Mongolian Dictionary of Buddhist Terminology*, Materials for Tibetan-Mongolian Dictionaries, vol. 1, Studia Tibetica no. 16, The Toyo Bunko, Tokyo.

ISHIKAWA, M.

1990   *A Critical Edition of the sGra sByor Bam po gNyis pa, An Old Basic Commentary on the Mahāvyutpatti*, Materials for Tibetan-Mongolian Dictionaries, vol. 2, Studia Tibetica no. 18, The Toyo Bunko, Tokyo.

JASCHKE, H. A.

1993   *A Tibetan-English Dictionary*, Rinsen Book Company, Kyoto.

JOHNSTON, W.

1973   *The Cloud of Unknowing and the Book of Privy Counselling*, Image Books, New York.

KAPSTEIN, M.

1985   "Religious Syncretism in 13th Century Tibet: The Limitless Ocean Cycle", *Soundings in Tibetan Civilization*, New Delhi, pp. 358-371.

1988   "Mi-pham's Theory of Interpretation", *Buddhist Hermeneutics*, D. Lopez, Jr. ed., University of Hawaii Press, Honolulu, pp. 149-174.

1989   "The Purificatory Gem and Its Cleansing: A Late Tibetan Polemical Discussion of Apocryphal Texts", *HR*, vol. 28, no. 3, pp. 217-244.

KARMAY, S. G.

1972   *The Treasury of Good Sayings: A Tibetan History of Bon*, London Oriental Series vol. 26, Oxford University Press, London.

1975a   *A General Introduction to the History and Doctrines of Bon*, MRDTB, n. 33, Tokyo, pp. 171-218.

1975b   "A Discussion of the Doctrinal Position of rDzogs-chen from the 10th to the 13th Centuries", *JA*, vol. 263, pp. 147-156.

1977   *A Catalogue of Bonpo Publications*, The Toyo Bunko, Tokyo.

1980a   "The Ordinance of lHa Bla-ma Ye-shes-'od", *Tibetan Studies in Honour of Hugh Richardson, Proceedings of the International Seminar on Tibetan Studies, Oxford 1979*, M. Aris and Aung San Suu Kyi eds., Aris & Phillips Ltd., Warminster, pp. 150-162.

1980b   "An Open Letter of Pho-brang Zhi-ba-'od", *TJ*, vol. 5, no. 3, pp. 1-28.

1981   "King Tsa/Dza and Vajrayāna", *Tantric and Taoist Studies in Honour of R. A. Stein*, M. Strickmann ed., vol. 1, Mélanges chinois et bouddhiques, vol. XX, Institut Belge des Hautes Études Chinoises, Bruxelles, pp. 192-211.

1983   "Un témoignage sur le Bon face au Bouddhisme à l'époque des rois tibétaines", *Contributions on Tibetan and Buddhist Religion and Philosophy, Proceedings of the Csoma de Körös Symposium*, Velm-Vienna, vol. 2, pp. 89-106.

1985   "The rDzogs-chen in its Earliest Texts: A Manuscript from Tun-Huang", *Soundings in Tibetan Civilization*, New Delhi, pp. 272-282.

1988a   *The Great Perfection: A Philosophical and Meditative Teaching of Tibetan Buddhism*, E. J. Brill, Leiden.

1988b   *Secret Visions of the Fifth Dalai Lama*, Serindia Publications, London.

1990   "The Decree of the Khro-chen King", *AO*, vol. LI, pp. 141-159.

1998   *The Little Luminous Boy: The Oral Tradition from the Land of Zhang Zhung Depicted on Two Tibetan Paintings*. Orchid Press, Bangkok.

KIMURA, R.

1981   "Le Dhyāna chinois au Tibet ancien après Mahāyāna", *JA*, vol. 269, pp. 183-192.

KING, R.

1995   *Early Advaita Vedānta and Buddhism: The Māhāyāna Context of the Gaudapādiya-Kārikā*. State University of New York. First Indian Edition as Sri Garib Das Oriental Series No. 234, Sri Satguru Publications, Delhi, 1997.

KLEIN, ANNE and GESHE TENZIN WANGYAL RINPOCHE

1995   "Bon and the Logic of the Non-Conceptual: Preliminary Reflections on *The Authenticity of Innate Awareness* (*gTan tshigs gal mdo rig pa'i tshad ma*)" in *Asiatische Studien/Etudes Asiatiques* XLIX 4, pp. 769-792.

KOLLMAR-PAULENZ, K.

1992-3   "Utopian Thought in Tibetan Buddhism: A Survey of the Śambhala Concept and its Sources", SCEAR, vol. 5/6, pp. 78-96.

KVÆRNE, P.

1971   "A Chronological Table of the Bon po: The bsTan rcis of Ñi ma bstan 'jin", *AO*, vol. XXXIII, pp. 205-282.

1973   "Bonpo Studies, the A Khrid System of Meditation", Part One, *Kailash*, vol. I, no. 1, pp. 19-50 , Part Two, "The Essential Teachings of the A Khrid System", *Kailash*, vol. I, no. 4, pp. 248-332.

1974   "The Canon of the Tibetan Bonpos", *IIJ*, vol. 16, The Hague, Part One, pp. 18-56, Part Two, pp. 96-144.

1975   "On the Concept of Sahaja in Indian Buddhist Tantric Literature", *Temenos*, vol. 11, pp. 88-135.

1976   "Who Are the Bonpos?", *TR*, vol. 11, no. 9, pp. 30-33.

1983   "The Great Perfection of the Tibetan Bonpos", *Early Ch'an in China and Tibet*, W. Lai and L. R. Lancaster eds., Berkeley Buddhist Series, No. 5, p. 367-392.

1985   *Tibet. Bon Religion: A Death Ritual of the Tibetan Bonpos*, Iconography of Religions XII, 13, E. J. Brill, Leiden.

1986   "Peintures tibétaines de la vie de sTon-pa-gÇen-rab", *Arts Asiatiques*, vol. XLI, Paris, pp. 36-81.

1988   "A New Chronological Table of the Bon Religion. The *bstan rcis* of Hor-bcun bsTan-'jin-blo-gros (1888-1975)", *Proceedings of the Fourth Seminar of the International Association for Tibetan Studies, Schloss Hohenkammer — Munich, 1985*, Kommission fürZentralasiatische Studien, Bayerische Akademie der Wissenschaften, München, pp. 241-244.

1989 "Śākyamuni in the Bon Religion", *Temenos*, vol. 25, pp. 33-40.

1990a "The Monastery of sNang-zhig of the Bon Religion in the rNga-ba District of Amdo", *Indo-Sino-Tibetica. Studi in onore di Luciano Petech*, P. Daffinà ed., Studi Orientali IX, Rome, pp. 207-221.

1990b "A Bonpo *bsTan-rtsis* from 1804", *Indo-Tibetan Studies, Papers in Honour and Appreciation of Professor David L. Snellgrove's Contribution to Indo-Tibetan Studies*, T. Skorupski ed., The Institute of Buddhist Studies, Tring, U.K., pp. 151-169.

1990c "The Bön of Tibet: The Historical Enigma of a Monastic Tradition", *The Renaissance of Tibetan Civilization*, C. von Führer-Haimendorf ed., Synergetic Press, Oracle, Arizona, pp. 114-119.

1994 "The Bon Religion of Tibet: A Survey of Research", *The Buddhist Forum, vol. III, 1991-1993.* Papers in Honour and Appreciation of Professor David Seyfort Ruegg's Contribution to Indological, Buddhist and Tibetan Studies, T. Skorupski & U. Pagel eds., SOAS, London, pp. 131-141.

1995 *The Bon Religion of Tibet*, Serindia Publications, London.

1996 "The Literature of Bon", *Tibetan Literature: Studies in Genre.* Essays in Honor of Geshe Lhun dup Sopa, J. I. Cabezón and R. R. Jackson eds., Snow Lion, Ithaca, New York, pp. 138-146.

KVÆRNE, P. and RIKEY, T. K.

1996 *The Stages of A-khrid Meditation: Dzogchen Practice of the Bon Tradition by Bru-sgom rGyal-ba g.yung-drung (1242-90)*, LTWA, Dharamsala, India.

LALOU, M.

1939 "Document tibétain sur l'expansion du Dhyāna chinois", *JA*, vol.231, pp. 505-523.

1952 "Rituel bon-po des funérailles royales", *JA*, vol. 240, pp.339-361.

1953 "Les textes bouddhiques au temps du Roi Khri-sroṅ-lde-bcan", *JA*, vol. 241, pp. 313-353.

LAMOTTE, É.

1988 "The Assessment of Textual Interpretation in Buddhism", *Buddhist Hermeneutics* D. Lopez Jr. ed., University of Hawaii Press, Honolulu, pp. 11-27.

LAU, D. D.

1963 *Lao-tzu, Tao Te Ching*, Penguin, Harmondsworth.

LAUFER, B.

1901 "Über ein tibetisches Geschichtswerk der Bonpo", *TP*, Série II, vol. II, E. J. Brill, Leiden; Kraus Reprint, Nendeln/Liechtenstein, 1975, pp. 24-44.

1916 "Loan-words in Tibetan", *TP*, vol. 17, pp. 402-552.

LOPEZ, D. S., Jr. (ed.)

1997 *Religions of Tibet in Practice*, Princeton University Press, Princeton, New Jersey.

LOSERIES, U.

1989   *Guru Padmasambhavas "Instruktion 'Die Kette der Anschauungen'" (Man-Ngag lTa ba'i Phreng ba)*, Ph. D. dissertation, University of Bonn.

MACDONALD, A.

1971   "Une lecture des Pelliot Tibétaines 1286, 1287, 1038, 1047 et 1290. Essai sur la formation et l'emploi des mythes politiques dans la religion royale de Sron-bcan sgam-po", *Études tibétaines dédiées à la mémoire de Marcelle Lalou*, A. Macdonald ed., Adrien Maisonneuve, Paris, pp. 190-391.

MALANDRA, W. W.

1983   *An Introduction to Ancient Iranian Religion*, University of Minnesota Press, Minneapolis.

MARTIN, D. P.

1991   *The Emergence of Bon and the Tibetan Polemical Tradition*, Ph. D. dissertation, Indiana University.

1994   *Mandala Cosmogony: Human Body, Good Thought and the Revelation of the Secret Mother Tantras of Bon*, Asiatische Forschungen Band 124, Harrassowitz Verlag, Wiesbaden.

1995   "'Ol-mo-lung-ring, the Original Holy Place", *TJ*, vol. 20, no. 1, pp. 48-82. Revised and expanded as "'Ol mo lung ring, the Original Holy Place", *Sacred Spaces and Powerful Places in Tibetan Religious Culture: A Collection of Essays*, T. Huber ed., LTWA, Dharamsala, 1998, pp. 258-301.

MAY, J.

1967   "Chojo", *Hôbôgirin*, Tokyo, pp. 353-360.

MAYER, R.

1994   "Scriptural Revelation in India and Tibet. Indian Precursor of the gTerma Tradition", *Proceedings of the Sixth Seminar of the International Association for Tibetan Studies, Fagernes 1992*, The Institute for Comparative Research in Human Culture, Oslo, vol. 2, pp. 533-544.

MIMAKI, K.

1982   *Blo gsal grub mtha'*, University of Kyoto, Kyoto.

1993   *Annotated Translation of the Chapter on the Yogācāra of the Blo gsal grub mtha'*, Part 1, Kyoto University, Kyoto.

1994a   "A Fourteenth Century Bon-po Doxography, the *Bon sgo gsal byed* by Tre ston rGyal mtshan dpal—A Preliminary Report toward a Critical Edition", *Proceedings of the Sixth Seminar of the International Association for Tibetan Studies, Fagernes 1992*, The Institute for Comparative Research in Human Culture, Oslo, vol. 2, pp. 570-579.

1994b   "Doxographie tibétaine et classifications indiennes", *Bouddhisme et cultures locales: Quelque cas de réciproques adaptations. Actes du colloque francojaponais de septembre 1991 édités par F. Fumimasa et G. Fussman*, EFEO, Paris, pp. 115-136.

MIMAKI, K. and AKAMATSU, A.

1985 "La Philosophie des Śaiva vue par un auteur Tibétain du 14è siècle", *Tantric and Taoist Studies in Honour of R. A. Stein*, M. Strickmann ed., vol. 3, Mélanges chinois et bouddhiques, vol. XXII, Institut Belge des Hautes Études Chinoises, Bruxelles, pp. 746-772.

MONIER-WILLIAMS, M.

1986 *Sanskrit-English Dictionary*, Meicho Fukyukai Co., Ltd. Tokyo.

MUKERJEE, R.

1971 *The Song of the Self Supreme (Aṣṭāvakragītā)*, Motilal Banarsidass, New Delhi.

NAGANO, Y.

1995 "Functions of a Written Tibetan Instrumental Particle, *-kyis*, Revisited", *New Horizons in Tibeto-Burman Morphosyntax*, Senri Ethnological Studies, vol. 41, Osaka, pp. 133-141.

NAGAO, G. M.

1991a "Connotations of the Word *Āśraya* (Basis) in the *Mahāyāna-Sūtralaṃkāra*", *Mādhyamika and Yogācāra: A Study of Mahāyāna Philosophies*, Collected papers of G. M. Nagao, edited, collated and translated by L. S. Kawamura in collaboration with G. M. Nagao, State University of New York Press, Albany, pp. 75-81.

1991b "Tranquil Flow of Mind: An Interpretation of *Upekṣā*", ibidem, pp. 91-102.

1991c "On the Theory of Buddha Body (*Buddha-kāya*)", ibidem, pp. 103-122.

1991d "The Buddhist World View as Elucidated in the Three-nature Theory and Its Similes", ibidem, pp. 61-74.

1992 "The Yogācāra Cognition Theory and Depth Psychology", *Études bouddhiques offertes à Jacques May*, *AS*, vol. 46, 1, pp. 307-322.

NAMKHAI, N.

1985 "Il canto dell'energia di Nyag-bla Padma bDud-'dul", *Orientalia Iosephi Tucci Memoriae Dicata*, G. Gnoli and L. Lanciotti eds., IsMEO, Rome, LVI, 3, pp. 1021-1028.

1995 *Drung, Deu and Bön: Narrations, Symbolic Languages and the Bön Tradition in Ancient Tibet*, LTWA, Dharamsala.

NAMKHAI, N. and PRATS, R.

1989 *Gaṅs ti se'i dkar c'ag: A Bon-po Story of the Sacred Mountain Ti-se and the Blue Lake Ma-paṅ*. Revised, collated and completed by R. Prats. Excerpts in English translated by Namkhai Norbu and Ramon Prats, *SOR*, vol. LXI, IsMEO, Rome

NEBESKY-WOJKOWITZ, R.

1956 *Oracles and Demons of Tibet*, Mouton & Co., The Hague.

NOBUMI, I.

1985   "Récits de la soumission de Maheśvara par Trilokavijâya — d'après les sources Chinoises et Japonaises — [Notes autour de Maheśvara-Śiva dans le Bouddhisme]", *Tantric and Taoist Studies in Honour of R. A. Stein*, M. Strickmann ed., vol. 3, Mélanges chinois et bouddhiques, vol. XXII, Institut Belge des Hautes Études Chinoises, Bruxelles, pp. 633-661.

OROFINO, G.

1985   *Insegnamenti tibetani su morte e liberazione*, Edizioni Mediterranee, Rome.

1990a   *Sacred Tibetan Teachings on Death and Liberation*, Prism Press, Bridport.

1990b   "The State of the Art in the Study on the Zhang Zhung Language", *Annali dell'Istituto Universitario Orientale*, Naples, pp. 83-85.

PADOUX, A.

1972   "Le Śivaïsme du Cachemire," in *L'Hindouisme: Textes recueillis et présentés par A. Esnoul*, Fayard/Denoël, Paris, pp. 479-492.

PALMER, E. H.

1974   *Oriental Mysticism: A Treatise on Sufiistic and Unitarian Theosophy of the Persians*, The Octagon Press Ltd., London.

PETECH, L.

1988   "Glosse agli Annali di Tun-Huang", *Selected Papers on Asian History*, SOR, vol. LX, IsMEO, Rome, pp. 261-299.

PRATS, R.

1978   "The Spiritual Lineage of the Dzogchen Tradition", *Tibetan Studies Presented at the Seminar of Young Tibetologists, Zurich, 1977*, M. Brauen and P. Kværne eds., Völkerkundemuseum der Universität Zürich, pp. 199-207.

1980   "Some Preliminary Considerations Arising from a Biographical Study of the Early *Gter-ston*", *Tibetan Studies in Honour of Hugh Richardson, Proceedings of the International Seminar on Tibetan Studies, Oxford 1979*, M. Aris and Aung San Suu Kyi eds., Aris & Phillips Ltd., Warminster, pp. 256-260.

1982   *Contributo allo studio biografico dei primi Gter-ston*, Serie Minor, vol. 17, Istituto Universitario Orientale, Seminario di Studi Asiatici, Naples.

1985   "The Aspiration-Prayer of the Ground, Path and Goal: An Inspired Piece on rDzogs-chen by 'Jigs-med-gling-pa", *Orientalia Iosephi Tucci Memoriae Dicata*, G. Gnoli and L. Lanciotti eds., IsMEO, Rome, LVI, 3, pp. 1159-1172.

1991   "On 'Contracted Words' and a List of Them Collected from a Bon-po Work", *EW*, vol. 41, pp. 231-237.

RIKEY, T. and RUSKIN, A.

1992   *A Manual of Key Buddhist Terms: Categorization of Buddhist Terminology with Commentary*, LTWA, Dharamsala.

ROERICH, G. N.
1949   *The Blue Annals*, RASB, Calcutta, 2 vols.

ROSSI, D.
1994   "The Nine Ways of the Bonpo Tradition: An Oral Presentation by a Con-
        temporary Bonpo Lama", *Proceedings of the Sixth Seminar of the Interna-
        tional Association for Tibetan Studies, Fagernes 1992*, The Institute for Com-
        parative Research in Human Culture, Oslo, vol. 2, p. 676-681.

RUEGG, D.-S.
1966   *The Life of Bu ston Rin po che with the Tibetan Text of the Bu ston rNam thar*,
        SOR, vol. XXXIV, IsMEO, Rome.
1969   *La Théorie du Tathāgatagarbha et du Gotra: Études sur la Sotériologie et la
        Gnoséologie du Bouddhisme*, EFEO, vol. LXX, Paris.
1971   "Le Dharmadhātustava de Nāgārjuna", *Études tibétaines dédiées à la mémoire
        de Marcelle Lalou*, A. Macdonald ed., Adrien Maisonneuve, Paris, pp. 448-
        471.
1980   "On the Reception and Early History of the dBu-ma (Madhyamaka) in
        Tibet", *Tibetan Studies in Honour of Hugh Richardson: Proceedings of the In-
        ternational Seminar on Tibetan Studies, Oxford 1979*, M. Aris and Aung San
        Suu Kyi eds., Aris & Phillips Ltd., Warminster, pp. 277-279.
1981   "Autour du *lTa ba'i khyad par* de Ye Śes sde (version de Touen-Houang,
        Pelliot tibétain 814)", *JA*, vol. 269, pp. 207-229.
1992   "Some Reflections on Translating Buddhist Philosophical Texts from San-
        skrit and Tibetan", *Études bouddhiques offertes à Jacques May*, *AS*, vol. 46, 1,
        pp. 367-391.

RYÔSHÔ, T.
1989   "A Historical Outiline of Japanese Research on the Chinese Chan Writ-
        ings from Dunhuang", *SCEAR*, vol. 2, pp. 141-169.

SANDERSON, A.
1990   "Śaivism and the Tantric Traditions", *The World's Religions: The Religions
        of Asia*, F. Hardy ed., Routledge, London, pp. 128-172.

SANGYE TANDAR, Tr. and GUARD, R.
1992   "The Twelve Deeds of Lord Shenrab", *TJ*, vol. XVII, no. 2, pp. 28-44.

SCHMITHAUSEN, L.
1973   "Zu D. Seyfort Ruegg's buch "La théorie du tathagatagarbha et du gotra"",
        Wiener Zeitschrift für die Kunde Südasiens und Archiv für Indische Philosophie,
        vol. 17, pp. 123-160.
1987   *Ālaya-vijñāna: On the Origin and Early Development of a Central Concept of
        Yogācāra Philosophy*, Studia Philologica Buddhica, Monograph Series IVb,
        The International Institute for Buddhist Studies, Tokyo.

SCHÜRMANN, R.
1978   *Meister Eckhart, Mystic and Philosopher,* Indiana University Press, Bloomington and London.

SHARMA, A.
1997   *The Rope and the Snake: A Metaphorical Exploration of Advaita Vedānta,* Manohar, New Delhi.

SIKLÓS, B.
1990   "Philosophical and Religious Taoism", *The World's Religions: The Religions of Asia,* F. Hardy ed., Routledge, London, pp. 10-19.

SILK, J.
1989   "A Note on the Opening Formula of Buddhist *Sūtras*", *JIABS,* vol. 12, no. 1, pp. 158-163.

SKORUPSKI, T.
1990   "The Religions of Tibet", *The World's Religions: The Religions of Asia,* F. Hardy ed., Routledge, London, pp. 273-278.

SMITH, E. G.
1970   "Introduction to 'Kongtrul's Encyclopaedia of Indo-Tibetan Culture'", *SPS,* International Academy of Indian Culture, vol. 80, New Delhi, pp. 1-78.

SNELLGROVE, D.
1967a   *The Nine Ways of Bon: Excerpts from the gZi brjid Edited and Translated,* London Oriental Series, vol. 18, Oxford University Press, London.

1967b   *Four Lamas of Dolpo,* Bruno Cassirer, Oxford. Second reprint, Himalayan Book Seller, Kathmandu, 1992.

1985   "Categories of Buddhist Tantras", *Orientalia Iosephi Tucci Memoriae Dicata,* G. Gnoli and L. Lanciotti eds., IsMEO, Rome, LVI, 3, pp. 1353-1384.

1987   *Indo-Tibetan Buddhism: Indian Buddhists and Their Tibetan Successors,* Serindia Publications, London.

SNELLGROVE, D. L. and RICHARDSON, H.
1968   *A Cultural History of Tibet,* Weidenfeld and Nicolson, London. Reprinted by Prajna Press, Boulder, 1980.

SOGYAL RINPOCHE
1994   *The Tibetan Book of Living and Dying,* P. Gaffney and A. Harvey eds., HarperSanFrancisco.

SØRENSEN, H.
1989   "Observations on the Characteristics of the Chinese Chan manuscripts from Dunhuang", *SCEAR,* vol. 2, pp. 115-139.

SPANIEN, A. and IMAEDA, Y.

1979 *Choix de Documents Tibétaines conservés à la Bibliothèque Nationale de Paris,* présentés par A. Spanien et Y. Imaeda, Paris, 2 vols.

SPARHAM, G.

1993 *Ocean of Eloquence: Tsongkhapa's Commentary on the Yogācāra Doctrine of Mind,* State University of New York Press, Albany.

STEIN, R. A.

1959 *Les Tribus anciennes des marches sino-tibétaines,* Paris.

1962 *La Civilisation Tibétaine,* Dunod, Paris.

1970 "Un document ancien relatif aux rites funéraires des Bon-po tibétains", *JA,* vol. 258, pp. 155-185.

1971a "Du Récit au Rituel dans les Manuscrits Tibétains de Touen-Houang", *Études tibétaines dédiées à la mémoire de Marcelle Lalou,* A. Macdonald ed., Adrien Maisonneuve, Paris, pp. 479-547.

1971b "Illumination Subite ou Saisie Simultanée. Note sur la Terminologie Chinoise et Tibétaine", *Revue de l'Histoire des Religions,* vol. CLXXIX, 1, Paris, pp. 3-30.

1971c "La langue Źań-Źuń du Bon organisé", *BEFEO,* vol. 58, pp. 231-254.

1972 *Vie et Chants de 'Brug-pa Kun-legs le Yogin,* Paris.

1973-4 "Récits autour du récit de Rudra", *Annuaire du Collège de France, Résumé des cours.*

1977 "La gueule du *makara*: un trait inexpliqué de certains objets rituels", *Essais sur l'Art du Tibet,* A. Macdonald and Y. Imaeda eds., Librairie d'Amérique et d'Orient, J. Maisonneuve, succ., Paris, pp. 53-62.

1980 "Une mention du manichéisme dans la choix du Bouddhisme comme religion d'état par le roi tibétain Khri-sroń lDe-bcan", *Indianisme et Bouddisme. Mélanges offerts à Mgr Etienne Lamotte,* Louvain, pp. 329-337.

1983 "Tibetica Antiqua I. Les deux vocabulaires des traductions Indo-Tibétaine et Sino-Tibétaine dans le manuscrits de Touen-Houang", *BEFEO* vol. 72, pp. 149-223.

1985a "Tibetica Antiqua III. A propos du mot *gcug-lag* et de la religion indigène", *BEFEO,* vol. LXXIV, Paris, pp. 83-133.

1985b "La mythologie hindouiste au Tibet", *Orientalia Iosephi Tucci Memoriae Dicata,* G. Gnoli and L. Lanciotti eds., IsMEO, Rome, LVI, 3, pp. 1407-1426.

1988 "Tibetica Antiqua V. La religion indigène et les *Bon*-po dans les manuscrits de Touen-Houang", *BEFEO,* vol. LXXVII, Paris, pp. 27-56.

1995 "La Soumission de Rudra et Autres Contes Tantriques", *JA,* vol. 283, no. 1, pp. 121-160.

STOUDT, J. J.

1968 *Jacob Boehme: His Life and Thought,* The Seabury Press, New York.

SUZUKI, D. T.

1934   *The Index to the Lankavatara Sutra* (Nanjio edition), The Sanskrit Buddhist Texts Publishing Society, Kyoto.

TENZIN NAMDAK

1992   *Bonpo Dzogchen Teachings According to Lopon Tenzin Namdak*, transcribed and edited by John Myrdhin Reynolds, Bonpo Translation Project, Vidyadhara Publications, San Diego and Amsterdam.

1993   *Heart Drops of Dharmakaya: Dzogchen Practice of the Bön Tradition*, Translation and commentary by Lopon Tenzin Namdak, Introduction by Per Kværne, Richard Dixey ed., Snow Lion Publications, Ithaca, New York.

TENZIN WANGYAL

1993   *Wonders of the Natural Mind: The Essence of Dzogchen in the Native Bon Tradition of Tibet*, Station Hill, New York.

THOMAS, F. W.

1933   "The Żań żuń language", *JRAS*, pp. 405-410.

1967   "The Żań żuń language", *AM*, vol. 13, pp. 211-217.

THURMAN, R.

1988   "Vajra Hermeneutics", *Buddhist Hermeneutics*, D. S. Lopez, Jr. ed., University of Hawaii Press, Honolulu, pp. 119-148.

TILLEMANS, T. J. F.

1988   "On *bdag, gźan* and Related Notions of Tibetan Grammar", *Proceedings of the Fourth Seminar of the International Association for Tibetan Studies, Schloss Hohenkammer — Munich, 1985*, Kommission für Zentralasiatische Studien, Bayerische Akademie der Wissenschaften, München, pp. 491-502.

TOKIWA, G.

1973   *A Dialogue on the Contemplation-Extinguished*, The Institute for Zen Studies, Kyoto.

TOUSSAINT, G. C.

1993   *Le Dict de Padma, Padma Thang Yig*, Bibliothèque de l'Institut des Hautes Études Chinoises, Paris. Translated from the French by K. Douglas and G. Bays, *The Life and Liberation of Padmasambhava*, Dharma Publishing, Berkeley, 1978, 2 vols.

TUCCI, G.

1949   *Tibetan Painted Scrolls*, Libreria dello Stato, Rome, 3 vols.

1956   *Preliminary Report on Two Scientific Expeditions in Nepal*, SOR, vol. X, no. 1, IsMEO, Rome.

1958   *Minor Buddhist Texts, Part II*, SOR, vol. IX, 2, IsMEO, Rome.

1980   *The Religions of Tibet*, translated from the German and Italian by Geoffrey
        Samuel, University of California Press, Berkeley and Los Angeles; a trans-
        lation of the author's "Die Religionen Tibets", in *Die Religionen Tibets und
        der Mongolei*, by G. Tucci and W. Heissig, Die Religionen der Menscheit,
        Band 20, W. Kohlhammer GmbH, Stuttgart, pp. v-291.

TULKU THONDUP R.

1986   *Hidden Teachings of Tibet: An Explanation of the Terma Tradition of Tibetan
        Buddhism*, Wisdom Publications, London. Reprinted by Wisdom Publica-
        tions, Boston, 1997.

1995   *Masters of Meditation and Miracles: The Longchen Nyingthig Lineage of Ti-
        betan Buddhism*, edited by H. Talbott, Shambhala, Boston and London.

UEYAMA, D.

1983   "The Study of Tibetan Ch'an Manuscripts Recovered from Tun-huang: A
        Review of the Field and its Prospects", *Early Ch'an in China and Tibet*, W.
        Lai and L. R. Lancaster eds., Berkeley Buddhist Series, No. 5, pp. 327-349.

URAY, G.

1964   "The Old Tibetan Verb *Bon*", *AOH*, vol. 17, pp. 323-334.

1983   "Tibet's Connections with Nestorianism and Manicheism in the 8th-10th
        Centuries", *Contributions on Tibetan Language, History and Culture I*, E.
        Steinkellner and H. Tauscher eds., Wien, pp. 399-429.

1985   "A Note on the Historical Geography of Ancient Tibet", *Orientalia Iosephi
        Tucci Memoriae Dicata*, G. Gnoli and L. Lanciotti eds., LVI, 3, IsMEO, Rome,
        pp. 1503-1510.

VAN DER KUIJP, L. W. J.

1986   Review of P. Kværne's *Tibet Bon Religion*, *AO*, vol. 47, pp. 202-208.

VITALI, R.

1996   *The Kingdoms of Gu.ge Pu.hrang According to mNga'.ris rgyal.rabs by Gu.ge
        mkhan.chen Ngag.dbang grags.pa*, Asian edition, Tho.ling gtsug.lag.khang
        lo.gcig.stong 'khor.ba'i rjes.dran.mdzad sgo'i go.sgrig tshogs.chung,
        Dharamsala, India.

VOHRA, R.

1988   "Ethno-Historicity of the Dards in Ladakh-Baltistan: Observations and
        Analysis", *Proceedings of the Fourth Seminar of the International Association
        for Tibetan Studies, Schloss Hohenkammer — Munich, 1985*, Kommission für
        Zentralasiatische Studien, Bayerische Akademie der Wissenschaften,
        München, pp. 529-546.

VOSTRIKOV, A. I.

1970   *Tibetan Historical Literature*, translated from the Russian by H. Chandra
        Gupta, Soviet Indology Series no. 4, Calcutta.

WADDEL, L. A.
1895   The Buddhism of Tibet or Lamaism, London.

WATSON, B.
1968   The Complete Works of Chuang Tzu, Columbia University Press, New York and London.

WAYMAN, A.
1973   The Buddhist Tantras, S. Weiser, New York.
1983   "Male, Female and the Androgyne per Buddhist Tantra, Jacob Boehme, and the Greek and Taoist Mysteries", Tantric and Taoist Studies in Honour of R. A. Stein, M. Strickmann ed., vol. 2, Mélanges chinois et bouddhiques, vol. XXI, Institut Belge des Hautes Études Chinoises, Bruxelles, pp. 592-631.
1988   "The Tibetan Negatives med and ma yin, and the Mañjuśrī-nama-saṃgīti, VI,19 Commentaries", Proceedings of the Fourth Seminar of the International Association for Tibetan Studies, Schloss Hohenkammer - Munich, 1985, Kommission für Zentralasiatische Studien, Bayerische Akademie der Wissenschaften, München, pp. 551-558.

WILLIAMS, P.
1989   Mahāyāna Buddhism: The Doctrinal Foundations, Routledge and Kegan Paul, London (reprinted by Routledge, London, 1996).

INDEXED GLOSSARY

I. Sanskrit Terms[1]

akaniṣṭha   (*'og min*), name of heaven, 81 n. 5

arūpadhātu   (*gzugs med khams*), the sphere without form, 53 n. 155; 81 n. 5

avyākṛita   (*lung ma bstan*), neutral, 54 n. 161

ālaya-vijñāna   (*kun gzhi rnam par shes pa*), the Basis-consciousness, 22 n. 25; 53

uḍḍiyāna   (*u rgyan, o rgyan*), birthplace of dGa' rab rDo rje, 23 n. 28

kāmadhātu   (*'dod khams*), the sphere of desire, 53 n. 155; 81 n. 5

guhyagarbha   (*gsang ba snying po*), name of *tantra*, 25

tathāgatagarbha   (*de bzhin gshegs pa'i snying po*), Buddha essence, 44 n. 115

tantra   (*rgyud*), category of teachings, 22; 24 n. 39; 28; 30; 40; 41 n. 108; 46 n. 127; 79 n. 3; 97 n. 4; 133, nn. 1, 2; 141; 153 n. 2; 271 n. 1

trāyastriṁśa   (*gsum cu rtsa gsum gyi gnas*), name of heaven, 215 n. 3

dṛishṭi   (*lta ba*), theory, view, 43 n. 110

nimitta   (*mtshan ma*), characterization, 60 n. 178

---

1. Entries are alphabetized as in Sanskrit and Tibetan. The definitions of terms refer to the meanings of terms as used in this work. Different meanings of given terms are reflected in separate entries; the same applies to compounded expressions based on the same term. Numbers refer only to the pages of the English text.

nirvāṇa (*mya ngan las 'das pa*), the state transcending suffering, 23 n. 28

prapañca (*spros pa*), diversification, 60 n. 178

bodhicitta (*byang chub kyi sems*), the Pure-and-Perfect-Mind, 56, 56 n. 169

bhikṣuṇī (*dge slong ma*), fully ordained Buddhist nun, 23

maṇḍala (*dkyil 'khor*), (sacred) circle, 47 n. 128

mahāyāna (*theg pa chen po*), the Great Vehicle, 38; 40; 56

mahāyoga (*rnal byor chen mo*), a class of *tantras*, 22; 24

yogācāra (*sems tsam pa*), Indian Buddhist philosophical school, 22 n. 25; 52

rūpadhātu (*gzugs khams*), the sphere of form, 53 n. 155; 81 n. 5

vāsanā (*bag chags*), (karmic) imprint, 53

sūtra (*mdo*), class of scriptures, 56

hetu (*gtan tshigs*), cause (of being), 123 n. 1

II. Tibetan Terms

ka (nas) dag pure from the beginning, 50; 53; 60 n. 180; 89; 95; 111; 193; 201; 243; 265

ka dag chen po great primordial purity, 55

ka (nas) dag (pa) primordial purity, 56; 58; 253

kun tu brtags pa'i ma rig pa the non-awareness that defines everything, 64

kun tu bzang po the All-Good, (the Primordial Teacher; also, gShen lha 'Od dkar), 28; 40; 44 n. 117; 50; 51; 55; 81; 85 n. 1; 87; 95; 103; 151; 155; 159 n. 1; 169; 193; 195; 197; 223; 225; 239; 257

kun tu bzang po'i dgongs pa the contemplation of Kun tu bZang po, 115; 141

kun tu bzang po'i ngang the Condition of Kun tu bZang po, 46 n. 122; 49; 50; 54; 63 n. 191; 157; 259

kun tu bzang po'i lta ba the View of Kun tu bZang po, 111; 203 n. 1

kun gzhi (kun gyi gzhi) the Basis of all, 40; 52; 53; 58; 59; 61; 65; 91; 173 n. 1; 175 nn. 3, 4; 221; 261; 263

kun la khyab (pa) all-encompassing, 261

klu subterranean beings, 27; 39; 177 n. 2

klong Expanse, 46 n. 124; 59; 261; 263

dkar chag catalogue, 30 n. 62; 32 n. 71; 61 n. 184

dkyil 'khor (1) disk, 83

dkyil 'khor (2) Circle, 245

bka' 'gyur the *corpus* of Bonpo canonical texts, 10; 30 n. 59; 31 nn. 67, 68; 32 n. 71; 74; 165 n. 3; 167

bka' brten	the *corpus* of ancillary literary production based upon 'the Word', 61 n. 184
bka' ma	(uninterruptedly transmitted) Word, 39; 79 n. 3
sku	Body, 52; 61; 99
sku gsum	the Three Bodies, 39; 49 n. 138; 85 n. 1; 97 n. 3; 107; 131
skye 'gag (gnyis) med (pa)	without birth and interruption, 60 n. 180; 93; 127; 129
skye ba'i gnas bzhi	the four locations of birth, 53 n. 158
skye (ba) med (pa)	unborn, without birth, 56; 60 n. 180; 93; 127
skye shi med pa	without birth and death, 45; 99
bskyed rim	the Generation stage (of meditative practices), 20 n. 19; 47 n. 128; 133 n. 2
khams gsum	the three spheres (of existence), 65; 241
khyad par chen po	the Great Difference, 51 n. 145; 197; 249
khyad par chen po'i gzhung	doctrine of the Great Difference, 50
khyad par med (pa)	without differentiation, 103; 175
khregs chod	one of the two most important practices of the Great Perfection, 68; 68 n. 212
'khor ba (1)	transmigration, 44; 44 n. 120; 48; 50; 53 n. 156; 54; 55 n. 164; 61; 62; 66; 95; 97; 109; 111 n. 1; 117; 155; 171; 191; 229 nn. 1, 3; 237; 251; 261; 271
'khor ba (2)	circle, 65
'khrul pa	delusion, 54; 55; 63 n. 189; 64; 65; 66; 67; 201; 217; 219 n. 3; 221 n. 1; 225; 231; 237 n. 1; 249
'khrul gzhi	the Basis (of) delusion, 55
gang zag nyi shu rtsa bzhi	the Twenty-four human beings (from Zhang Zhung who inherited the Aural transmission of the Great Perfection), 28; 159 n. 2
go mi chod pa	useless, 67
gyi ling	fine and thoroughbred horse, 203 n. 1; 259
grol ba	deliverance, 67
glo bur	accidental, 59; 64
dgag sgrub med (pa)	without obstruction and achievement, 189
dge bsnyen gyi theg pa	the Vehicle of Virtuous Devotees, (the Fifth Vehicle, first Vehicle of the Fruit), 20 n. 19
dge bshes	a degree of learning, (the Tibetan equivalent of Doctor of Philosophy), 10; 10 n. 3; 35; 73 n. 2; 90 n. 3
dgongs rgyud	mind(-to-mind) transmission, 28; 159
dgongs gter	treasure text hidden in and revealed out of the mind of realized teachers, 31

ngang	Condition, 40; 57; 58; 60; 83; 93 n. 2; 117; 123 n. 2; 125; 127; 129; 137; 155; 175; 181; 221; 231; 261; 269
ngo bo	essence, 52; 55; 57; 60; 93 n. 1; 183; 225
dngos grub	(supernatural) accomplishment, 135; 247
dngos po	substantiality, 171 n. 3
dngos po med (pa)	insubstantial, 267
mngal	womb, (one of the four locations of birth) 53 n. 158
mngon shes drug	six precognitions, 67 n. 208
snga dar	earlier propagation of the Bonpo doctrine, 27
sngags sde	the section of Formulas, 32 n. 71; 61 n. 184; cf. *rgyud sde*
sngags pa	*tantric* practitioner, 10 n. 3
sngon 'gro	preliminary practices, 10 n. 3
gcan gzan	animals of prey, 171 n. 1
gcig gi ngang	the Condition of One, 201; 267
gcig rgyud	transmission of knowledge during the lifetime of one teacher to one single disciple, 28
gcig pu	singleness, 197
bcos slad med (pa)	untainted and unaltered, 99
chags pa	attachment, 211; 223; 233
chags (pa) med (pa)	unbegotten, 267
chad (pa'i) lta (ba)	the nihilistic view, nihilism, 113 n. 3; 147 n. 2; 227; 229; 239; 251; 255
chu bur mig	eyeballs, 259 n. 4
chu srin	crocodile, 145; 147 n. 3
'ja' lus	rainbow body, 68
rjes dran drug	six subsequent recollections, 67 n. 208
brjod (du) med, brjod bral	ineffable, 81; 127
nyams	experience, 46 n. 123
nyams len pa	practitioner, 139 n. 1
nyon mongs med pa	devoid of afflictions, 60 n. 178
gnyis med	'not two', non-dual, 44; 60 n. 180; 62; 117; 251; 253; 255; 259; 267
gnyis (su) med (pa)	non-duality, without duality, 45; 56; 57; 123; 175 n. 4; 181; 203; 209; 211; 221 n. 3; 227; 241; 255
mnyam (pa)	equal, equalized, 63; 195; 203
mnyam pa, mnyam nyid	equality, 63; 117; 137; 197; 225; 231; 249
mnyam pa gcig	single equality, 203
mnyam pa chen po	great equality, 155
mnyam pa'i rgyal po	king of equality, 205

mnyam pa'i ngang	the Condition of equality, 251
mnyam pa'i don	the state of equality, 205
rnying ma	the Old School of Tibetan Buddhism, 10 n. 3; 21; 23; 33; 37; 38; 41 n. 108
rnying ma pa	doctrinal systems and followers of the Old School, 21; 24; 24 n. 40; 34
snyan rgyud	the Aural transmission, (one of the three Bonpo systems of the Great Perfection, originating from Zhang Zhung), 26; 35; 79 n. 1
snying rje	loving kindness, 83; 149; 241
snying thig	system of transmission of *rDzogs chen* teachings developed within the *rNying ma* tradition, 41 n. 108
snying po	quintessence, 243; 245; 267
ti se	Mount Kailash, 18
ting nge 'dzin	meditative absorption, 48; (eighty components of -), 52
ting nge 'dzin (gyi) dgongs pa	meditative contemplation, 87
gtan tshigs	cause (of being), 123 n. 1; 253; 255
gtan tshigs gsum	the three causes, 123
gti mug	stupidity, (one of the five poisons), 53 n. 157
gter ma	treasure text, 20 n. 19; 27 n. 47; 30; 39; 45; 45 n. 121; 52 n. 153; 66 n. 205; 165
gter shad	the mark of separation between verses or sentences found in treasure texts, ($\frac{\circ}{\circ}$), 167
rtag pa	eternity, 209
rtag pa('i lta ba)	the eternalist view, eternalism, 113 n. 1; 147 n. 2; 227; 229; 251; 255
rtags	token, 56; 83; 93; 205
rtog pa med (pa)	without conceptuality, 267
rtogs pa	realization, 40; 48; 51; 60; 68; 103 n. 2; 137; 139; 181
lta ba	view, 17; 37; 39; 40; 41; 43; 46; 46 n. 122; 47; 51 n. 145; 61; 67
lta (blta) ru (rgyu) med (pa)	without investigation, 91; 179; 193; 195; 269
stag gzig	a country traditionally situated in the West, from where Bonpo teachings are said to have been introduced in Zhang Zhung, and through the latter brought into Tibet, 18; 27
stong pa	empty, 57; 60; 61; 65; 95; 121; 123; 125; 205 n. 1
stong pa (nyid)	emptiness, 57; 59; 60 n. 180; 62; 85 n. 1; 93 n. 2; 111 n. 2; 113; 117; 181; 183; 185 n. 2; 227; 251; 257
ston pa	teacher, (also, *the* Teacher, *i.e.* gShen rab Mi bo che), 18; 34 n. 76; 87

brten 'gyur	the Bonpo *corpus* of commentaries and doctrinal treatises related to the canonical scriptures, 31 n. 67
bstan du med pa	without description, 267
thar pa	liberation, 68
thig le (1)	Essence, 65; 261; 263; 265
thig le (2)	sphere, 60 n. 180; 217 n. 2
thig le nyag gcig	Single Essence, 54; 60 n. 180; 79; 93; 95; 97; 101; 107; 117; 119; 121; 125; 127; 129; 137; 139; 141; 153; 155; 157
thugs	Mind, 61; Heart, 55 n. 167; 103; 145; 169
thugs rje	compassion, 81; 83; 85; 87; 131; 151
thugs rje'i ston pa	the Compassionate Teacher, (*i.e.* gShen lha 'Od dkar), 40; 49; 81; 169
thugs nyid	the Heart itself, the Mind-Itself, 55 n. 167
theg pa (rim) dgu	the Nine Vehicles, (one of the two main classifications of Bonpo tenets), 21; 32; 34; 45 n. 121; 141; 153
thod rgal	one of the two most important practices of the Great Perfection, 35; 68; 68 n. 212; 241 n. 2
mtha' (dang) bral	without extremes, 113; without limits, 125; 199; without demarcation, 137
mtha' bral chen po	great separation from extremes, 113
mthong tshor	perceptions, 233
da log dra	inverted *da* (ཌ), the sign indicating the consonant-group *-gs*, 76
dang po'i ye shes	the original Wisdom, 103
dang po'i sangs rgyas	the original Enlightenment, 107
dam tshig	commitment, 40; 133; 149; 197
dug lnga	the five poisons, 40; 53 n. 157; 97 n. 4
dus kun tu dri ma ma bgos pa	at all times wearing no stains, (an interpretation of the term *kun tu bzang po*), 49
dus gsum	the three times, (past, present and future), 103; 141; 175; 241
de'i ngang	the Condition of That, 81; 175
de('i) don	the state of That, 217; 221; 223; 247; 253
don (1)	state, 107; 115; 119; 127; 207; 211; 217; 241
don (2)	meaning, sense, 56; 93 n. 1; 101; 137; 179; 187; 191; 197; 221
don (3)	point, 113
don gyi 'od gsal	the Clear Light which is the meaning, 61
don dam bon nyid	Absolute Reality, 127
drang srong gyi theg pa	the Vehicle of Ascetics, (the Sixth Vehicle, second Vehicle of the Fruit), 20 n. 19

drod gsher	heat and humidity, (one of the four locations of birth), 53 n. 158
gdags su med (pa)	inexpressible, 99
gdags su med pa'i kun tu bzang po	the inexpressible Kun tu bZang po, 49; 177 n. 1
gdags su yod pa'i kun tu bzang po	the expressible Kun tu bZang po, 49
bdag nyid	Identity, 40; 58; 93 n. 2; 123; 221
bdag nyid chen po	Great Identity, 123 n. 3; 175; 181; 221
bdag gzhan	self and other, 63 n. 194
bdag sems	the mind of the self, 243
bde (ba) chen (po)	Great Bliss, 263
bde ba (chen po)'i klong	the Expanse of great bliss, 207; the blissful Expanse, 261
bde ba chen po'i don	the state of great bliss, 221
bde ba'i ngang	the Condition of bliss, 263
bder gshegs	the 'Well-gone Ones', 145
bder gshegs dgu	the 'Nine Well-gone Ones', (the first nine teachers in the lineage of the Zhang Zhung Aural transmission of the Great Perfection), 28; 159
mdo sde	*sūtra*, (one of the four Bonpo canonical sections), 31
'dus 'bral med (pa)	neither separated nor unified, 117
'dus ma byas	uncompounded, 111; 121
'dod khams	the sphere of desire, 53 n. 155; 81 n. 5; 215 n. 3
'dod chags	desire, (one of the five poisons), 53 n. 157
rdo med gser gling, rin chen gser gling	the golden island without (other kinds of) stones, 137 n. 1; 205
sde	canonical sections or series of scriptures, 31
sder chags	clawed animals, 171 n. 1
brda	symbol, 191 n. 1
bsdus yig / skung yig	contracted/hidden words, 76
nang man ngag dmar khrid	second section of the *Zhang Zhung snyan rgyud*, 29
nam mkha' (1)	space, 46 n. 124; 56; 59
nam mkha' (2)	sky, 46 n. 124; 93; 105; 107; 121; 125; 143; 161 n. 3; 205 n. 1; 261; 265
nam mkha'i klong	the Expanse of Space, 46 n. 124
gnad byang	focal-point, 79 n. 4; 157
gnas pa'i sa gsum	the three places of existence, (*i.e.* the three spheres (*khams gsum*) of desire (*'dod khams*), form (*gzugs khams*) and absence of form (*gzugs med khams*)), 52
gnas tshul	Manner of Being, 64
gnas lugs	Way of Being, 50 n. 143; 58; 64; 66; 67 n. 208; 185 n. 6; 227 n.1

bar pa   mediator, 191

bu   son, 61; 62

bon (1)   the religious tradition, 10 n. 3; 17; 19; 20; 20 n. 19;
                                    23 n. 33; 24 n. 40; 27; 28 n. 53; 31 n. 67; 33 n. 74; 34;
                                    37; 43; 44 nn. 118, 120; 49 n. 137; 53 n. 157; 66 n.
                                    205; 141 n. 1; 153 n. 1; 211 n. 1

bon (2)   the state of being, (i.e., the Absolute Reality), 89; 127

bon (gyi) sku   Body of Reality, 49; 52 n. 150; 60 n. 180; 85 n. 1; 97
                                    n. 3; 129; 137; 227; 241; 263; 265

bon (can)   phenomenon, phenomena, 44 n. 120; 50; 51 n. 148;
                                    57; 89; 127; 155; 175 n. 4; 185 n. 3; 189; 191 n. 1;
                                    197; 225; 229 n. 1; 243; 261

bon nyid   Reality, 44; 48; 49; 51; 56; 61; 81; 93; 95 n. 1; 103 n.
                                    2; 127; 133; 199; 211; 229; 231; 245; 257

bon po   tenets and instructions related to, and followers
                                    of the Bon religion, 10; 10 n. 3; 17 n. 1; 19; 20; 21;
                                    23; 24; 24 n. 40; 27 n. 47; 28; 29; 30; 31 nn. 67, 68;
                                    32 n. 71; 34; 34 n. 76; 35; 37; 37 n. 86; 45 n. 121; 53;
                                    68 n. 215; 73; 81 n. 5; 97 n. 4; 165; 167; 271 n. 1

byang chub (kyi) sems   the Pure-and-Perfect-Mind, 40; 51; 55; 56; 57; 58;
                                    59; 79; 95; 97; 99; 101; 105; 107; 109; 111 n. 2; 121;
                                    123; 141; 153; 155; 157; 195; 197; 207; 225; 229; 243;
                                    263

byang chub sems gab pa dgu skor   a fundamental treasure text of the Great Perfec-
                                    tion revealed by gShen chen Klu dga' in 1017, 30;
                                    30 n. 61

byung tshor   feelings, 217

blang dor med pa   without acceptance and rejection, 119; 137

blo ('khrul pa'i blo, phyin ci   thoughts, 46; mind, 63 n. 189; 143; 149; 203; 249;
    log gi blo, rnam rtog blo,   263; deluded mind, 63; 64; fallacious mind, 64;
    zhen pa'i blo)   conceptual mind, 207; biased mind, 259

dbang   empowerment, 40; 133

dbang po rab   excellent spiritual capacity, 68

dbu chen   Tibetan printing script, 73

dbu med   Tibetan cursive script, 74; 165; 166

dbus gter   Central Treasure, (one of the three main group-
                                    ings of treasure texts), 27 n. 47

dbyings   Dimension, 55 n. 166; 57; 58 n. 175; 59; 60 nn. 179,
                                    180; 61; 65; 81; 93; 127; 185 n. 5; 191; 231; 233; 257;
                                    261

dbyer (ba) med (pa)   inseparability, inseparable, 56; 62; 65; 85 n. 1; 125

'bum sde   one of the four Bonpo canonical sections, 31

'byung ba lnga   the five elements, 66; 177

zhi ba'i don skor	Peaceful State cycle, (a classification of teachings related to the *sPyi spungs Tantras*), 30
zhe sdang	aversion, (one of the five poisons), 53 n. 157
zhen pa	partiality, 57
gzha' ('ja') tshon	rainbow, 63; 121; 161; 217
gzhi	Basis, 43; 51; 52; 54; 55; 58; 60 n. 180; 61; 64; 65; 95 n. 1; 185 n. 6; 187 n. 1; 195; 203; 207
gzhi'i kun tu bzang po	Kun tu bZang po of the Basis, 49; 177 n. 1
gzhi'i rang 'byung ye shes	Self-Originated Primordial Wisdom of the Basis, 49; 103 n. 1; 177 n. 1; 185 n. 5
gzhung	doctrine, 50; 179; 189; 249
zo chu'i rgyun ma	the flow of water-buckets, 63
gzi brjid	*'Dus pa rin po che dri ma med pa gzi brjid rab tu 'bar ba'i mdo*, (the long-version biography of gShen rab Mi bo che), 34 nn. 75, 76
gzugs khams	the sphere of form, 53 n. 155; 81 n. 5
gzugs med khams	the sphere without form 53 n. 155; 81 n. 5
gzung (bzung) 'dzin	grasping and grasped, 63 n. 193; 97; 113; 125
gzung 'dzin med (pa)	without grasping and grasped, 137; 189
'ug pa	owl, 259 n. 3
'og min	residence of gShen lha 'Od dkar, 81
'od gsal	Clear Light, 55 n. 162; 95; 127; 135; 223
yang dag don	the real sense, 91; 121
yang rtse bla med kyi theg pa	the Unsurpassable Supreme Vehicle, (the Ninth Vehicle, fifth Vehicle of the Fruit), 20 n. 19; 34; 45 n. 121
yang gsang gnas lugs phug gcod	fourth section of the *Zhang Zhung snyan rgyud*, 29
yi dam mchog lnga	the Five Tutelary Deities (of Bon), 10 n. 3
yid bzhin nor bu	the Wish-fulfilling Gem, 213 n. 1
ye khri mtha' sel	a cycle of Great Perfection teachings attributed to Dran pa Nam mkha' (8th century), 29
ye ci bzhin ma'i sangs rgyas	the Primordially Enlightened (one), (i.e. the Primordial Teacher Kun tu bZang po), 85
ye nyid kyi ston pa	the Primordial Teacher, 28; 50; 81; 85 n. 1
ye shes	Primordial Wisdom, 52; 59; 61; 60 n. 180; 65; 66; 83; 93; 95 n. 1; 127; 129; 191; 233; 235; 241; 243; 263; Wisdom, 103; 129; 139
ye shes lnga	the Five Wisdoms, 40; 97 n. 4; 129
ye shes zang thal	transparent Primordial Wisdom, 223
ye gshen gyi theg pa	The Vehicle of the Primordial gShen, (the Eighth Vehicle, fourth Vehicle of the Fruit), 20 n. 19; 47; 47 n. 128; 133 n. 2

ye sangs rgyas pa	Primordial Enlightenment, 50; 54; 55 n. 164; 64; 67; 89; 95; 103; 107; 179; 199 n. 1; 207; 261; 265
yod med	existence and non-existence, 229; 251
yon tan	Qualities, 61; 101
g.yung drung	everlasting, 17 n. 2; 207; 209; 219; 269
g.yung drung sku	Everlasting Body, 263
g.yung drung don	the Everlasting State, 209; 211; 213 n. 1; 215; 219; 221 n. 2
g.yung drung bon	the Everlasting Bon, (the doctrinal tenets expounded by gShen rab Mi bo che, and classified as 'the Word' (*bka'*)), 17 n. 2; 34
g.yung drung sems	the Everlasting Mind, 223; 229
g.yeng ba lnga	the five diversions, 241 n. 1
g.yo ba	active, 59; 83
rang grol	self-liberation, 97 n. 4; self-released, 171
rang 'byung	self-originated, 89; 97; 107; 135; 261
rang 'byung ye shes	Self-Originated Primordial Wisdom, 60; 60 n. 179; 61; 89; 157
rang 'byung (gi) rig pa	Self-Originated Awareness, 81
rang bzhin	the (Ultimate) Nature, 40; 43; 45; 51 n. 145; 54; 56; 58; 60; 61; 64; 66; 93 n. 2; 123 n. 2; 173 n. 2; 175 n. 2; 177; 179; 181; 185; 191 n. 1; 193; 195; 201; 203; 207; 217 n. 2; 221; 225; 237 n. 1; 253; 265; 267
rang bzhin med pa	devoid of (inherent) nature, 50; 57; 58; 63 n. 188; 83; 95; 97 n. 4; 99; 195; 229 n. 2; 233 n.1
rang rig	Self-Awareness, 91; 117; 151; 231
rang rig (pa'i) ye shes	Primordial Wisdom of Self-Awareness, 61; 87; 89; 95 n. 1; 123 n. 2; 145; 157; 173 nn. 1, 3; 231 n. 1
rang shes rig gi rgyal po	the King of Self-Knowledge, 66
rab byung	the Tibetan cycle of sixty years, 35
ri rgyal lhun po	Mount Meru, 215
rig pa	Awareness, 44; 62; 65; 85; 161 n. 3; 191 n. 1; 233; 241
ris med pa	non-sectarian movement flourished in Eastern Tibet during the late 19th century, 21 n. 21
ru tra	see p. 147 n. 3
re dog med pa	without hope or apprehension, 137
rol pa	manifestation, 51 n. 148; 53 n. 154; 58; 113; 187 n. 1
rol pa chen po	Great Manifestation, Great Play, 51; 231
lam	path, 44; 101; 135; 153; 217 nn. 3, 4, 5
lam lnga	the five paths (stemming from the five poisons), 53 n. 157; 97
lung	precepts, 28; 141; 153; 171 n. 4; 185; 265; 271

gser gyi grang ma	(cold) gold dust, 215
lha	deity, 27; 47; 48; 49; 81 n. 1; 133 nn. 1, 2; 153; 177 n. 2
lhag mthong	superior seeing, 48
lhan gcig skyes pa'i ma rig pa	the non-awareness simultaneously born (with sentient beings), 64
lhun (gyis) grub (pa), lhun grub	spontaneous accomplishment, 56; 58; 139; spontaneously accomplished, 44; 53; 55; 58; 65; 91; 101; 107; 175; 197; 205; 223; 227 n. 1; 245
lhun rdzogs	spontaneous perfection, spontaneously perfected, 45; 91; 101; 131
lhun rdzogs chen po	great, spontaneous perfection, 131; 133; 135
lho gter	Southern Treasure, (one of the three main groupings of Bonpo treasure texts), 30; 45 n. 121
lho brag ma'i skor	the cycles of the *bsGrags pa skor gsum* and *Yang rtse klong chen* discovered by gZhod ston dNgos grub Grags pa, 27 n. 47
a dkar gyi theg pa	the Vehicle of the White A, (the Seventh Vehicle, third Vehicle of the Fruit), 20 n. 19; 46 n. 127; 133 n. 2
a khrid	one of the three Bonpo systems of transmission of the Great Perfection, 26; 34
a khrid thun mtshams	the eighty retreat-sessions of the *A khrid*, (meditative training system developed by dGongs mdzod Ri khrod Chen po (1038-1096)), 26
a khrid thun mtshams bco lnga brgyad bcu pa	the fifteen retreat-sessions of the *A khrid*, (meditative training system developed by Bru chen rGyal ba g.Yung drung (1242-1290) as a simplified form of the *a khrid thun mtshams brgyad bcu pa*), 26
u du 'bar ba'i me tog	the Udumbara flower, 215
e ma ho	expression of wonder, 79; 95; 97; 101; 107; 113; 117; 119; 121; 125; 127; 139; 151

INDICES OF NAMES